LAST QUARTER

LAST QUARTER

The Next Twenty-five Years
in Asia and the Pacific

MALCOLM BOOKER

MELBOURNE UNIVERSITY PRESS

1978

First published 1978

Printed in Australia by
Academy Press Pty Ltd for
Melbourne University Press, Carlton, Victoria 3053
U.S.A. and Canada: International Scholarly Book Services, Inc.,
Box 555, Forest Grove, Oregon 97116
Great Britain, Europe, the Middle East, Africa and the Caribbean:
International Book Distributors Ltd (Prentice-Hall International)
66 Wood Lane End, Hemel Hempstead,
Hertfordshire HP2 4RG, England

National Library of Australia Cataloguing in Publication data

Booker, Malcolm Richard, 1915–
    Last quarter
    Index
    Bibliography
    ISBN 0 522 84151 1

    1. Asia—Foreign relations. 2. Asia—Foreign economic rela-
tions. 3. Pacific area—Foreign relations. 4. Pacific area—
Foreign economic relations. I. Title.

327'.5

Whosoever commands the sea commands the trade; whosoever commands the trade of the world commands the riches of the world, and consequently the world itself.

Sir Walter Raleigh (1552–1618)

Contents

Introduction

The poor international repute of Australians may not be altogether justified. They are not all grasping and racist; nor are they all vulgarians. Self-righteousness may seem to be a dominant national characteristic but there are some who can recognize virtue in others. Although our larrikin politicians of left and right attract a good deal of notice overseas they are not wholly representative of the people. Not all our demonstrators are publicity seekers interfering in others' business: some have real concern for the evils in our own society. There are also some who are aware that disregard for the feelings and aspirations of our neighbours might put our own interests in jeopardy.

The attitudes which have earnt for us such ill will were developed in the days when we regarded ourselves as an outpost of the Anglo–Saxon powers and assured of their protection. This confidence has vanished, but no alternative idea has yet taken its place. Out of habit we behave as though we were still invulnerable and superior, but there is nevertheless a deep unease and perplexity. Our political leaders, tied as they are to the ideas of the past, have no guidance to offer. This is true even of the so-called left wing; in other countries this is often the source of useful new ideas, but in Australia it is trapped in shibboleths. Australia badly needs a radical element in its politics, but there is none in sight; all parties huddle in the centre, concerned only to avoid disturbing the complacency of the electorate.

Distance is the main problem. It may have ceased to be strategically vital but in the world of ideas it is still a handicap. The inability of Australians to develop a clear view of their position in the world is due to ignorance about what is actually happening overseas. They usually become aware of one set of problems at the point when it is about to be superseded by different ones; so that such efforts as they make towards adjustment are often irrelevant

1

to current needs. They argue about the importance of maintaining a balance between the superpowers in the Indian Ocean at a time when the possibility of such a balance has passed. They call for strong Australian action to curtail the proliferation of nuclear weapons long after the time when an Australian initiative could have any effect. They discuss the energy crisis as though it were still a matter of whether one source of power is preferable to another, whereas the real question is whether the maximum exploitation of all forms will be sufficient to avoid massive starvation in the poor countries in the next twenty-five years.

In the field of economic relations we have belatedly become concerned about the high tariffs we maintain on low technology goods produced by our Asian neighbours, without realizing that many of them are now passing to levels of technology higher than our own: they produce not only shirts more cheaply than we can, but also cars, electronic equipment and engineering products. The question for the future is not so much whether they will have access to our small market, but whether we will be excluded from their vast one.

In the field of defence our lack of knowledge of the outside world has made it impossible for us to devise a coherent strategic doctrine or a realistic defence structure. Governments spend large sums of money on equipment which would have been useful in the wars of the past but which can have no value in the future.

This handicap of ignorance is partly self-inflicted. The flow of information and ideas into Australia is through Western channels and therefore cannot give us a true picture of developments in the region in which we live. The media maintain few Australian representatives in Asia, and rely mainly for their news on foreign press organizations.

In these circumstances it is particularly important for Australian governments to make special efforts to gather information of a more reliable kind. It is one of the primary tasks of a foreign service to do this and in the years after the end of the war considerable progress was made in building up an adequate organization to serve the purpose. We developed in Asia a diplomatic service which was second to none in expert knowledge and dedication. For the first time in history Australian governments received objective information and advice which was relatively free of American, British or European bias. This was not always listened to, but in some notable instances it led to policies which were realistically related to Australian circumstances and requirements.

This promising development has stopped. The Fraser government has crippled the foreign service by applying much higher manpower cuts than elsewhere in the public service. It has weakened its morale in a multitude of different ways: it has forced experienced and independent-minded officers into retirement; it has placed the leadership of the department in the hands of officers not distinguished by their capacity for positive thought; and by stopping all recruitment it has cut the service off from the best minds of the younger generation. At a time when the Australian government urgently needs information about the rapidly changing international scene it has greatly reduced the effectiveness of its most reliable professional source.

A potent cause of distortions in Australian policy in the past thirty years has been the reliance by governments on overseas 'intelligence'. This has flooded in from the Americans, who have used it to persuade Australian Cabinet Ministers and senior officers to accept their own way of thinking. It has always come attractively packaged, and made available only to people who have been subjected to screening rituals that outdo the most arcane societies of freemasons. In passing on this intelligence to politicians the Americans have been particularly adept in persuading them of its superior authenticity, and most have preferred to believe it rather than information coming from mundane sources such as the Department of Foreign Affairs. Prime Ministers in particular have taken to American intelligence as to a drug and it has often had disturbing effects on their judgement and political behaviour. Senior defence and foreign affairs officials have also been heavily addicted and whenever the supply has diminished—as it did briefly during the early days of the Whitlam government—they show acute withdrawal symptoms. Ministers are importuned with arguments that a continued supply of information is essential to the nation, and that it must be maintained at almost any cost.

One of the most useless, if not the most damaging, developments in the Australian public service in recent years has been the elaboration of intelligence organizations—designed mostly to ingurgitate and regurgitate American secret information, mixed with a smattering from British sources. Data from Australian sources, if included, is usually discounted. The consequence is that the information which goes to ministers and senior officials concerned with foreign relations—whether political, defence or economic—is slanted in the direction of preserving the interests of foreign countries rather than Australia's own. The cost to the Australian people of dependence on it during the Korean and Vietnam wars is now a matter of public record.

When the Whitlam government appointed Mr Justice Hope to conduct an enquiry into the whole range of intelligence services there was an expectation that there would be some rationalization and reduction of this vast apparatus. The bizarre result has instead been the creation of yet another intelligence authority, located in the Prime Minister's Department, and thus able to pour its concentrated product direct into the Cabinet's bloodstream.

It is not an exaggeration to say that no Australian government will be able to see the outside world clearly until this apparatus is dispersed. In the making of policy the need for secret intelligence is only marginal, and should in any case be used only when the source is untainted by the interests of other powers. For the Australian government to base its policies on a flow of tendentious and misleading 'intelligence' is dangerous and could be suicidal.

Secret intelligence organizations tend to be staffed by persons of unbalanced judgement—mature and responsible people who find their way into them quickly leave them—and they tend to corruption and deception. If they are necessary at all—and for a country like Australia this is questionable—they should be strictly supervised and repeatedly purged.

The need for reliable and exhaustive information about the outside world would still remain and to provide this a properly organized foreign service is essential. The current weakness of the Department of Foreign Affairs is an important cause of the unhealthy importance attributed to foreign intelligence. If it is to be rebuilt into an effective organ of information and advice the first requirement is to understand the causes of its recent failures.

The Fraser government was able to strike at the Department of Foreign Affairs with impunity because it is widely disliked. This is only partly the fault of the diplomatic officers themselves: it is their role to remind ministers and other departments of the realities of world affairs, which they would often prefer to ignore. It is also their responsibility to draw attention to any damage to Australia's wider international interests which might follow from policies adopted in areas not of direct concern to the diplomatic service —in matters of trade, for example. Such advice inevitably arouses resentment, but this situation is not peculiar to Australia: in most countries the foreign service is the least popular of all the organs of government. In Australia the problem has been worse because the foreign service lacked a historical status and prestige; and because its officers presented their advice without the necessary tact and humility. Not all of them have understood the important distinction between proffering useful advice and interfering in matters beyond their competence. Seeing the damage that the policies of other departments have sometimes done to Australia's broad interests foreign service officers have often attempted to take over the direction of those policies. These attempts have usually failed and the result has been to ensure that their advice is ignored.

An effective foreign service needs to have wide horizons but small ambitions. It should seek to gather for the benefit of its government information across the whole spectrum of human affairs—reporting not only in the traditional fields of diplomacy and politics but in international economic relations, defence and strategy, international law, world environmental problems, and all other matters which affect the relations between governments and peoples. To do this effectively its officers need to be trained in a wide range of disciplines and many languages; they must know where to find the best information and report it lucidly and briefly. They need to be able to analyse current situations and identify emerging trends; they should, when appropriate, offer advice without fear or favour; and finally they should ensure that their reports are presented in such a form that they speedily reach the people in their own government, both ministers and officials, who need the information for the proper consideration of policy.

These tasks would absorb the available energies of the foreign service, even if it were greatly reinforced beyond its present strength. It should, therefore, cease attempts to take over functions properly belonging to others. It should contribute advice to the Attorney-General's Department on matters of international law; to the Trade Department and Treasury on economic relations; to the Department of Immigration on migration; and so on. It should seek to be consulted in discussions on policy in all these areas and, where appropriate, co-ordinate the activities of other departments when several of them are involved in related aspects of a particular international problem; but it should not usurp the authority of other departments in their own fields. If it gives good information and advice it will be listened to; if it tries to trespass on the responsibilities of others it will be disregarded. A foreign service cannot run the country's foreign relations. This can only be done by the government—which must take its decisions in the light of both domestic and international considerations. But its decisions will be better attuned to the country 's interests if in making them it has available to it the advice of a competent and trusted foreign service.

The other important function of a foreign service is to promote the international policies and objectives of its own government. The smaller and more vulnerable the country the more important is this role: in Australia's case it is no exaggeration to say that the foreign service is its first line of defence. But it can only be effective if it has a coherent and rational set of policies to promote. Unfortunately this has so far been lacking: the Australian government and people still have no clear understanding of where their international interests lie.

Experience suggests that no present Australian political party is likely to develop an appropriate set of policies. This will only come when the Australian people are sufficiently informed about the nature of the world and their own position in it to impose on the politicians a consensus as to what their relationships should be with other countries. This book has been written in the hope that it will provide some of the relevant information.

One problem is that most Australians appear to believe that the historical process has stopped—that the problems of the future will continue to be the same as the present: tension in the Middle East and Africa, sporadic terrorism, inflation and unemployment, environmental pollution and other relatively manageable matters. There is little realization that fundamental shifts are occurring which are likely in the next twenty-five years to change the nature of the world beyond recognition, or that mankind will be lucky if this change is accomplished without catastrophe. The world has had thirty years of stability; it cannot expect another thirty.

The main developments which are undermining this stability are already visible to those who study the evidence: the withdrawal of American power and the expansion of Russian; the population growth, which will lead to a doubling of population by the end of the century in the countries least able to afford it; and the acquisition by an increasing number of countries of the capacity to produce nuclear weapons. It is certain that Australia in the next twenty-five years will face difficulties in maintaining its independence beyond anything it has so far encountered. It is now generally accepted in Australia that the American alliance will not in future provide a sufficient basis for our security, and that diplomatic, economic and defence policies based on the assumption that the Americans would protect us are no longer valid. But there is almost total confusion as to what should take their place.

In this book I suggest that Australia has only one realistic option. It is too weak to survive alone. Its security is inescapably bound up with its neighbours in south-east Asia. If they fall under the domination of a great power so also will Australia. But they also are too weak to stand alone. Their only chance—and ours—is to join together in developing the collective strength necessary to resist the pressure of all outside powers. This will not be easy: all the countries in the region face grievous social, political and economic problems; and the greater likelihood is that they will successively fall into the orbit of one or another of the great powers, until ultimately the rivalry between the latter will be resolved in favour of one.

If Australia is to contribute to the development of a regional security system its first and urgent task is to seek good relations with its neighbours. These are at present worse than usual because of the economic policies of the Fraser government and the insulting attitude of certain Labor politicians. Before there can be any improvement the Australian people must make it clear to their elected representatives that they will no longer acquiesce in policies and attitudes that are inimical to our national interests. It is said that people get the politicians they deserve: if this is true of the present situation in Australia our deserts must be grievously low. One thing is certain—the behaviour of politicians will not improve until better standards are insisted on by the people: it is urgent for Australia's survival that they should so insist.

Once reconciled with our neighbours, our next task would be to help them overcome their difficulties and develop their combined strength. Because of our small market and inferior technology we can at present give them little direct economic assistance. By lowering our tariffs we could avoid deliberate damage, but we should also help to promote international arrangements which would give them a better share of the world's wealth. We should encourage, rather than obstruct, the diversion to them of new sources of wealth, such as the resources of the deep sea bed. Their handicap is not only lack of capital and resources, but low managerial and administrative ability. Again, because of our own poor standards we cannot assist directly, but we should support international arrangements which might help to remedy this deficiency. Good management could make the difference between famine and survival for millions of people in the next quarter of a century and this precious resource needs to be nurtured and developed above all others.

The most useful contribution that Australia could make would be in the defence field. Our armed forces are locked in an archaic structure and equipped largely with irrelevant weapons; but they are disciplined, well-trained and, except at the top, intelligent. In a region where the armed forces, with some exceptions, are poorly organized and trained we could give help by example and even, if we could shake off our own backward doctrines, give leadership in developing concepts for the collective defence of the whole region. If we could follow the example of smaller countries like Sweden and move to the front line of technology we might even provide them with the modern weapons which will be essential to their defence.

Finally, we should give whole-hearted support to the Association of Southeast Asian Nations in establishing a zone of peace and neutrality in the region. We are, as it happens, in a position to contribute to making this concept into a practical reality. No such zone could be effectively established unless there existed means of surveillance and control. Because of the existence on Australian soil of communication and satellite tracking stations we could provide the means to maintain constant observation of the whole area.

There has been a campaign by certain members of the Labor Party and the trade unions to abolish these stations and to prevent the building of new ones. This is the height of absurdity. They constitute a unique and valuable capability and could be used to serve Australian national interests, the security of the region, and the strategic stability of the world. The essential requirement is that they should not serve the interests of the United States alone—which is at present the case in respect of the most important of the stations —but made available to the whole international community.

A group of nations in the region of south-east Asia and the south-west Pacific, collectively armed with the right kind of weapons and disposing of the most modern means of surveillance and inspection, would have a realistic chance of establishing a neutral zone which the great powers might find it easier to respect than attempt to destroy. There would then be a possibility of the emergence of a new and more stable balance of power; the closing of the Russian pincers round China would be prevented; China would have the chance to develop its full potential, but since it could not get control of south-east Asia it would not itself become a global threat; and Japan, since its access to the resources of south-east Asia and the Indian Ocean would be assured, need not fear economic strangulation.

The United States would stand to gain enormously from a zone of armed neutrality in south-east Asia and if the proposal could be shown to have real prospects it might attract their support. Since Nixon's day the Americans have accepted that they should not seek to continue to exercise global strategic control, and they have adopted the only logical alternative—a classical balance of power policy. They are at present relying on China and Japan to counterbalance the steadily expanding Soviet power but, for reasons which are outlined in the following pages, this policy is dangerous and could be self-defeating. If any one of these nations achieved control of Asia and the western Pacific the global balance would be decisively tilted against the United States. If this shift is to be prevented a strong barrier to the extension of the power of all of them must be erected.

The geographical place for this is the nexus of islands and waterways which links the Indian and Pacific Oceans. The countries in the area have the resources to erect a barrier which could hold in any circumstances short of a nuclear holocaust. There are encouraging signs that the political will to do so is also developing, but the vital question is whether they will have the time. The Russians clearly see themselves as engaged in a race against time not so much, as many believe, to control the Indian Ocean, but to break into the South China Sea and the central Pacific. Once they have done this the chance of erecting the barrier will have passed.

In the following pages I give a good deal of attention to Russia's growth in global power because I believe that this will be the most important single factor in world affairs in the final quarter of this century. This should not be regarded as indicating hostility to the Soviet Union. There have been many examples in history of nations suddenly entering upon a dynamic expansionary phase, and this is clearly true of the Russians at the present time. I have tried to describe this process as objectively as possible. As they extend their power they will have an increasingly important influence on Australia's own future. It will, therefore, be prudent for us to show nothing but the most scrupulous friendship and courtesy towards them.

There will be in the next ten to fifteen years a potentially disastrous conjunction of circumstances: there will be a shortage of energy precisely when the population explosion is gathering force; there will be in the hands of many nations weapons of the most advanced types with, by then, the trained manpower to use them; and there will be up to ten additional countries with nuclear weapons systems already in their hands or the means to acquire them at short notice. Sharp economic distress in the mid-1980s is now virtually inevitable, with the likelihood of widespread famine. The competition for resources will be bitter and will involve the superpowers no less than the poor nations. The old alternatives of starvation or war might reappear, and it cannot be assumed that the countries with the weapons to fight will not use them— especially if risk-taking is encouraged by global strategic instability. It is vital, therefore, that a stable international system be constructed before the tempest strikes.

Disaster *could* be avoided. If mankind pooled its abilities and resources on a genuinely global scale, and if the necessary priority were given to producing low-cost food and low-cost energy (the two are inescapably related) there would not only be sufficient for all, but the foundation could be laid for a twenty-first century of unprecedented affluence and well-being. But few of the world's leaders seem even to have grasped the nature of the problem: they speak only of palliatives—of marginal increases in aid and credits for developing countries, and of tariff adjustments and commodities agreements, of technical training schemes and transfers of technology. These have been talked about for thirty years and if they had been resolutely applied they would have been useful. But it is now too late for patchwork adjustments to be effective. The oil-producing countries of the Middle East did the world a service by giving a warning of what was to come, but because of the relative ease with which the affluent world overcame the difficulties caused by the rise in the price of oil the warning has already been largely forgotten. Resources which will be desperately needed in the next twenty years are being consumed with undiminished profligacy by the wealthy nations—in the apparent belief that when the crisis comes they will be able to take care of themselves. Simple arithmetic—some of which is quoted in Chapter 9—could tell them otherwise.

Although it is proper to hope that the worst will not happen, Australians would be wise to prepare for it. From our point of view the worst would be that one of the great powers—it would not much matter which one—should take over south-east Asia. We would then have to fall into its orbit and we would be wise to do so without useless resistance. Our resources would be exploited in the interests of our masters and our migration laws would be rewritten to serve their purposes. If we were clever, hard-working and humble we might still have a tolerable existence, but none of the potential winners of the contest for dominion over our area would have any reason to show us more consideration than we have been accustomed to show others.

Believing that it might gain them votes the politicians have assured the people that no threat to Australia's independence is in sight. But, even more foolishly, they have said that forward defence is no longer necessary. This book is intended to show that the threat is serious and might be imminent. It also draws attention to what should indeed be sufficiently obvious: that if Australia can be defended at all it is only by keeping the threat as far as possible from our own shores.

1

New Empire in the Indian Ocean

Recent developments in the Indian Ocean have rightly become a matter of concern for the Australian people. This region is now vital to global equilibrium and the countries in it are likely to be increasingly affected by the contest for strategic control.

In Australia discussion has been focused on an out-dated issue: whether the United States should maintain in the Indian Ocean a 'balance' with the Soviet naval forces. Such a balance has not existed since 1971, and seems unlikely ever to exist again. It is not easy to measure exactly the strengths of different navies; but by 1977 the relationship, by any standards, was heavily in favour of the Soviet Union. This gap must be expected to widen.

Not only do the Russians continuously maintain stronger naval forces in the Indian Ocean than the Americans, but they have built up logistical facilities which would be capable of supporting a greatly expanded effort. As a result of their intervention in the war between Ethiopia and Somalia they will be able to dominate the west coast of the Red Sea.

They also have naval facilities in the ports of the Peoples' Republic of Yemen to which they have given substantial economic, political and military support. Through client States on both sides of the southern end of the Red Sea the Soviet Union is thus in a good position to control the entrance to that sea and also to the Suez Canal. Naval facilities have also been developed on the island of Socotra in the Gulf of Aden.

Russia has, in addition, developed a chain of supply points and anchorages around the coast of Africa and in the western Indian Ocean off the British islands of the Seychelles, Mauritius and the Chagos Archipelago.

The reopening of the Suez Canal in 1975 greatly facilitated the deployment of the Soviet navy in the Indian Ocean. The sailing distance from the main Soviet naval base in the Black Sea was reduced from about 10 000 miles to only 3000, and even in the case of Russia's northern fleets the distance was substantially reduced. The advantage to the Soviet Union is all the greater in that all its warships are able to pass through the canal, whereas the major vessels in the American navy, such as the nuclear aircraft carriers, are too large to do so.

In the Persian Gulf area the Soviet Union has taken advantage of its close relationship with Iraq to obtain the use of the port of Umm Qasr, at the head of the gulf. It is not, however, in such a favourable position at the mouth of the gulf—the straits of Hormuz—as in the case of the Red Sea. Iran controls the northern side and has developed strong military facilities in the straits area; while the southern side is controlled by Saudi Arabia and the United Arab Emirates, who are strongly anti-Russian.

In the Persian Gulf area the Americans might seem to be in a stronger position than the Russians, in that they have shore facilities on the island of Bahrein, inside the gulf, and on the island of Masirah in the southern approach to the gulf. The American presence on these islands, however, arouses a good deal of political opposition and their availability in a crisis would be uncertain. In the case of Masirah, British control of the island, on which the American use depends, is due shortly to end.

In the Indian Ocean area as a whole the facilities available to the United States are very limited compared with the Soviet Union. The only significant base is at Diego Garcia, in the central ocean. If this were developed to its fullest extent and were made the headquarters of an American carrier task force it might eventually serve to counterbalance Russian influence; but it is clear that the American government has no intention of making such an expensive commitment. It is estimated that it would require the addition of three aircraft carriers to the United States Navy.

The extent of the Soviet naval build-up demonstrates that the Indian Ocean has become a major strategic priority for the Russians, whereas the United States now regards it as an area of minor importance in its own global strategy. This means that even without armed conflict the Russians will be able progressively to extend their influence among the politically unstable and economically weak littoral States. As in the past, the Russians will no doubt meet with setbacks in their relations with these States but it would be unwise to expect that these would lead them to abandon their overall programme, or that there is likely to be any permanent check to the expansion of their activities.

Much has been said about the political influence that can be exerted by a great power which maintains a strong military presence in an area, but it needs to be remembered that such influence depends ultimately upon whether the great power concerned does indeed offer a believable military threat in the area. In the case of the Soviet Union it clearly has a number of options for military action—if the rewards and the risks seemed worthwhile. It might be instructive to examine these options, not in order to suggest that the Soviet Union will take any of them, but to illustrate the possibilities that the countries of the area must take into account in their dealings with the Russians.

Except for the oil-rich states, all the countries of the region are still in need of outside economic help. The problems of India are discussed in the following chapter, but the difficulties of other countries of the sub-continent seem as insoluble. Democracy has everywhere failed to provide effective government and in many areas the standard of life is lower than at any time since the collapse of the Mogul empire in the middle of the eighteenth century. In spite of the veneer of Westernization the past still dominates the present and the deep divisions among the people are unlikely to be resolved without further conflict and instability. This will inevitably provide opportunities for outside interference, of which the Soviet Union is likely to be the principal beneficiary. Its main competitor in the region will not be the United States but China, and it is in this circumstance that the real possibility of war resides.

The line-up is already becoming clear. Apart from its hold over the Horn of Africa and Yemen the Soviet Union has strong influence in States closer to home—Iraq and Afghanistan. Moreover, the Soviet-Indian alliance must be expected to become closer. After the defeat of Indira Gandhi in early 1977 there was an attempt by the new Prime Minister, Morarji Desai, to draw India back into a non-aligned position; but India has already become too dependent upon the Russians for this to be feasible and, in view of its continuing political and social instability, this dependence is likely to increase. The only way that this trend might be reversed would be for the Americans to outbid the Soviet Union in offering military and economic support. It is clear that no American administration is likely in the foreseeable future to be willing to do this.

In the western Indian Ocean and Africa the Chinese try to counter Russian influence wherever the opportunity offers, but the advantage in those areas lies clearly with the Russians. On the eastern side in north-eastern India—Bangladesh, Assam and Burma —the advantage is with the Chinese, and this is the part of the region of most use in facilitating their access to south-east Asia. Lying uncomfortably in the middle are the Pakistanis, who have nowhere to turn but to China.

It might not at present seem likely that the competition between Russia and China will result in actual takeovers of territory by these powers. But such possibilities are very much in the minds of the peoples of the area, and on historical grounds alone they cannot be ruled out.

Afghanistan has a key role in the western sector. In recent times its strategic importance has tended to be overlooked. Foreign invaders of the Indian sub-continent have come through Afghanistan since the time of Alexander of Macedon, and no doubt long before. The ancient route still exists from Samarkand (now in Russian territory) to Kabul, the capital of Afghanistan, thence through the Khyber Pass to Peshawar (in Pakistan) and on to the capital at Islamabad. Another route goes southward to Quetta and on to Karachi—two of Pakistan's most important cities. The possibility that Russian armies might one day use these routes for an invasion of their country is never far from the minds of Pakistan's defence planners. The fear is reinforced by their distrust of Afghanistan. The Afghans claim territory in north-west and south Pakistan and have fomented rebellion among the Pathan and Baluchi peoples ever since Pakistan became independent. It is, therefore, easy for Pakistanis to believe that Afghanistan would be ready to co-operate with the Russians in the dismemberment of Pakistan.

Even if the Afghans sought to prevent Russian use of their territory for a move against Pakistan they would have little hope of doing so. Their armed forces are small and dependent on Russian equipment, supplies and training. Their primitive economy is closely linked to the Soviet Union and if the Russians wished they could exert severe economic as well as military pressure. The present Afghan government seeks to maintain an independent attitude vis-à-vis the Soviet Union, but it is unlikely that it would be able to resist determined Russian pressure. The prospect would in any case be very tempting to the Afghans of regaining access to the Indian

Ocean—and perhaps possession of Karachi, which in the fifteenth century was an important Afghan city. When it is remembered that before the coming of the Moguls the Afghans ruled north India from the Indus valley to Bengal, it is not difficult to conceive that the Russians might one day use the Afghans to help extend their own sway over the area.

Pakistan's present territory consists principally of a narrow strip running the length of the valley of the Indus and its tributaries. If a combined attack were made from Afghanistan in the west and India in the east she would have no hope of survival. Her desire to develop friendly relations with China is thus understandable. Under present circumstances it would be difficult for China to give direct military assistance. The only border between the two countries is that which runs through the western Himalayas in Pakistan-held Kashmir and there are no militarily useful routes across it. (A road is being constructed through the Karakoram range into the eastern Chinese province of Sinkiang, but it passes through difficult terrain and it is not known how useful it would be in an emergency.) It is thus easy to understand Pakistan's desire to secure control of the whole of Kashmir, since it would give her a more extended and more secure land frontier with China. This would not only improve China's capacity to give direct military support but would also enable Chinese forces to threaten the Indian province of East Punjab. But the terrain is unsuitable for large-scale military operations and Pakistan's best hope would be that China would mount a diversionary thrust into India at the eastern end of the Himalayas.

The prospects for a successful Chinese invasion would be much more promising on the eastern side than in Kashmir. During the border war between India and China in 1962 the Indian forces were badly defeated and although little notice of the fact was taken in the west this meant that the way was open for a Chinese invasion of the Brahmaputra valley. The Chinese did not at the time follow up their victory, but it cannot be ruled out that they might do so in the future, especially in response to combined Soviet-Indian pressure on Pakistan. It would not be a difficult military undertaking for Chinese forces to link up with Bangladesh territory. This would sever Assam and its other border provinces from India and enable the Chinese to draw this territory into their own sphere. (See p. 48 for a discussion of Chinese political penetration of this area.)

It is no doubt with such possibilities in mind that the Chinese have since the end of World War II maintained guerrilla groups

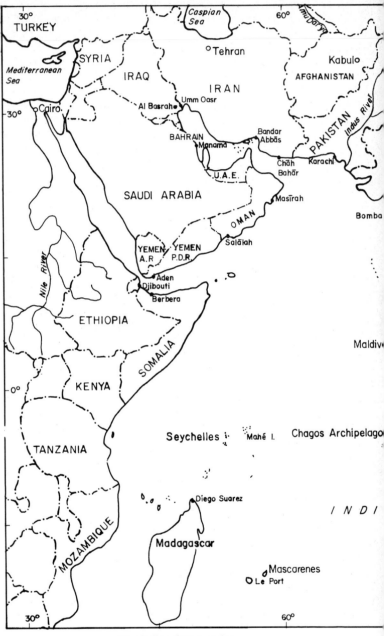

The Indian Ocean region

in northern Burma. Their intention to continue to deploy these units was demonstrated at the time that Hua Kuo-feng became chairman of the Chinese Communist Party. Among the first visitors he received in Peking after taking office were the leader and deputy leader of the Burmese Communist Party, which is dependent on the support of Chinese elements. The Burmese government has sought continuously to persuade the Chinese to withdraw this support, but they are unlikely to succeed. It is certain that Chinese military experts are thoroughly familiar with the terrain and that operations could be quickly developed to support a thrust into northeast India and to the Bay of Bengal. Since the collapse of Burma would be likely to follow, this would bring the Chinese virtually to the borders of Malaysia and Thailand.

China is working hard to expand its influence in Bangladesh. In January 1977 General Ziaur Rahman, who was already the effective ruler of Bangladesh, visited Peking and was met at the airport by Chairman Hua Kuo–feng. Two agreements of great economic importance were signed: one providing for substantial Chinese economic and technical aid, and another envisaging an exchange of trade in 1977 worth US$14 million. These agreements have been followed by a steadily increasing Chinese presence in Bangladesh.

Conflicts directly involving Russia and China are not the only dangerous possibilities in the region. The Pakistanis fear that India and Afghanistan might themselves launch a combined attack, and it is for this reason that they are seeking close co-operation with Iran and Turkey. They are also offering increased support to CENTO, the mutual security organization which consists of Turkey, Iran, Pakistan and the United Kingdom.

The United States is not a full member of CENTO but it participates in the work of the committees concerned with the security of the area. Its association with the organization, and its large-scale supply of arms to its members, are nowadays the principal manifestations of American presence in the area. They are usually regarded as the best guarantee that the United States would resist any Russian attempt to disturb the status quo. The Americans have made massive arms sales to Iran in recent years and it appears that in their view the development of Iran as an important military power would contribute to the security and stability of the region. It is anticipated that within a few years Iran will have armed forces second in the region only to India, and that its equipment and weapons will be more modern than India's.

It may be doubted, however, that Iran will ever develop sufficient strength to be able to resist a Russian attack, especially if the countries on both its flanks—Iraq and Afghanistan—remain subservient to the Soviet Union. It will, moreover, be in the same dilemma as all other countries who equip their forces with foreign arms—in a conflict it would be dependent upon the willingness and the ability of the United States to provide them with the spares and replacements without which their new weapons would become quickly useless.

Saudi Arabia is the most anti-Russian of all the States in the area and it is also making large purchases of arms from America. It seems to be a natural ally of Iran's, but deep enmities persist between the two countries and it is unlikely that effective military co-operation could be developed between them at least for some time to come. It is doubtful, in any case, whether, either jointly or singly, they would be able to defend themselves against the Russians.

Nevertheless, a direct assault on these two countries by the Soviet Union is perhaps the least likely possibility. Because of the weakness of the countries in the Indian sub-continent it would seem an easier option for the Russians first to establish themselves in that area rather than on the Persian Gulf. Once they had done so Iran and Saudi Arabia would have no choice but to yield to their pressure.

Pakistan's strategic vulnerability is unfortunate because if it were not for this she might have the best prospects of any State in the sub-continent. Since the unnatural link with east Bengal has been severed she no longer has to support the economic burden of that grievously poor territory and can devote herself to developing the wealth of the Indus valley. Her rate of population growth is high, but manageable, and industrialization has expanded fourfold since 1960. Foreign trade is also growing steadily. The cost of its defence forces is, however, a serious drain on its economy. It maintains an army of nearly 600 000 men, and a moderately strong air force. These forces are relatively well trained and well equipped, but in terms of the security that they provide it is doubtful whether their cost is justified. If this money were available for internal development it is possible that the country's domestic difficulties might be more easily overcome.

The political situation is confused and uncertain. The Westminster type of government inherited from the British at the time of independence failed from the outset to meet the country's needs. President Bhutto won an election in 1977 by means that are widely regarded as fraudulent although probably he could in any case have gained a majority. He was a choleric and suspicious man and did not have the temperament to heal the divisions in his country or become the trusted leader it needs. The racial and cultural origins of the people are diverse—Pathan, Punjabi, Sindi, Baluchi, Persian and Turkish—but ninety-eight per cent are Moslem and there is not the same rancour between the communities as in India. The stage seems to be set for the emergence of a strong national leader, but if one exists he remains for the present in the wings. Bhutto was dismissed from office by a military coup led by General Zia-ul Haq, and imprisoned. But the coup leaders show no more signs than their military predecessors—Ayub Khan and Yahya Khan—of being capable of bringing about a reconciliation within Pakistan.

In spite of its political problems Pakistan is well favoured compared with Bangladesh—the State formed from East Pakistan after the 1971 India–Pakistan war. Bangladesh's strategic situation is hopeless. Except for a short border with Burma it is surrounded by India. There are no natural boundaries separating its territory from India and it is much too poor to be able to maintain the kind of defence forces it would need to make itself secure. Its present forces are vestigial and are likely to remain so.

The poverty of Bangladesh is, ironically enough, due to the richness of its soil. Its territory is made up of the great deltas of the Ganges and Brahmaputra rivers and the fertility of the land favoured a high population growth. In the time of the Moguls the area was one of the richest in India and was still rich at the heyday of British rule. Sheer numbers ultimately overwhelmed the resources of the area. There are at present seventy-five million people crowded into an area about twice the size of Tasmania. The situation has been made worse in recent years by a succession of natural disasters caused by floods and gales in the northern corner of the Bay of Bengal. Malnutrition is endemic and the average life expectancy is among the lowest in the world. Jute, of which Bangladesh produces half the world's quota, is practically its only source of external income and its economy is therefore at the mercy of the wide swings that occur in the price of this fibre. The country customarily has an enormous balance of payments deficit and is heavily dependent on foreign aid and credits. Since its separation from West Pakistan it has not succeeded in establishing a stable system of government, and until this is done it is unlikely that there will be any real improvement in the economic and social state of the country. In any event it will continue for decades to be dependent on outside help, with all the opportunities that this will provide for external interference.

Burma is another country whose weakness might have critical importance for the stability of the eastern Indian Ocean. For fifteen years it has stagnated under a military régime headed by General Ne Win. Little has been done to develop the potential agricultural wealth of the Irrawaddy delta, mining has been neglected and industry is minimal. During the time of British rule intense hostility developed between the Burmans of the delta and the upland tribes —the Shans, Karens and Kachins—and this persists. There are several guerrilla movements which derive their strength from these tribes and, in spite of years of effort, the government has been unable to eliminate them.

The strongest dissident group is the Burma Communist Party which, as mentioned above, has been supported since the end of World War II by the Chinese Communists. There is a great fear of the Chinese among the Burmese people and it is generally realized that little resistance could be offered to a Chinese takeover. The government is in no position to defend the extensive border with China because the frontier areas are occupied by dissident tribes. Ne Win has refused outside military help—fearing that this would involve interference in Burma's internal affairs—but Burma's own forces are not sufficient even to establish the government's authority inside the country.

Another country in the Bay of Bengal which might become increasingly subject to Chinese influence is Sri Lanka (formerly Ceylon). Its economy is still heavily dependent on the export of tea, but its earnings from this source are steadily declining. Efforts to diversify the economy have met with little real success and overseas trade is stagnant. Relatively little progress has so far been made towards industrialization. The national income per head is even lower than in India. Over the years Ceylon has accepted aid from both Western and communist countries, but recently China has become the principal benefactor. Chinese influence is not entirely welcome to the Ceylonese people, but the government is in no position to reject Peking's offers of help. In some quarters, moreover, China's support is welcomed as a counterweight to India, which is still deeply distrusted. The Russians have recently sought to develop their relations with the Ceylonese, but for the present the Chinese are predominant.

In regard to Russia's wider interests in the Indian Ocean, relationships with black African countries are increasingly important. Here again the overall picture is one of internal weakness and instability.

In the north the overthrow of Emperor Haile Selassie of Ethiopia in 1975 initiated a prolonged period of disorder, during which the previously strong American presence was practically extinguished and the Russians moved in to take their place.

By the end of 1977, however, the Soviet Union appeared to be in a serious dilemma. In 1974 they had entered into a treaty of friendship with the People's Republic of Somalia, and had invested considerable resources in building up a base for use by their own forces at Berbera, a strategically important harbour in Somali territory outside the southern entrance to the Red Sea. But the Somali government was giving military backing to the Somali rebels in the Ogaden province of Ethiopia, and for a while it seemed that the Russians were helping opposing sides in the same war. Naturally enough this was resented by the Somali government and in November 1977 it expelled the Russians and refused access by their forces to Berbera.

No doubt the Russians had foreseen this reaction and they quickly transferred their operations to Aden, on the opposite side of the entrance to the Red Sea. This port is in the territory of South Yemen (which is a 'People's Republic' firmly under the influence of the Soviet Union). The Russians also foresaw that domination of Ethiopia would be a more important strategic prize than control of Somalia; and in any case that in the end the Somalis would have no alternative but to accept their return.

After expelling the Russians in 1977 the Somalis appealed to the United Sates for military help. This was refused. President Carter's only response was to call for the withdrawal of Soviet and Cuban military forces from Ethiopia 'as soon as the Ethiopian forces had re-established control over their own territory'. He said that the United States would not give defensive military assistance or economic aid unless Somalia gave a clear commitment to respect the boundaries both of Ethiopia and of Kenya (which also has a large Somali minority).

With the help of about 1000 Soviet advisers and 10 000 Cuban troops the Ethiopians were able to put down the rebellion in Ogaden, and in March the Somali government withdrew its own forces from Ethiopian territory. The Ethiopian government, no doubt inspired to do so by the Russians, undertook that its forces would not invade Somalia. Within a few months of having expelled the Russians from their country the Somalis were therefore in the position of being beholden to the Soviet Union for preventing an invasion of their own territory.

A continuing embarrassment for the Russians has been the revolt in Eritrea against Ethiopian rule. This revolt has been going on for several years and in the past has received assistance from the Cubans. The territory includes the port of Massawa, which lies inside the Red Sea and which the Russians would no doubt like to control. Somalia had few friends in Africa in its quarrel with Ethiopia but Eritrea has wide support, especially among the Arab countries. It will not therefore be as easy politically for the Russians and Cubans to help the Ethiopians to re-impose their rule. In fact the Cubans announced that they would not intervene militarily in Eritrea. Since it now has a firm strategic grip on the Horn of Africa the Soviet Union can, however, be expected to bring about a settlement which will suit its own interests.

South of the Horn of Africa is the Republic of Kenya which was for a time regarded as one of the stable countries in Africa. The founding leader, Jomo Kenyatta, is now over eighty, however, and there are signs that after he passes from the scene there will be a revival of tribal and religious friction in the country. The Russians are undoubtedly watching the situation closely and will be quick to take advantage of any opportunities that arise to extend their influence.

The country in east Africa offering some present prospect for stability is Tanzania. It is a one-party State under President Julius Nyerere, who has governed with skill and firmness since 1964. He has accepted aid from both Western and communist powers but has so far been able to maintain a policy of resolute non-alignment. The country is, however, poor in resources and the high rate of population growth threatens to overwhelm the government's developmental efforts. Small defence forces are being built up, but their main purpose appears to be to defend the country against neighbouring Uganda, whose policies under Idi Amin became increasingly eccentric in 1976–77. Tanzania is one of the African countries which accepted substantial Chinese help—for the construction of the Tanzam railway between Tanzania and Zambia. Its economic dependence upon the Soviet Union has, however, progressively increased since 1976, and with the steady growth of Russian influence in neighbouring States its ability to maintain an effectively non-aligned posture will be under strain.

Mozambique, the southernmost country on the eastern seaboard of Africa, is passing steadily into the Russian orbit. During the visit to the country by President Podgorny in April 1977 a treaty of friendship was signed which has led to close military co-operation between the two countries. This has included the provision of arms for the guerrillas fighting in Rhodesia.

Mozambique has always been important in relation to Rhodesia, whose access to the sea is through the ports of Lourenço Marques and Beira. During Portuguese rule, which ended in 1975, the supplies which were able to reach Rhodesia through these ports

partly nullified the sanctions imposed on that territory by the United
Nations Security Council. In 1977 Mozambique applied a blockade
on supplies to Rhodesia, and in compensation for the economic loss
thereby suffered it has received substantial subventions from the
oil-rich states and from the Soviet Union. Largely because of its
traditional entrepot trade Mozambique was one of the more
prosperous countries in Africa. The decline of this trade, however,
is likely to increase its dependence on the Soviet Union, to whom
it is likely to prove a strategically valuable ally.

The importance of South Africa in regard to the Indian Ocean
was formerly very considerable, especially in relation to the British
possessions east of Suez. The naval base at Simonstown was
originally developed for use by the British navy, but in 1955 the
British government transferred the base to the South African
government. It is not likely to have great strategic value for any
other power, and its importance has been further diminished by
the reopening of the Suez Canal.

South Africa is not itself likely to play an active role in the Indian
Ocean. It is becoming increasingly embattled in its struggle with
black Africa. In its own territory the white South Africans are
outnumbered five times by blacks and they face the hostility in the
rest of Africa of 300 million. Their armed forces are at present
surprisingly small—they have an army of only about 50 000 men
and small naval and air forces; but it seems probable that increasing
resources will have to be expended on maintaining both internal
and external security. Although their economy is at present strong
their future prospects cannot be regarded with optimism.

The conflict between whites and blacks in Africa is increasingly
serving the interests of the Soviet Union. With their collaborators
the Cubans they have become accepted as the principal supporters
of the African groups who are trying to rid Africa of white rule
and economic domination. In this role they have greatly out-
distanced the Chinese, especially since the latter backed the losing
side in the civil war in Angola. The Chinese can still be a nuisance
to the Russians in Africa but they are no longer serious competitors.
The treaties of friendship and co-operation which the Soviet Union
has signed with Angola and Mozambique will give it many
opportunities for powerfully extending its political, economic and
military influence throughout the continent. It is, moreover, evident
that the Western powers are decreasingly willing, with the possible
exception of France, to maintain the effort necessary to counter
Russian influence.

A rearguard action against the spread of Russian influence in

Africa was nevertheless conducted in the Central African Republic of Zaire. In early 1977 a rebellion broke out in the mineral-rich southern province of Shaba (formerly Katanga) which was clearly supported, if not inspired by, the Russians and Cubans operating from neighbouring Angolan territory. The government of Zaire, under President Mobutu, received speedy supplies of arms and material from France and the United States. Moroccan troops were transported by the French air force to stiffen local forces, and American arms and equipment were also flown in. The rebellion was suppressed but it flared up again in 1978 with the loss of many European lives. Because of its influence in Angola Russia is in a position, through its Angolan and Cuban proxies, to stir up local strife whenever the opportunity again offers.

The only European country to maintain an effective continuing presence in the general region of Africa and the Indian Ocean is France. Ships of the French navy are always on station in the region, visiting on a fairly regular basis former French territories and existing colonies.

The largest of these territories is the Indian Ocean island of Madagascar, which became the Republic of Malagasy on securing its independence in 1958. The French continued to have rights of access to the excellent harbour at Diégo–Suarez but in 1976 the Malagasy government gave notice of termination of this arrangement. The French nevertheless maintain a strong influence. The Malagasy economy is mainly agricultural and remains closely tied to France. Its eight million population is made up of an extraordinary ethnic variety—French, Portuguese, Chinese, Indians and about twenty Malagasy ethnic groups. There has recently been considerable political turbulence and this seems likely to grow.

To the north-east of Malagasy lies the Comoro Archipelago. This was formerly a French colony but three of its four islands have opted for independence. The fourth, Mayotte, wishes to remain part of the French community, and there are plans to develop a naval base on the island to offset the loss to the French navy of Diégo–Suarez.

One of the oldest French colonies in the region is the island of Réunion, which has belonged to France continuously since 1642. It lies about 700 kilometres east of Madagascar. Since the war it has had the status of an overseas department of France. It has become over-populated, however, and its vulnerable economy is heavily dependent on sugar. The local communist party is strong and active, and is well disposed to the Soviet Union.

The territory of greatest strategic importance in the region to the French is perhaps the tiny territory of the Afars and the Issas (formerly known as French Somaliland). It consists of only 23 000 square kilometres, with a population of less than 200 000. It is situated on the western side of the southern entrance to the Red Sea and contains the important harbour of Djibouti. Since the reopening of the Suez Canal this has become a significant rival to Aden as a bunkering port for traffic through the canal and the Red Sea. It is the main headquarters for the French navy in the Indian Ocean region. In 1977 it received its formal independence (as the Republic of Djibouti) but France will undoubtedly do its best to maintain its influence in the territory and access for the French navy to the port of Djibouti (although whether this will be possible in the face of pressure from Soviet-dominated Ethiopia is perhaps open to question).

Since the time of de Gaulle French governments have given considerable public emphasis to their ability to maintain good relations with the Soviet Union and have seen themselves as setting an example in this regard to the rest of the world. In view of their own need to maintain good relations with Arab countries—because of their dependence on the oil of the Middle East—they have been careful not to put themselves in opposition to Soviet policies in these countries. It is, therefore, ironical that in black Africa and the Indian Ocean France is now increasingly in the position of being the only European country offering resistance to the spread of Russian influence. It does this not only by deploying naval forces but by encouraging and helping the former French and Belgian territories in Africa to resist communist and Russian influence. Its support of Zaire in 1977–78 was a case in point, an additional motive being that the minerals of this province are important for the French economy.

Unlike the French, the British have virtually given up the attempt to maintain any direct influence in the region; and the spread of Russian power has been facilitated by the ease with which the Soviet Union has been able to move into positions formerly occupied by the British Empire. The scattered British possessions which remain have been combined into what is now called the Indian Ocean Territory, but these islands now seldom see a British warship. The only island of continuing strategic importance is Diego Garcia, the site of the American base (mentioned above).

Within the region the country which is offering the most strenuous resistance to the spread of Russian influence is Saudi Arabia. It is using its oil revenues to give economic support to all the Arab and near-Arab world. In places like Somalia and the Yemen it does so in direct competition with the Russians and it apparently hopes that it will ultimately be able to draw them out of the Soviet orbit. But Saudi Arabia's own vulnerability imposes sharp limits on its influence. If it appeared that Russian interests were being seriously threatened the Soviet navy would no doubt make its presence felt to good effect. It could apply a partial or even a total blockade on the country without having to take any direct military action against Saudi territory.

Although it is now generally recognized that the United States has yielded dominance in the Indian Ocean and Africa to the Soviet Union, it is assumed that any direct military action by the Russians is unlikely because it would still be countered by the United States. This assumption needs careful examination.

The key to successful United States resistance to Russian moves would be its capability to make graduated responses. In the past it had this capability, and this was why it was able to check Russian moves against Berlin in 1948 and during the Cuban crisis of 1962. This capability is now increasingly in doubt. If present trends continue America might find itself in the position that it must either stand by while the Russians undertake a local military strike, or initiate a general nuclear attack. Since it must be taken as axiomatic that the United States would not resort to nuclear war unless its own territory were directly threatened, the possibility of an unopposed Soviet strike must therefore be regarded as real.

The Russians would of course be careful never to give the Americans a clear-cut *casus belli*. Suppose, for example, that the anti-Russian activities of Saudi Arabia described above did in fact become a serious embarrassment to the Soviet Union. The first moves towards a blockade could be made by proxy—say, by South Yemen in the Gulf of Aden, concerted with Iraq in the Persian Gulf. America's first response would no doubt be to try to act similarly by proxy. It would presumably encourage Iran to counter Iraqi moves in the Persian Gulf. The Russians could, however, readily reinforce Iraq. The United States would in turn have to reinforce Iran, but to do so the Americans would have to risk a major naval confrontation. Since the Soviet Navy could be expected at this point to have strong forces in the approaches to the Persian Gulf and the Gulf of Aden the American navy would be unlikely to win the engagement.

It is possible that, given time, the Americans might eventually be able to mobilize sufficient forces in the area to outweigh the Russians. But it is already clear that they could only do so by uncovering other vulnerable areas, such as the Middle East and the north Pacific.

The strategic situation in the north Pacific will be discussed in Chapter 3, but it might be useful here to consider briefly the relationship between the Middle East conflict and the Indian Ocean.

The United States maintains a strong naval force in the Mediterranean to support the southern flank of NATO and to ensure the continued existence of Israel. The large nuclear aircraft–carriers form the backbone of this force and in tonnage the American fleet normally exceeds the Russian. There is growing concern in the United States, however, about the vulnerability of these huge carriers and doubt whether in a conflict they would be sufficient to enable the American fleet to maintain control of the eastern Mediterranean. Their continued presence is nevertheless essential to give credibility to their role in the defence of the southern NATO countries and Israel. This credibility would be weakened if they were moved to the Indian Ocean.

They are too large to use the Suez Canal. If, for example, they were deployed in the Gulf of Oman, in order to ensure access to Iran, they would be many steaming days from the Mediterranean. It would be sensible for the Russians to initiate pressure on Saudi Arabia at a time of renewed crisis in the Arab–Israeli conflict and this, of course, would make the American dilemma all the more acute. Priority would have to be given to maintaining the United States navy in the Mediterranean at full strength over any attempt to reinforce Iran. The difficulty the Americans face in maintaining control of the Mediterranean was exemplified during the Yom Kippur war in 1973. This is not the place to discuss the Arab–Israeli conflict, but it is important to remember that its strategic environment changed as a result of that war. The Soviet Union mobilized sufficient strength to challenge the control of the Mediterranean by the United States navy, and forced the Americans to make the Israelis desist from the destruction of the Egyptian forces on the west bank of the Suez Canal. The Egyptians were able to maintain military control of the canal zone and reopen the canal.

The Soviet Union might, however, face fewer risks if it initiated action farther to the east—through Afghanistan to Pakistan. It could in this case also begin by proxy: it could encourage the Afghans to seize Baluchistan—which they already claim—and this would bring them to the Arabian Sea. It is unlikely that the Americans would take major risks to help Pakistani forces retain Baluchistan. Certainly they would not go to war. But the result of an Afghan takeover of Baluchistan would be that the Russians

would have access to ports and air bases commanding the approaches to the Persian Gulf—thereby acquiring a similar position in that area to the one they already hold in the Gulf of Aden.

Let us suppose, however, that the above analysis underestimates the strength of the American response: suppose that the United States navy mobilized sufficient forces in the Gulf of Aden and the Gulf of Oman to force the Russians to yield control of the sea. The Americans would then no doubt be able to reinforce Saudi Arabia and Iran (or Pakistan as the case may be). But the strategic advantage would still be with the Soviet Union. Persia has many times in its history been invaded from the region between the Caspian Sea and the Oxus and it would not be difficult for Soviet forces to follow the same route in a full-scale invasion of Iran. Saudi Arabia could at the same time be attacked through Iraq. Afghanistan could be quickly reinforced from across its common border with Russia. The Americans would thus be faced in either contingency with a war in territory as remote from its own as Vietnam—and ultimately as unwinnable.

The capacity of the Soviet Union to gain control by a relatively minor military effort of this vital region can, therefore, scarcely be doubted. But it might be asked whether they would wish to do so, and if so why.

The answer is apparent. If in the next twenty years the Russians could regulate the flow of Middle Eastern oil to Western Europe they would have a more powerful weapon than the entire forces of the Warsaw Pact. Apart from the risks of a direct assault on the NATO countries, Soviet interests would be better served by forcing Western Europe into their economic orbit while its productive capacity was still intact, rather than acquiring a war-devastated continent. The threat of denying them the oil of the Middle East—on which they will continue to be dependent at least until the end of the century—would be sufficient to enforce the co-operation of the west-European countries. The fact that the Soviet Union is likely in the coming decade to be itself in increasing need of external oil supplies would of course be an added incentive for a Russian move into the Persian Gulf area.

The oil resources of the Middle East merely give added point to ambitions that the Russians have nourished since the time of the czars. Plans for a thrust into the region undoubtedly exist in the Soviet war ministries, as they did in imperial days. At the end of the nineteenth century British policy was much influenced by the fear that the Russians would launch an attack on northern India through the ancient invasion routes along the valley of the Oxus.

This was an important motive in their entering into an alliance with the Japanese—thereby encouraging them in their own competition with Russia. Nowadays, however, neither Britain nor Japan have sufficient military strength to impose any restraints on Russian expansion.

Current Soviet military doctrine is quite compatible with the kind of moves described above. Almost all Western commentators assume that Russia's main strategic preoccupation is with the north Atlantic, and many go so far as to suggest that provided NATO forces are maintained at sufficient strength to balance the Warsaw Pact forces the rest of the world is safe. Australian commentators, with their traditional propensity for looking for danger steadily in the wrong direction, are almost unanimous in subscribing to this view. A study of Soviet global strategy suggests that the Russians have quite different plans in mind.

Little attention is given to what the Russians themselves say about their strategy because it is assumed that they cannot be believed. The same mistake was made between the two world wars about Hitler; if closer attention had been paid to what he said and wrote the rest of Europe and the United States would have been more prepared in 1939 to counter German aggression.

It is first necessary to keep in mind that in spite of *détente* the Soviet Union still adheres to the view that while capitalism exists wars are inevitable and will continue to occur until the final destruction of 'imperialism'. This view was reaffirmed in the 1968 edition of *Soviet Military Strategy*, the authoritative work on military doctrine written by no less a person than Marshal of the Soviet Union V. D. Sokolovsky. The practical consequences of this doctrine can be readily seen: in order to ensure Russia's readiness for these inevitable wars it devotes a higher proportion of its national income to military expenditure than any other country in the world.

It might be thought that Russia's vast forces are intended for purely defensive purposes, and Soviet propaganda certainly seeks to give this impression. But it is belied by the overall structure of their forces.

It may be presumed that the *strategic* nuclear armaments are for defensive purposes. Unless a madman comes to power the Soviet Union is no more likely to initiate global nuclear war than the United States. But the expansion of Soviet military strength goes beyond what is necessary for strategic equivalence with the United States. In this respect the contrast with the United States is marked. American defence expenditure is being increasingly concentrated on maintaining technological superiority in nuclear weapons and their means of delivery, and providing for the defence of the United States itself. The resources devoted to maintaining American military strength overseas are declining. The days have passed in which America could deploy ground forces anywhere in the world and be able to protect and support them with overwhelming sea and air cover. In the case of the Russians, however, their capability to take military action beyond their own borders is steadily increasing.

Western commentators acknowledge that the strength of the Soviet armed forces is growing relative to those available to the West, but they often conclude that this is not a matter for concern. It is an article of faith that Western technology is superior to Russian and therefore that any quantitative advantage could be offset by the qualitative superiority of Western armaments. It is also assumed that the purpose of the Soviet Union in building up its military strength is to increase its political influence, and that the Russian leaders are too cautious to initiate military action.

Both these assumptions are questionable. The West has in the past had some unpleasant surprises in regard to the technological capacity of the communist countries. The rockets first developed by the Russians for space exploration were much more powerful than the Americans' and if war had broken out at that time this would have had great military importance. In the case of China, nuclear weapons were developed several years sooner than Western observers had thought possible. There may be similar surprises in the future. The overall industrial development of the communist countries may be backward, but defence technology is given the highest priority and there is no reason to believe that Soviet and Chinese scientists are less intelligent than the Americans or Europeans.

Some commentators drew comfort from what they regarded as the inefficient structure of the Soviet armed forces. They pointed to the lack of large aircraft carriers and relative inferiority in long-range bombers. It was concluded from this that the Russians would not be able to conduct major operations at any distance from their own territory because they would be unable to provide the necessary air support, and from this it was deduced that the Russians had no intention of conducting such operations.

This argument reflects a typical bias in Western thinking—that the next war will be fought under the same conditions as the last. In the last war the aircraft carrier dominated the seas and was vital in defeating Japan. But the large aircraft carriers may be going the same way as the battleships: they are enormously costly and increasingly vulnerable. The accuracy of the newest missiles means that carriers can be attacked from long distances and in a way that could overwhelm the carrier's own defences. The position could thus arise that the huge American nuclear-powered carriers of the Nimitz class could be immobilized by their own vulnerability.

It is in the development of missile forces that the greatest Russian expansion has occurred. In 1977 the Soviet navy had nearly 150 nuclear-powered submarines capable of firing nuclear and non-nuclear missiles and another 170 diesel-powered boats. It had a multitude of large and small missile-armed ships. The newest Soviet bombers are short-range aircraft compared with the American, but they are also armed with powerful missiles, and can be refuelled in the air. Aircraft carriers are being built which are only 40 000 tons (the American Nimitz class is about 96 000 tons) and they will be equipped with short-range vertical–take-off aircraft. But they will be ideal for giving air and missile support for local operations in regions distant from the Soviet Union. The Russians are concentrating on what they regard as the weapon of the future —the missile—and they are developing it in all its forms and with all possible means of delivery.

Russia's capability to transport troops and military supplies to distant places is also being steadily increased, and it must be remembered that in the ten years from 1968 to 1978 the Soviet merchant marine increased from one of the smallest to one of the largest and most modern in the world. In addition, Russia has fishing fleets that are larger than those of any other country.

If the strategic problems of the Soviet Union are looked at from a Russian point of view present trends in the development of the Russian armed forces are readily understandable. It is reasonable to assume, in spite of their propaganda to the contrary, that the Soviet leaders no longer genuinely fear that the United States or any Western country will initiate a nuclear attack on Russia. But they would like to be assured of more than this: they would like to be certain that the Americans would not attack them even if they took military action against another country. They therefore maintain, and continuously develop and improve, their ability to inflict vast nuclear destruction on the United States. But their forces are being developed beyond what is necessary to ensure maximum damage to the United States itself. They are designed also to counter any attempt American forces might make to interfere with Soviet operations elsewhere in the world.

Returning to the admittedly extreme case of a Russian invasion of Iran it may be assumed that they would first ensure that there would be no nuclear attack on the Soviet Union by making clear their readiness to make retaliatory strikes against the United States and western Europe; and they would immobilize the American aircraft carriers by shadowing them with nuclear-armed submarines. Their sea-to-air missile-firing ships would ensure that there would be no interference from long-range American bombers. They would be able to deny to the Americans any possibility of asserting sea or air control in the area, and would thus be able to pursue their local military operations with relative impunity. They could do this even if the global naval and air strength of the United States remained quantitatively greater than that of the Soviet Union— because the *denial* of the sea and air to hostile forces requires less strength than to *control* them.

Evidence that Russian thinking was turning in the direction of such possibilities was given in the 1968 edition of *Soviet Military Strategy*. Like so many official Russian writings its meaning can best be understood by holding it up, as it were, to a mirror. The second chapter of the book is devoted to the 'Military Strategy of Imperialist Countries' and in the 1968 edition extensive consideration is given to alleged Western preparations for 'limited wars', which are strongly denounced. The Americans are accused of giving increased attention to the development of conventional forces and tactical atomic weapons in order to be able to use armed force to retain their control of countries from which they draw essential resources, or which they wish to use as 'military springboards' against the socialist bloc. The warning is given that such limited wars are 'fraught with a tremendous danger of escalating into general war, especially if tactical nuclear weapons are used'.

The Russians' own interest in the means and tactics required for limited war is shown, however, by the extensive discussion in that chapter of the preparations allegedly being made by the Americans, which in fact turn out to be remarkably similar to their own. It seems clear that the accusations made against the Americans are intended, at least partly, to justify their own preparations. In the 1968 edition of *Soviet Military Strategy* it was stated that:

> The armed forces of the socialist camp must be prepared for small-scale local wars which might be unleashed by the imperialists. The experience of such wars which have repeatedly arisen during the post war period shows that they are conducted by ways and means which differ from those used in world wars. Therefore, Soviet military strategy calls for the study of means for conducting such wars in order to prevent them from developing into a world war and to bring quick victory over the enemy. (p. 188)

It can readily be seen, therefore, that if the Russians were to take military action in a third country it would be presented as being in defence against a move by the United States, or by one of its proxies. If they invaded Iran it would doubtless be argued that this was being done to counter American-inspired hostility by Iran, or perhaps more plausibly by Saudi Arabia. It would be contrary to communist doctrine for the Soviet Union to engage in aggressive war, but the grounds have been well prepared for Soviet propagandists to claim in almost any circumstances that Russia was acting in self-defence.

The global ambitions of the Soviet Union are strikingly exhibited in the writings of Admiral Sergei Gorshkov, the commander-in-chief of the Russian navy. In a series of articles published in 1972 and 1973 he explained in detail the purposes for which the new Soviet naval forces were being developed. He described the disadvantages which Russia had suffered in the past because it lacked a 'blue water' navy—that is, naval forces which could operate beyond the Baltic Sea, the Black Sea and the frozen waters of the north-west Pacific. In his final article, significantly entitled 'Some Problems in Mastering the World Ocean' he declared that the United States had created a situation in which the socialist countries were surrounded from the sea, but in which it 'did not experience a similar danger'. This situation was entirely unacceptable to the Soviet Union: it could no longer agree to the age-long domination of the seas and oceans by the traditional Western sea powers. (See *Red Star Rising at Sea*, p. 128.)

Gorshkov pointed out that in order to overcome this domination it was not necessary to copy the Western countries, but to follow 'our own national path which best corresponds to the specific tasks facing the Soviet Navy'. He gave first emphasis to nuclear-powered and missile-armed submarines. The ballistic missiles of submarines provided an assured capability of destroying the strategic targets of the enemy, and their cruise missiles were 'a most important weapon for destroying surface targets'. These permitted the delivery of powerful and accurate attacks from great ranges against the enemy's major surface ships (*op. cit.*, p. 129).

Gorshkov wrote that although the Soviet navy was based on nuclear-powered submarines 'a modern navy cannot be only an underwater navy' (*op. cit.*, p. 130). While giving priority to the development of submarine forces, numerous types of surface ships were being built which, in addition to providing support for the submarines, were 'intended to accomplish a wide range of missions both in peacetime and in war'. He added:

It is the Navy which is . . . capable in peacetime of visibly demonstrating to the peoples of friendly and hostile countries not only the power of military equipment and the perfection of naval ships, embodying the technical and economic might of the State, but also *its readiness to use this force in defence of state interests of our nation or for the security of the Socialist countries.* (my emphasis) (*op. cit.*, p. 131)

He echoes the accusation in *Soviet Military Strategy* that the waging of local wars remains an invariable part of 'imperialist' policy, and says that this factor is particularly important in regard to the navy's mission. He continues, 'The constant upgrading of its readiness for immediate combat operations . . . is a most important precondition determining the development of the navy'.

As early as 1968 Gorshkov had declared that: 'The flag of the Soviet Navy flies over the oceans of the world. Sooner or later the United States will understand that it no longer has mastery of the sea.' The implications of the growth in Soviet naval power do not receive much attention in Australia; but it is clear that the Americans are increasingly coming to understand them. The energy policy which President Carter announced at the beginning of his term of office has not yet been implemented, but there is no doubt about the seriousness of the need for such a policy. The programme laid down by Carter was intended to eliminate American dependence upon the oil of the Middle East, or upon any sources of energy outside direct American territorial control. He declared that unless this were done the Americans 'would endanger their freedom as a nation'. He sought to ensure that the United States would not be drawn into military action overseas in order to secure energy supplies for its own needs. The consciousness of the dangerous vulnerability of the whole Middle East region to Russian pressure was clearly the main inspiration of the Carter policy.

It was suggested above that an attack against Pakistan might provoke a diversionary Chinese thrust into eastern India and to the Bay of Bengal. It is conceivable that the possibility of a Russian move in the Red Sea–Persian Gulf region might lead to the same reaction. That the Chinese dislike the spread of Russian power in the western Indian Ocean is shown by the support they give to anti-Russian elements in their daily propaganda—even to such unlikely bedfellows as President Mobutu of Zaire. Such a Chinese move might not serve to stop the Russians in the west, but it would put the Chinese in a stronger position to resist their expansion towards the eastern side of the Indian Ocean region.

What might be the consequences of these developments for Australia?

The appearance of the Chinese on the Bay of Bengal would not have much immediate impact on Australia although the long-term effect, in increasing Chinese influence over south-east Asia, would be great, and this will be discussed in the following chapter. The repercussions of Russian control of the Persian Gulf might, however, be severe. Australia draws a substantial percentage of its oil requirements from that area and the failure of successive governments to devise a sensible energy policy means that this dependence is likely to continue, at least for some years. Even more damaging than interference with the flow of oil could be the effect on our trade with western Europe. This still constitutes a valuable part of our total trade and if Europe were deprived of the oil of the Persian Gulf, or forced drastically to re-orient their economies towards the Soviet bloc by the threat of such deprivation, an abrupt contraction might occur in this trade.

There is, of course, nothing Australia itself could do to prevent such developments. Our only hope would be to ameliorate as much as possible the adverse consequences for ourselves. How best could we do this?

Clearly our only sensible policy would be non-intervention in any military conflicts in the Indian Ocean. We should join no more lost causes. There need be no reason for Russia or China to strike directly against our interests, and if we dealt skilfully with them we might be able to lessen the indirect damage. We might, for example, be able to secure Russian co-operation in allowing our trade with Europe to continue, especially since this might be as useful to a Soviet-controlled Western European economy as it is to the present European community. The Chinese would have nothing to gain from interfering with our trading activities, such as they are, in the Bay of Bengal. Nor is there any reason why they would wish to prevent the continuance of normal relations with Burma and Bangladesh—provided, of course, that we made it clear that we were not hostile to their interests in those countries.

Neither Russia nor China would gain from blocking for any length of time the ebb and flow of trade through the Indian Ocean, and if we were sufficiently alert and flexible there might be prospects of profitable dealings with the new Soviet Empire on the Arabian Sea. We would gain nothing by an attitude of hostility, whereas a policy of careful neutrality might earn useful dividends.

A country which might find itself in a much worse dilemma than ourselves is India. In a conflict between Russia and China it would have no prospect of remaining neutral. The price that it would have to pay for its present dependence on Russia would certainly include military resistance to the Chinese—which would, of course, increase India's military dependence on Soviet supplies. The Indians would be required to fight for the Russians by proxy in the same way as the Cubans. They would have no option but to allow the Soviet navy to use any ports that it needed and perhaps even to accept Cuban and Russian 'volunteer' forces.

Nehru told the Indian people that if they could not stay out of a future war they should be sure to join the winning side. If the Indians were wise they would follow this precept without procrastination. They might thereby gain some of their own objectives —such as the reabsorption of Pakistan and Kashmir—and even be allowed a degree of internal autonomy. This latter would be all the more likely in that the Russians would gain nothing from accepting any responsibility for solving India's internal problems. But their dream of leading an independent and non-aligned Indian Ocean community would be gone for ever.

An area which may ultimately have even greater strategic importance than the Red Sea and the Arabian Gulf is that of the Indonesian and Malaysian islands and the straits lying between the Indian and Pacific oceans. The resources of the region are potentially far greater than the Middle East and it may well become the focal area of competition between Russia and China. This possibility will be discussed in succeeding chapters.

2

The Problem of India

It is thirty years since India gained its independence from the British but none of its basic problems have been solved. The standard of life of many of the people is below that of farm animals in other countries. It has developed an industrial sector based on the most advanced technology but this has benefited only a tiny proportion of the population. Social antagonisms going back three thousand years still persist, and religious and regional differences which have developed during the country's long and turbulent history are unreconciled.

India has one of the most conservative societies known to history. The caste system which still governs most aspects of Hindu life was introduced by the Aryans who came to India 1500 years B.C. The worship of the cow goes back to the same period. The two great Indian epics—the Mahabharata and the Ramayana—deal with Aryan life in the period 1000 years before Christ and the powerful influence that these still have over the religious and cultural life of the people is evident on all sides.

Caste is not unique to the Indian people but in no other society has it persisted in such an elaborate form over such a long period. In origin it was based on racial prejudice—from which mankind seems never to have been free. The Aryans appear first to have developed it to preserve themselves from intermixture with the peoples of the country which they had invaded. In Sanskrit (which was the language of the Aryans) the word for caste means colour, which suggests that the indigenous people of India were regarded as inferior because they were darker in complexion than the Aryans. From this basis an elaborate system of social distinctions was developed. The Brahmins, or priests, came to be the superior caste, then followed the kshatriyas, or warriors, the vaishyas, or peasant cultivators, and the shudras, who were regarded as menials. A further category later emerged of outcastes who were looked down upon by all the others and whose mere approach was (and in some communities still is) regarded as polluting.

Several attempts have been made throughout the historical period in India to get rid of the caste system but all have so far failed. The first important attempt was made by Buddha over 500 years before Christ. He rejected the whole concept of caste and this understandably enabled him to win many millions of adherents from the lower groups. The great age of Buddhism was inaugurated in 260 B.C., when the Emperor Ashoka was converted to the faith, and for a time it seemed as though this egalitarian doctrine would be established not only in India but throughout Asia. It had a powerful influence even over Greek thought and culture. The upper Hindu castes, however, clung to their own religion during the period of the Ashoka empire—understandably since this was the basis of their claim to superiority—and over the centuries gradually re-established their religious and political pre-eminence. From the fifth century A.D. Buddhism began to decline, and by the time Marco Polo visited India it had practically disappeared from the country of its origin.

Meanwhile, however, the caste system had come under pressure from another egalitarian religion. In the year 1000 A.D. the first of the invaders from Afghanistan arrived—Mahmud of Ghazni—and he spread the Moslem religion by force into northern India. He was succeeded by other Moslem invaders and by the thirteenth century the Sultanate of Delhi dominated most of northern India. The governing group was made up mostly of Afghans, Turks, Persians and Arabs. But the Hindu upper castes were not greatly affected by the religion of the conquerors and retained their privileged social position. The ruling group of Moslems were themselves highly class-conscious, and this led them to respect the claims of the upper caste Hindus (as the British did centuries later). Nevertheless Islamic sects developed which appealed directly to the masses and they turned to the new religion, as they had formerly to Buddhism, to escape from their inferior status. Out of this ferment came such groups as the Sikhs, who called for the abolition not only of castes but of distinctions between Moslem and Hindu.

Eventually about one-quarter of the people of the sub-continent became converted to Islam or to the egalitarian sects.

The social predominance of the Brahmin caste has nevertheless continued in India until the present day. One of the unfortunate consequences of the separation from India of the Moslem States of Pakistan and Bangladesh is that the egalitarian influence of Islam has been substantially removed from Indian society. Eighty-two per cent of the population are Hindu. The Moslems remaining in India, and the adherents of other minority religions, do not attempt to challenge the social superiority of the Brahmins. Almost all the important leaders of modern India have been from the higher castes. Mahatma Gandhi, Jawarharlal Nehru and their followers denounced caste distinctions but they have remained substantially unshaken. Westernized Indians might sometimes appear to disregard them but they still powerfully affect the lives of the vast majority of the people.

It was hoped by many that the coming of Western-style democracy to India would bring greater social equality. But democracy has failed to solve any of the country's other problems and there is no likelihood that it will lead to the abolition of castes. The constitution purportedly abolished caste discrimination and untouchability but their continuing existence is everywhere apparent.

The gulf between the ruling classes and the masses thus remains India's basic problem. Officially literacy is claimed to be about thirty per cent but among the inferior castes it is much lower. India has many educational institutions serving the commercial and ruling classes but primary education for the masses has been neglected. The constitution provides for universal adult suffrage but secular political ideas have barely touched the minds of the ordinary people. They react to their rulers in the same way as they have in the past—according to their religious beliefs and their physical necessities.

The career of Mahatma Gandhi illustrated this. His international fame is based on the contribution he made to the political objective of ridding India of British rule, but his hold over the masses rested on a religious appeal. He genuinely believed that the liberation from the British would mean little without the moral and religious regeneration of the people. He was a religious reformer in the Bhakti tradition, which had produced a succession of reforming sects in India over the previous 500 years. He preached a gospel of universal brotherhood, non-violence and poverty. His strongest appeal was to the outcastes, whom he called 'the sons of God' (harijans). Although he sought to improve the standard of life of the masses he rejected the materialist pursuit of wealth. He refused to accept that progress lay only in industrialization and urbanization and tried to revive the village as the true centre of Indian social, religious and economic activity. He believed that progress lay not in destroying the enemy, whether foreign or internal, but by converting him by moral example and persuasion.

The irony is that he succeeded with the foreign enemy but failed with the internal. His assassination by an orthodox Brahmin symbolized the betrayal of his ideas by his own people.

The degradation of Indian villages has continued; the modern rulers of India have concentrated their efforts on expanding industralization as the best means of progress—thereby creating urban slums of horrific size. After a series of famines increased attention was eventually given to agriculture and as a result of the introduction of new crop varieties productivity has in some areas increased. But food production is still far below real needs.

In 1977 the government was embarrassed by surpluses of grain which could not be properly stored. The extraordinary phenomenon appeared of India offering grain to other countries—while millions of its own people remained at starvation level. More food was lost through infestation in storage than the entire annual production of Australia—about eighteen per cent of India's own production. The country which in 1976 produced an atomic explosive device could not provide efficient means of storing the country's food supplies. In spite of the relatively favourable conditions of 1977–78 the basic ills remained: backward agriculture, over-population, social and religious blocks to the efficient use of land and animals, and lack of capital for rural development. In several areas famine is a continuing threat. Although the wealth of the commercial and governing classes exceeds that in many Western countries the national annual income per head is only US$150.

India today presents a picture which in almost all respects is the opposite of the Ghandian ideal. It still awaits the social revolution without which it seems impossible for its basic problems to be solved.

Does it seem likely that such a revolution might soon occur? Is a peasant-based revolution—which would seem to offer the people of India their best hope for relief from their sufferings—now possible? Unfortunately, no; or not without outside help. The repressive power of the Hindu upper classes is enormous; and the ancient divisions among the people make it unlikely that a mass movement could be organized in the way that Mao Tse-tung was able to organize the people of China. The materialist philosophy of communism has made little impact on the Hindu masses (except for the untouchables); and other Western political philosophies—such as social democracy—have become a pastime of the privileged classes.

The futility of internal revolutionary movements is exemplified by that led by Jayaprakash Narayan. J.P. (as he is known) was a follower of Gandhi and a close associate of Nehru and led a movement which was based on Gandhian ideals of morality, welfare and non-violence. He called for a 'total revolution' of Indian society and accumulated a considerable following among the lower Hindu castes. Originally a supporter of Indira Gandhi, he turned against her because of her authoritarian methods. He was arrested towards the end of her reign but his movement undoubtedly played an important part in her defeat in the 1977 elections. He was released by the new government but owing to illness has since been unable to play an active political role. He appeals from time to time to the conscience of the Janata government in its dealings with the Naxalite rebels in West Bengal and for better treatment generally for the untouchables, but his interventions have little practical effect. Since he is himself an upper caste Hindu and the leadership of the movement is dominated by members of the higher castes, it has never won wide support among the untouchable communities.

The man with the largest mass following in India is Jagjivan Ram, the present leader of the untouchables, who are today estimated to number between 80 and 120 million people out of a population of 600 million. He is not, however, a revolutionary. He accepts the principle of non-violence and in any case he could never hope to extend his appeal beyond his own community.

B. R. Ambedkar, the leader of the outcastes at the time of independence, believed in the possibility of reconciliation between the castes and gave his full support to the Congress Party and to Nehru. But at the end of his life he became deeply disillusioned with the corrupt politics of the party and retired to a Buddhist monastery. Jagjivan Ram succeeded him and for some years continued co-operation with Congress. He broke away shortly before the 1977 election, and has joined the present government coalition. The relationship is, however, uneasy. The Home Minister in the Janata government, Charan Singh, is a Sikh and has a reputation for hostility towards the untouchables. He has been accused of condoning violence towards them. The Prime Minister, Morarji Desai, is regarded as a deeply religious man of the highest moral standards. He frequently calls for humane treatment of the untouchables. But he has the upper caste Hindu's unshakeable conviction that the lot of the untouchables is ordained by God, and that there is little therefore that man can do about it. Since this conviction is shared by the vast majority of his countrymen—including, let it be said, many of the untouchables—the prospect of a radical improvement in the plight of this vast community seems as remote as ever.

For the present most of the untouchables keep to the path of non-violence. But in Bihar and West Bengal an extreme group—the Naxalites—have been steadily increasing in strength. They claim a Marxist-Leninist ideology and are pledged to redress the wrongs of the untouchables by force. Their appeal is based on a promise of revenge against the upper castes for the misery and subjection in which the untouchables live. Disorder instigated by the Naxalites in Bihar and West Bengal is now endemic and it is increasingly spreading to other parts of India.

It might have been thought that the untouchables could have made common cause with the Moslems in India, who are the next most important minority (numbering over 60 million) and who are, from the Hindu point of view, also outcastes. They are, however, better off economically than the untouchables, and they are unlikely to endanger their own interests by supporting rebellion.

The other main sects who, like the Moslems, are in principle egalitarian, are the Sikhs and the Christians. But they also have relatively privileged positions and would be reluctant to engage in any struggle other than to safeguard those positions.

In short, Indian society has not so far succeeded in adapting to the modern world. Western ideas and methods have not solved the country's problems and the hope that they will do so has all but disappeared.

The explanation for this failure may be that such ideas have never been adequately adapted to Indian needs. The contrast in this respect with Japan and China is marked and instructive. Both these countries have successfully drawn upon Western philosophies and science to modernize their political and economic structures; but they have done so on a foundation of strong national and social traditions. This has given them sufficient confidence (although less in the case of China than of Japan) to take what was required from the West without suffering a loss of national integrity and morale. Because of the lack in India of this self-confidence the assimilation of Western ideas and methods has been both less efficient in its results and more damaging to the social and political fabric of the country. An unbridgeable gulf has developed between the industrialized and partly Westernized cities and the still primitive countryside. Gandhi's hope for a revival of the traditional crafts and industries of Indian villages has not been realized and efforts to introduce from the West simple forms of mechanization and improved methods of cultivation have made only modest impact.

The reason why Gandhi's concepts have failed lies possibly in the fact that they were themselves an uneasy blend of East and West. The attempt he and his followers and successors made to purify Indian society in the light of ethical standards learnt in the West in the end undermined Indian self-respect.

Gandhi's own career was marked by a fundamental ambiguity: he won a mass following by adopting the guise of a religious leader but, unlike such leaders in the past, he did not establish a new sect. His influence, therefore, faded quickly after his death, and the moral regeneration which he sought to bring about is as remote as ever. It has often been said that his moral influence was compromised by his purely political objectives, many of which he succeeded in achieving; but this need not have been so: most successful religious leaders in history have exhibited great political skill. His failure seems rather to have been due to the fact that both his religion and his politics were in the last resort inappropriate to India's needs.

Paradoxically Gandhi's moral influence was greater in the West than in his own country. The British hastened their withdrawal from India because he persuaded many of them that it was morally wrong to remain. Gandhian ideals are being increasingly offered as the remedy for the terrorism which has become such an affliction throughout the world. But in India itself they have had little effect in loosening the grip of superstition and corruption in which the country is still held.

Nehru's failure, although he never sought to be a religious leader, was of a similar kind. He was educated as an English gentleman and since, under the British Raj, this had become the ideal of the Indian aristocratic classes he was very acceptable to them. He was a consummate politician and an intelligent and articulate man; but in India, he was, as V.S. Naipaul has said, 'a displaced person'. India's problems could not be solved by ameliorist philosophies developed in the nineteenth century by the English upper classes. He manipulated with great deftness the Westminster style of government which was installed in India at the time of independence; but it was a shadow-play. By the time of his death its failure to solve India's problems was already apparent. His foreign policy, which had won him great international acclaim, was also in disrepute.

Mahatma Gandhi, Nehru, and Nehru's daughter, Indira Gandhi, dominated the politics of India for nearly half a century: between them they demonstrated that India cannot be saved by foreign ideas and methods.

Towards the end of Indira Gandhi's reign a new Raj began to emerge which had many of the characteristics of the Mogul empire: government was increasingly concentrated in the hands of a ruling élite whose decisions and actions were only notionally responsive to the popular will. This process appeared to receive a setback at the 1977 elections, when Indira Gandhi and the Congress Party were voted out of office. But the Janata government led by Morarji Desai was itself dominated by a strong coalition of conservative forces. When the euphoria of its first few months evaporated it became clear that the new government had no new remedies to offer for India's ills. It seems inevitable, whether or not Indira Gandhi returns to power, that the trend will continue towards an authoritarian régime based on the models of the past.

The empires of India's historical period were all governed on the principle of divide and rule. Under the Moguls the informer was an essential instrument of government and he remained so under the British. The role of the agent was to detect dissidence in its early stages, so that it could be isolated and quelled with a minimum of effort. Since few such movements were able to attract wide support their suppression was usually easy. These empires ultimately collapsed, not because of popular uprising, but because of a loss of will on the part of the rulers themselves.

Under Indira Gandhi Indian gaols were full of people who were there because the agents of the central government had reported them to be trouble-makers. It is easy to be censorious about her methods but faced as she was with growing resistance—for example, in the vital area of birth control—she had little alternative but to resort to repressive methods. Years of persuasion and propaganda had made little impact on the rigid social attitudes of the masses and it is understandable that she felt justified in taking positive action to save future generations from starvation. In the event Indira Gandhi decided—either because of miscalculation or loss of will— to put her government to the hazard of an election, and she was defeated. Coercion in this instance therefore failed; nevertheless firm action to reduce the birth-rate must be taken if there is to be any prospect of avoiding recurrent famine, or of raising the standards of living of the Indian masses above the present primitive level.

A contributory factor in depressing the standards of life of the Indian people is the high level of defence expenditure and the unproductive investment in developing nuclear explosives—undertaken because of the ambition of the ruling group to make India the leading power in the Indian Ocean region. The armed forces total over one million men and the recurring cost of equipping them with modern arms absorbs a large proportion of the central government's annual budget.

When the Indians first exploded a nuclear device the government claimed that it was for peaceful purposes only, but no one outside India took this seriously. No safe use for nuclear explosives for developmental purposes has yet been found, and the crowded Indian sub-continent seems to be one of the least likely regions in the world where their use would be feasible. It is clear that the device was exploded to let the world know that India was capable, if it wished, of acquiring nuclear armaments. The protestations of Indira Gandhi and her successors that India would not develop nuclear weapons have not, nor have been intended, to diminish this impression.

Objectively seen, the development by India of a nuclear explosive was unwise, even in the country's own interests. It has undoubtedly encouraged other countries to prepare, openly or secretly, to acquire a similar capability. India's aspirations to be the leader of the region have not been promoted—they have been undermined. Its moral authority, by which some of its modern leaders have set great store, has been greatly diminished by the patent insincerity of its protestations concerning its nuclear experiments. In the past it was possible to envisage a non-aligned and non-nuclear community of nations with India at its head; the greater likelihood now is a defensive grouping of other countries against India. None of its neighbours would trust a country actually or potentially armed with nuclear weapons.

As far as India's own security is concerned the gains are illusory. In spite of its advanced technology it cannot afford a credible nuclear capability. No country could risk using nuclear weapons unless it had the means to deter a retaliatory attack against itself. This would require a counter-strike capability not only against the immediate enemy but against the nuclear superpowers—any of whom might otherwise intervene. The delivery systems which India would need are vastly more costly—at any rate at the present stage of technology—than the nuclear explosives themselves. Without such systems India's nuclear capability could be eliminated by a major nuclear power without cost to itself.

In addition to increasing India's strategic isolation, her large expenditures on nuclear developments have added to India's economic difficulties and increased its dependence on others. If it were to exert real leadership in the region it needed first to remedy its own economic weaknesses. There is now little prospect of its being able to do this.

In the past India has been able to survive its recurrent economic crises because of aid from the United States and other Western countries. In recent years, however, it has become increasingly dependent on the Soviet Union, which will in future have an important influence on India's economic well-being. A treaty for economic co-operation was first signed in 1955 and in the following twenty years trade between the two countries increased one hundredfold. There is extensive collaboration between the two countries in the industrial field, especially in defence-related industries. The Russians have provided substantial military aid and the Indian defence forces are now to a considerable extent dependent on Soviet equipment, especially for such vital elements as submarines, front-line aircraft and missiles.

The significance of India's relationship with the Soviet Union in contributing to the expansion of Russian power in the Indian Ocean was discussed in the previous chapter. India's standing in the non-aligned movement has also been drastically affected by this relationship.

In Nehru's day non-alignment was the cornerstone of Indian foreign policy. In 1954 he promulgated the Five Principles of Co-existence (the Panh Shila), which were based on the proposition that as many countries as possible should avoid committing themselves to either of the great power blocs. He believed that this would help to reduce the danger of another global war because the superpowers would be less likely to undertake military action if other countries insisted on maintaining their neutrality towards both of them. India played an important role in rallying to the support of this doctrine many of the countries of Asia, Africa and Latin America, and for some years held a position of undisputed leadership in the group. The war with Pakistan in 1971 led, however, to an abrupt abandonment by India of its own stated principles. It signed a treaty with the Soviet Union which was indistinguishable in its effect from ANZUS and similar treaties signed between the United States and its allies.

Under Indira Gandhi the government of India maintained that the treaty did not affect India's non-aligned status, but this was plainly untrue: article 9 states that in the event of a military attack by a third party on one of the signatories consultation would be held to 'remove the conflict'. Obviously the conflict could not be 'removed' without military means, so that this article makes the treaty at least as much a military alliance as ANZUS.

Irrespective of the terms of the treaty, the extensive defence co-operation which has developed between the two countries in recent years has placed India firmly within the strategic ambit of the Soviet Union. India could not contemplate any military action, even against its immediate neighbours, without being assured of Russian logistic backing; and it could not, of course, make any move hostile to Soviet interests without risk of military and economic disaster.

It might be thought that the close relationship between India and Russia could lead to a social revolution inspired by Soviet communism. The ironical truth is that the Indian upper classes are relying increasingly on Russian help to keep them in power. Russia's own plans in the Indian Ocean would be best served by a stable and reliable India and it has no interest in encouraging revolution; the weapons which it supplies to the Indian armed forces (and therefore to the upper castes) are perhaps the best insurance that it will not occur.

There is, however, some possibility of a Chinese type revolution in the north-eastern quarter of the sub-continent. In view of China's strategic interest in this area it would undoubtedly welcome the emergence of a peasant revolutionary movement on Maoist lines.

Their penetration of northern Burma has enabled the Chinese to aid the dissidents in Nagaland, a territory which is strategically placed between Burma and Assam. The rebel leader A. Z. Phizo, who has called for complete independence for Nagaland, refused to compromise either with Indira Gandhi or Morarji Desai. Naga guerilla fighters are being trained by the Chinese in northern Burma and in China itself. The Chinese are also helping dissidents in the other four Indian provinces lying between the Burmese border and Bangladesh—Mizoram, Manipur, Tripura and Meghalaya.

The role of the Marxist Communist Party (CPM) in this area is of special significance. It made considerable gains in key States in India during the 1970s, and in West Bengal won an absolute majority of seats. It broke away several years ago from the Moscow-oriented Communist Party of India (CPI), which collaborated closely with the Congress Party during the closing period of Indira Gandhi's reign. Officially the Marxists are neutral in the dispute between the Soviet Union and China, but they lean more towards Peking than to Moscow. It is believed that some of its leaders receive Chinese assistance. The party has won a powerful political position in the States on both sides of Bangladesh. As well as in the States on the Burmese border it has strong influence in Arunachal Pradesh (the former north-east frontier province) which has a long border with China, and in Assam; and on the west side of Bangladesh, in addition to controlling West Bengal it has gained substantial representation in Bihar, Uttar Pradesh, and as far afield as the Punjab. In most of this region it entered into governmental alliances with the Janata Party, but the relationship was inherently unstable. The CPM's programme calls, for example, for radical land reform, but if they tried to implement this it would bring them into sharp conflict with the conservative upper caste landholders, who are supporters of the Janata Party. On the other hand, if they make no positive moves to implement their pledges of reform they are likely to find that the initiative will pass into the hands of the extremist Naxalites, who have formed their own party—the Communist Party of India—Marxist Leninist (CPML). In their main stronghold—West Bengal—the CPM leaders seem determined to maintain their reforming impetus, and have proclaimed that the alternative to the Congress Party throughout India is not Janata but the CPM. But elsewhere the party is not yet strong enough to act without the co-operation of the Janata Party.

The Naxalites suffered brutal repression during the régime of Indira Gandhi, but after her defeat many were released from prison. Their attitude is clear: they call themselves Maoists and seek the violent overthrow of existing society. Their strength is increasing among the untouchable communities throughout the north-east, who constitute almost half the untouchables in all India, and they openly look to China for support.

The Chinese have always been careful to maintain friendly relations with the Himalayan kingdom of Nepal and in recent times they have actively sought to develop their influence in the country. In this case, however, they give their support to the rulers rather than to the dissident masses. They have acclaimed King Birendra's proposal for an international declaration of Nepal as a 'zone of peace', and when Teng Hsiao-ping visited the country in February 1978 he said that China was 'ready to assume appropriate commitments arising therefrom'. Help was also promised in the development of Nepal's economy. The most significant aspect of Teng's visit was, however, the interest he showed in the proposal to build a canal across the thirty-kilometre strip of territory which separates Nepal from Bangladesh. This is part of a plan to develop the enormous snow-fed water resources of Nepal and make them available to Bangladesh. This would greatly enhance the strategic importance of Nepal, and the scheme is naturally opposed by the

Indians, who also refuse to allow transit of Nepalese goods across Indian territory to Bangladesh ports. The canal scheme has the support, however, of the Americans and the British, and the Chinese will no doubt give it strong encouragement.

A chain of territory is thus open to Chinese political influence from northern Burma, through the eastern states of India, Bangladesh and Nepal and from West Bengal to the borders of Pakistan in the Pubjab. If there is indeed a possibility that the Chinese might one day seek to counter Russian influence in the Indian Ocean region, as was suggested in Chapter I, by extending their own power to the Bay of Bengal, they would have an invaluable political base in north-eastern India.

It would be rash to predict what will happen in this part of the world in the next twenty-five years, but one thing can safely be said: the fate during this time of the unfortunate people of the Indian sub-continent will not be decided by their own efforts but, as often in their history, by the outcome of the contest between empires from beyond their northern borders.

3

Russian Expansion in the Pacific

In the Indian Ocean the Soviet Union has been able to move into the vacuum left by the withdrawal of British power, and it clearly hopes that it will be able to do the same in the western Pacific as American strength declines. In doing so, however, it is faced with greater obstacles than in the Indian Ocean, and it will be some years before it can expect to have the strategic control formerly exercised by the United States.

On the face of it, American power in the western Pacific is still formidable. In bases in Japan and Okinawa there were in 1978 over 40 000 American servicemen and about 150 combat aircraft The American Seventh fleet, based principally on Subic Bay in the Philippines, normally consists of three aircraft carriers, twenty other major surface vessels and six submarines. Clark Field is still available to the American Air Force, and serves as the main base for air surveillance of the South China Sea. In Korea the American ground force of 30 000 men is being withdrawn over a five-year period but sixty fighter-bomber aircraft continue to be stationed near the dividing line between South and North Korea. The political pressure in Japan and the Philippines for the withdrawal of the American forces has diminished in recent years and if the Americans wished to do so they would probably be able to maintain for some time longer their present strength without unmanageable local opposition.

There is reason to doubt, however, whether these forces would be sufficient to maintain sea and air control of the region in the face of the growing Soviet capability to deny it. The large Soviet submarine fleet has been described on page 32. This is two and a half times larger than the American underwater fleet. In 1977 the deployment into the Pacific had begun of the Russian 'Delta' class submarine, which is equipped with a nuclear-armed missile with a range of 4500 miles (which the Americans cannot yet match). The Russians have a total of about eighty modern missile-firing surface ships, some of which are the most powerful of their class in the world. A substantial proportion of these is stationed in the Pacific.

It is the missile capability of the Soviet navy that is bringing increasingly into question the usefulness of the large United States aircraft carriers. Although heavily protected by their own means of defence and by escort vessels they may be vulnerable to attack by submarines or ships which launch their missiles from beyond the range of the carriers' aircraft. The bases from which the American forces operate, including those in Guam, Hawaii and on the west coast of the United States, are also within range of Russian sea-borne missiles. It would be reasonable to assume, therefore, that the Soviet Union may already have sufficient naval strength in the western Pacific to neutralize the American naval and air forces in any outbreak of hostilities.

It was no doubt with this situation in mind that in 1977 the Chief of U.S. Naval Operations, Admiral James L. Holloway, said that the American navy could be sure of maintaining control of the sea in the Pacific only inside a line drawn from Hawaii to Alaska. At the time this statement was discounted in America and overseas as unduly alarmist; but if the build-up of Soviet naval forces continues it might prove to have been optimistic. Much emphasis has been placed on the superiority in tonnage of the American ships in the area; it is also argued that reinforcements would be quickly available from the Third Fleet, which is based on Pearl Harbor and which includes six carriers; but it seems doubtful whether the combined power of the two fleets would now be sufficient to assert control over the western Pacific in the face of the Soviet capability for massive and flexible missile attack; and even doubtful whether the United States would have sufficient forces to ensure that the Hawaii-Alaska line was not breached.

This does not mean that in present circumstances the Russians would have unfettered freedom for offensive action. Although they may have the means for sea *denial* they do not have the kind of forces necessary for sea *control*. The Americans have in the Pacific about fifty submarines, of which two-thirds are nuclear-powered, and a substantial force of missile-firing ships. Provided that the aircraft carriers could be safely deployed, they would be able to contribute about 800 combat aircraft. Even if the Russians were able to penetrate the eastern Pacific these American forces should be sufficient to maintain effective control.

There are other navies in the Pacific of which the Soviet navy would have to take account. The Chinese have over fifty submarines and, although none is at present nuclear-powered, a number are being built. There is also a growing fleet of destroyers and missile-launching ships. Although not at present a formidable force, the Chinese navy is being steadily developed.

Because of Japan's careful avoidance of publicity regarding its Self-Defence Force, it is not generally realized that it also disposes of a significant naval force. There are well over a hundred surface vessels, of which forty-six are destroyers or similar ships, and sixteen submarines. There are no aircraft carriers, but there is a land-based bomber force of over a hundred craft, which is principally designed to interdict hostile naval operations in the approaches to Japan.

Bearing in mind the forces already deployed in the Pacific, it might be useful to illustrate the problems of 'denial' and 'control' by reference to some hypothetical possibilities.

Let us suppose that the North Koreans attack South Korea and, as in 1950, succeed initially in overwhelming the forces stationed there. The South Koreans would then need, and presumably would call for, reinforcements from the United States. In attempting to provide these the Americans would face greater difficulties than in 1951, when they had unchallenged control of the sea surrounding the Korean peninsula. If the Russians decided to prevent such reinforcements arriving they could mount a missile attack against American transport ships, aircraft and bases from submarines, missile-firing ships and, using their new 'Backfire' missile-armed bomber, from land bases in their own territory. They would also have the support of over two hundred modern combat aircraft from North Korea. If the Americans persisted in the attempt to reinforce South Korea they would need to re-establish sea and air control in the Sea of Japan, the East China Sea, and the Yellow Sea. To do this would involve a major confrontation between the bulk of American forces in the Pacific and the Soviet and North Korean missile forces, and could put at risk not only the existing American position in the western Pacific but the U.S. navy's capacity to defend the Pacific approaches to North America.

Let us suppose, however, that the tide of the Korean battle flowed

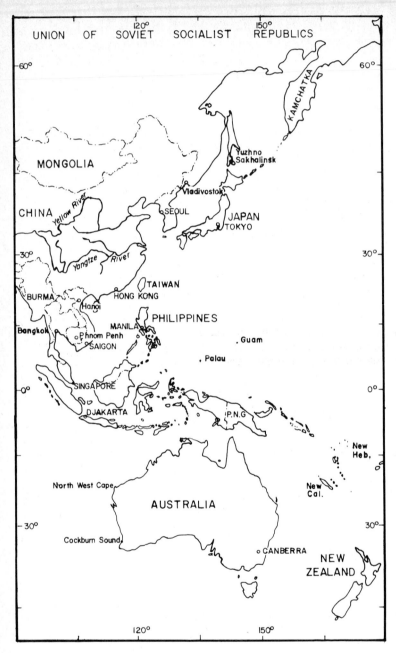

The Western Pacific region

in the opposite direction. The Russians might decide to assist Kim Il Sung. They have a short common border with Korea but to be effective reinforcements would have to be sent by sea and air. Since they do not have sufficient strength to *control* the Sea of Japan or the air above it the Russians would face strong interdiction from American submarines, attack aircraft based in South Korea and Japan, and missile-firing surface vessels. They would thus find themselves in the same dilemma as the Americans.

There are clear signs that the Russians are conscious of the weaknesses in their strategic position in the Pacific, and that they are working at several different levels to remedy them. They do not intend merely to reproduce the American forces structure. They have seen that even though the United States is vastly richer than the Soviet Union it can no longer afford, or is no longer prepared to accept, the cost of deploying naval, air and land forces on a sufficient scale to maintain global control. The Russians are likely to resort to more economical, and more traditional, methods. They are building up mobile, hard-hitting forces which would be capable of establishing local superiority in widely dispersed parts of the world. Because they will not have global control of the sea and air, however, they will need land bases of the traditional kind in locations of strategic importance. Such bases will be necessary to provide naval and air facilities to enable quick deployment of forces, and to give sufficient logistical backing to allow them to operate effectively without reinforcement from the Soviet Union once hostilities began.

Unfortunately for the Soviet Union, bases are less easily found in the Pacific than in the Indian Ocean. The Russians' increased interest in the islands of the South Pacific is doubtless related to the search for facilities in that region and it is possible that they will ultimately be able to make arrangements with one of the local governments which would provide a useful focal point for their activities. This area is too remote, however, to contribute significantly to Russia's major strategic needs. It is clear that south-east Asia is the area which is being regarded increasingly by the Russians as of prime strategic importance. Their interest in Vietnam is understandable and they are obviously ready to expend considerable resources in bringing the country into their orbit. Cam Ranh Bay, which was developed into a major sea and air base by the Americans, provides ready-made facilities for the Russians, and secure occupation of this would enable them to exert control over the South China Sea—which is of vital strategic importance to China and to the countries of south-east Asia.

In the competition for influence in Vietnam at the end of the war the Soviet Union started with some advantages. It was the communist country which had given most assistance in the form of weapons and materials, and it was able to exploit the historic Vietnamese suspicion of the Chinese. In the early days after the end of the war it provided substantial aid to the new régime and Soviet advisers and technicians were widely in evidence. At the Fourth Congress of the Vietnamese Workers' Party (renamed the Vietnam Communist Party) held in 1976 a large Russian delegation led by Mikhail Suslov (a deputy president of the Soviet Union) strengthened the impression of dominant Soviet influence. At this time there had been little movement towards reconciliation between Vietnam and the United States and it seemed that the country was moving steadily into the Russian orbit.

But the fourth party congress proved to be a turning point in Vietnamese attitudes. They adopted policies which suggested that they intended to avoid undue dependence upon the Soviet Union. In the economic field they established the basis for expanded trade with Western countries. The report adopted by the congress stated that the aim of trade was to obtain modern technology, which was needed to promote productive efficiency. Joint ventures with foreign countries were welcomed and guarantees were given against nationalization. On foreign policy the usual obeisance was made to co-operation with fraternal communist countries ('on the basis of Marxist-Leninism and proletarian internationalism') but the congress also called for the 'establishment and widening of normal relations with all countries irrespective of their social systems'. Co-operation would be 'on the basis of respect for each other's independence, sovereignty and territorial integrity, equality, mutual benefit and peaceful co-existence'. Significantly, this echoed the non-aligned language of the Yugoslavs.

The first Western country to enter into substantial relations with Vietnam was France, which had provided some aid from the time the new régime was first established. In 1977 economic relations were expanded. The Vietnamese Prime Minister visited France in April and agreements were signed providing for credits for the purchase of French goods and for technical and industrial co-operation. An agreement was also reached which was of particular importance in regard to Vietnam's links with the outside world: Air France was given landing rights in Hanoi for its services between Paris and Far Eastern capitals.

The non-communist country with whom economic relations have most rapidly expanded is Japan. In 1976 its exports to Vietnam exceeded those of France by almost eight times. The Japanese had maintained business contacts with Hanoi during the war and were in a good position to expand contacts after the north's victory. In spite of an unresolved dispute about the repayment of a loan to the former Saigon régime the Japanese have made substantial amounts of reconstruction aid available. Commercial credits have also been freely forthcoming and there is a steady inflow of Japanese capital investment. (Japan has acted quickly to establish a strong economic position not only in Vietnam but in Laos and Kampuchea, no doubt seeing the countries of Indo-China as an outlet for exports and also a valuable additional source of coal and timber and other raw materials.)

In April 1977 guidelines on foreign investment were issued by the Vietnamese which are unusually liberal compared with other socialist countries and are clearly aimed at attracting further Japanese and Western capital. High priority is given to oil exploration, and co-operation in this field is being sought with several foreign companies, including the Broken Hill Proprietary of Australia. Rich oil deposits are believed to exist in the South China Sea and Vietnam asserted its claim to exploit these by declaring a 200-mile reources zone in May 1977. This claim extended to the Paracel and Spratly Islands—which are, however, also claimed by China, the Philippines and Taiwan.

The Vietnamese are thus widely extending their international contacts, hoping by this means to reduce their dependence on the Soviet Union, and perhaps also believing that they might in case of need be able to call on international political support. The Carter Administration withdrew the American veto on their membership of the United Nations in 1977, but even before they became full members they had been active in a number of its subsidiary organizations. Unlike the members of the Soviet bloc, Vietnam sought and obtained membership of the World Bank, the International Monetary Fund and the Asian Development Bank. The country received substantial aid from these institutions and also from the United Nations Development Programme.

Both Vietnam and China were for a long time reticent about their relations with each other but in the middle of 1978 open hostility developed over the ill-treatment of ethnic Chinese living in Vietnam; and there were rumours of armed conflict along the border. In their own media they became highly critical of the new republic, which is in marked contrast to the effusive reports which they frequently publish concerning Kampuchea (formerly Cambodia) and Laos.

There are signs in fact that the Chinese are actively seeking to extend their influence in these smaller Indo-Chinese countries, in order to combat the influence of the Russians and the Vietnamese. The outcome of this competition will have great importance for the future of south-east Asia. The whole course of the fighting in Indo-China since the end of World War II showed the vital importance of Laos and Kampuchea to the security of Vietnam. The French were defeated at Dien Bien Phu in 1954 because the Vietminh forces were able to outflank the French forces through Laos; and later the use of the territory of both Laos and Kampuchea by the communist forces led ultimately to the overthrow of the South Vietnam régime. Having won control of Vietnam by the use of these territories the new régime will be well aware of the danger to itself which would exist if they were in hostile hands. It is, therefore, faced with an acute dilemma. At the Party congress in December 1976 the new régime strongly asserted its respect for the independence and territorial integrity of other countries and, in view of the vast problems it faces internally, it is reasonable to assume that it would have preferred to devote its attention to these rather than quarrelling with its neighbours.

Since the friendship of Laos is essential to Vietnamese security the pressure which China, by virtue of geography, is able to exert on Laos causes much uneasiness in Vietnam. During the long period of fighting in Indo-China, the Chinese built roads running deep into Laos from the Chinese province of Yunnan. The Chinese are, ironically enough, cultivating the same relations with anti-Vietnamese tribal groups as were cultivated by the Americans—the Meo of the hill regions of Laos. The Pathet Lao régime was installed in power by the Vietnamese and this is still resented by the non-Lao tribes. It is possible that if the Chinese were to decide on a military takeover of Laos they could do so in a way that appeared to be in response to an appeal from the Meo.

For the present the Chinese are, at the State to State level, doing their best to conciliate the Pathet Lao government. On the first anniversary of the founding of the Peoples' Democratic Republic of Laos the Peking newspapers published warm praise of the new régime. An editorial in *Renmin Ribao* of 2 December 1976 said:

> As close neighbours linked by the same mountains and rivers, China and Laos share weal and woe. There is a long-standing traditional friendship between the peoples of the two countries . . . In the future, the Chinese people will continue to unite with the Lao people in struggle and advance with them.

The present government of Laos is too much beholden to the Vietnamese to respond with the same warmth. It has maintained close relations with Vietnam and has taken attitudes in foreign policy conspicuously different from China's. It has been vehemently critical of the Association of South East Asian Nations (ASEAN consisting of Indonesia, Malaysia, Singapore, Thailand and the Philippines) whereas the Chinese are giving encouragement to this group. It is also much more critical of the United States than is China. During a visit to Burma in January 1977 the Laotian president, Souphanouvong, subscribed to a communiqué which strongly implied criticism of China for its continued support of the Burmese Communist Party. It stated that

> the two sides considered that it would be conducive to the general cause of peace and friendship if each country in the region undertook scrupulously not to interfere in each other's internal affairs and not to allow their territory to be used by any force, indigenous or foreign, as a base of direct or indirect aggression against each other.

The Laotians are actively cultivating relations with the Soviet Union. Soon after independence a succession of Lao leaders visited Moscow and there is a visible and active Russian presence in Vientiane, the Laotian capital. Economic and technical assistance is being provided also by East Germany and other countries of the East European bloc. Close contacts have been developed with India, which is seen as a friend of Russia and an opponent of China.

The Laotians are unlikely to be happy about the success the Chinese have had in establishing close relations with Kampuchea. The régime installed in Phnom Penh in 1975 by the Kampuchean Revolutionary Army moved quickly to assert its independence from Vietnam. In retrospect it seems that the success of the revolution may have owed more to Chinese than to Russian or Vietnamese assistance. In the early stages of the new régime almost the only link with the outside world was with Peking. At the end of 1976 a strong Chinese economic delegation visited Phnom Penh and agreements were signed for the provision of Chinese equipment and for co-operation in science and technology. The economic programme promulgated by the government shows strong Chinese influence, being expressed in terms which reflect Chinese usage. Official statements declare that the Revolutionary Organisation (as the governing group is known) has laid down a policy which stresses 'taking agriculture as the foundation to promote the development of industry'. It puts emphasis on the development of light industry to meet the people's daily needs, promote the development of agriculture production, and in this way gradually accumulate funds for the development of heavy industry. (This is indeed a sensible prescription for a country at Kampuchea's state of development, and it contrasts markedly with the over-emphasis on industrialization and urbanization customary in countries under Western influence.) During the visit of the economic mission the Kampucheans pledged themselves to the struggle against 'hegemonism' (which is the Chinese term for Russian imperialism) although the government has so far refrained from an openly anti-Russian line.

When Pol Pot, the head of the revolutionary government, visited Peking in October 1977 he was given a fulsome reception. He spoke of the 'great, unbreakable and everlasting militant solidarity and revolutionary friendship between our two Parties, our two peoples and our two governments'.

At the beginning of 1978 open warfare broke out between Vietnam and Kampuchea. It was not possible to obtain reliable information as to its nature and scope but it seems certain that Vietnam acted to maintain military control of the north-south communications across the border in Kampuchea and Laos. The Kampucheans retaliated with attacks not only on the Vietnamese forces but on civilians, and it must be assumed that they were assisted in doing so by the Chinese. It is believed that in the following months considerable numbers of Chinese military advisers and 'worker soldiers' were flown into Kampuchea, together with equipment. These were sent to assist not only in reorganizing the armed forces but in rebuilding Kampuchea's transport infrastructure.

Peking propaganda blamed Vietnam for aggression against Kampuchea and called upon Hanoi to accept Phnom Penh's proposals for a settlement. These were that Vietnam should desist from its invasion of Kampuchean territory, abandon its attempts to subvert the government in Phnom Penh, and renounce its plans to bring Kampuchea under Vietnamese domination in an 'Indo-China Federation'.

In the same period the quarrel between China and Vietnam regarding the ill-treatment of the ethnic Chinese intensified, and Peking's increasingly threatening statements may have been intended partly to put pressure upon Hanoi to desist in its campaign against Kampuchea. In June 1978 the Chinese government retaliated against the Vietnamese delay in allowing the establishment of a consulate in Ho Chi Minh City (formerly Saigon) by closing the three Vietnamese consulates in south China. There were at the same time widespread rumours, which the Chinese did not discourage, that Chinese forces in the Vietnamese border area were being reinforced.

There were many stories in the international press at this period about the atrocities committed by the new Kampuchean rulers, both against their own people and also in attacks across the borders on the Vietnamese and the Thais. There seems no doubt that in seeking to establish their authority inside the country and in the border regions the revolutionary authorities behaved with great ruthlessness. But reports that over a million Kampucheans were murdered, including those published in a succession of books, should be treated with scepticism. They were based mainly on refugees' accounts, which are notoriously unreliable; and there is a strong possibility that a good deal of 'disinformation' was planted on the Western press by countries which dislike the new Kampuchean régime, including the Soviet Union.

At the time of writing it was clear that the Soviet-Chinese competition in Indo-China was intensifying. But it was difficult to predict the outcome. It seemed unlikely that the Chinese would risk military action against Vietnam but if they could establish a strong and permanent presence in Kampuchea the effect on the future balance in the area would be important. They would have, as it were, a forward base from which to check the spread of Russian influence, and they would also be able to prevent a Vietnamese takeover. Current trends in Chinese policies convey a clear message both to Moscow and Hanoi: that they will oppose any expansion by Vietnam into Indo-China, whether spontaneously undertaken by the Vietnamese or instigated by the Soviet Union.

The Chinese also seem determined to obstruct Vietnamese penetration of Thailand. There are considerable numbers of Vietnamese in north-east Thailand who established themselves during the Indo-Chinese war and they are regarded by the Thai authorities as a subversive threat. But the leaders of the guerrilla groups who cause most trouble in the north-east and north of Thailand appear to be Chinese or Sino–Thai. Their propaganda reflects Chinese themes and they receive support from a radio station which has operated from southern China since 1962.

The main success of the insurgents has so far been in appealing to the non-Thai peoples in the areas bordering on Laos and also to the hill tribes of the north. The danger that they will develop wider appeal is, however, considerable. Following the overthrow of the short-lived democratic régime in Bangkok in October 1976 by a military coup, a number of intellectuals and students joined the Communist Party of Thailand, thus broadening its political base and increasing its appeal to the Thai people. The decision in 1977 of the Socialist Party of Thailand (which is believed to draw on Russian support) to ally itself with the communists also increases the possibility of the development of a nation-wide revolutionary movement.

The military régimes that have governed Thailand throughout most of its recent history have failed to adapt to the requirements of the modern world. Under these régimes the ruling class has become enormously rich, while the standards of life of the people have declined. Although many parts of the country are very fertile, the available resources are being overwhelmed because of the uncontrolled birth-rate, which is one of the highest in the world.

Thailand is an example of the failure of Western ideas of development. Since the end of World War II it has received considerable quantities of foreign aid, the main consequences of which have been gross economic distortions. The forced pace of industrialization has meant that the city of Bangkok has grown to enormous proportions. Formerly one of the most charming cities in Asia, it is now a bloated monster, with the worst traffic and one of the highest crime rates in the world. The best hope for the future would be for a massive transfer of resources back to the countryside, and a determined effort to raise rural productivity and standards of living. There is little hope that the present rulers would have either the will or the capacity to do this.

The only man who might be able to accomplish such a transformation is the King. He is regarded almost as a god by the rural masses and he is one of the few members of the Thai ruling class who understands and sympathizes with their needs. But he is virtually a prisoner of the generals who run the country and it is hard to see how any change can occur except by revolution from below. The possibility that such a revolution, if organized and led on Maoist lines, might succeed is increased by the incompetence and lack of fighting spirit of the armed forces.

In these circumstances Thailand might well become a crucial arena for the contest for influence in mainland south-east Asia between the Chinese, the Russians and the Vietnamese. The Russians cannot compete directly and must work through a proxy. The obvious candidate for this role is Vietnam; nevertheless it must be doubted whether the Vietnamese would wish to assist in bringing about a revolution in Thailand of which the main beneficiary would be the Soviet Union. It seems likely that the Vietnamese would avoid any action that might lead to a collapse in Thailand until they could be sure of securing for themselves a dominant influence. They no doubt believe that if they could achieve this they would have a good chance of keeping both the Russians and the Chinese out of what they would like to regard as their own sphere of influence.

The rewards for the Russians in gaining control over the Vietnamese are so considerable as to make it likely that they will make a strong effort to do so. Apart from the control which this would give them of the South China Sea, they would be able to use the best disciplined people in south-east Asia in their competition with the Chinese. This would overcome the disadvantage imposed by their geographical remoteness from the area and would help them achieve one of their main aims—to block the extension of Chinese influence to the Straits of Malacca.

The Vietnamese are in a difficult situation. On the one hand they need Russian help to resist the Chinese pressure already developing through Laos and Kampuchea; and on the other the price of this help might be the loss of their hard-won independence. If the Russians gained strategic control of Indo–China and the South China Sea they would be likely to exploit their control much more ruthlessly than the United States ever sought to do. If the Vietnamese attempted any resistance to the Soviet Union they would this time be completely on their own. There is little substance in the often expressed fear that Vietnam will take over south-east Asia; the country will be hard put to it to preserve its own independence in the face of Russian and Chinese pressures.

The best hope for Vietnam, and indeed for all the countries of south-east Asia, is that the competition between Russia and China in the area will limit the power of both. In the short run there is some prospect of this. The resources of the Soviet Union are not limitless and it still has much to do to consolidate its expansion into Africa and the Indian Ocean; it seems likely that it would wish to complete this undertaking before engaging in the more difficult task of establishing itself in south-east Asia. China also is not yet ready for any strong forward move. The new Chinese leadership is now well established, and its determination to make China's weight felt in the world is becoming daily more apparent; but it accepts that China's power will ultimately depend upon its being able to achieve levels of productivity and economic wealth comparable to Western countries. It can therefore be expected in the coming years to devote its main efforts to internal problems.

It is possible, therefore, that the countries of south-east Asia may have a breathing space in which to build up their individual and collective strength against the day when, inevitably, it will again be the arena for great power competition and conflict.

Because of their political weakness little can be expected of Burma and Thailand. But Malaysia presents a more hopeful picture. It has so far survived internal racial and social stresses more successfully than expected and is now among the world's fastest growing economies. If it is given the time Vietnam also has good prospects of rapid economic development. These two countries are therefore the natural leaders of mainland south-east Asia and if they could develop close accord there might be some hope for maintaining the region's independence.

At the non-aligned summit meeting in August 1976 there was sharp friction between the two countries, arising especially out of Vietnam's criticism of ASEAN, but it is significant that in May 1977 the Malaysian Foreign Minister was the first leader from an ASEAN country to visit Hanoi. Arrangements were made for the provision by Malaysia of technical assistance in restoring Vietnam's rubber industry, and also in the field of communications, including road-building. In the following month the Vietnamese Foreign Minister said that although it was unrealistic to speak of Vietnam becoming a member of ASEAN, Vietnam wished to develop good bilateral relations with all south-east Asian countries, whether they were members of ASEAN or not. He seemed at that time to be ready to contemplate the creation of a new organization in which Vietnam would be included. In an interview published in the *Far Eastern Economic Review* of 24 June 1977 he was quoted as saying: 'When it is a question of the co-operation of nine South-east Asian countries [he was referring to Laos, Cambodia and Burma, as well as Vietnam, as possible new members] a new formula has to be worked out to assure equality between the five ASEAN members and the four other nations'. He added: 'ASEAN has its own established rules. Some would need to be changed: others eliminated. Basic new components would have to be introduced to meet the new situation in south-east Asia in a new spirit'. This somewhat lofty attitude was not well received in some ASEAN circles, but it indicated a substantial change in the attitude of the Vietnamese since the non-aligned meeting of the previous year. It certainly suggested that Vietnam was no longer prepared to echo Russia's condemnation of ASEAN.

Co-operation between Vietnam and ASEAN does not depend only on Vietnam. In addition to ideological distrust of a communist régime there is concern among the ASEAN countries about the size of the Vietnamese armed forces—the largest and best armed in south-east Asia. The Indonesians are particularly suspicious—although this may be partly due to the feeling that the Vietnamese might diminish their own role in the region.

Since the new leadership took over in Peking the competition between China and Russia has sharpened noticeably. The Chinese exhibit obvious anxiety that the Russians might be able to complete the encirclement of China before she has been able to develop sufficient strength to combat it. A constant barrage of anti-Russian propaganda is poured out by the Chinese media. This is aimed principally at creating suspicion and distrust of the Russians throughout the world, but a strong attempt is being made to undermine the loyalty of the non-Russian minorities inside the Soviet Union, especially of those living close to the border between the two countries. The Soviet government is accused of 'ruthless exploitation and plunder' of the central Asia republics. Propaganda aimed at stimulating opposition is regularly beamed by radio from the Chinese province of Sinkiang. In the north a similar campaign is being directed towards Outer Mongolia, in an attempt to weaken that country's attachment to the Soviet Union.

The anti-Russian activities of the Chinese elsewhere in the world are extraordinary in their range. Wherever the Russians are active the Chinese are there trying to counter their influence—in Africa, the Middle East, the Indian Ocean, Latin America, and the Pacific. They offer some economic and military aid but their resources cannot match the Russians and their main effort is devoted to propaganda. Whenever a country has a grievance against Russia the Chinese will take it up, no matter how ideologically incompatible the government concerned might be. Western Europe, Japan, and anti-communist régimes like Saudi Arabia and Iran, are nowadays offered sympathy and encouragement in their efforts to resist Soviet pressure. There is evident alarm in Peking at the gradual decline in the global power of the United States and warnings are constantly directed towards America of the dangers in allowing Russian expansion to proceed unchecked. The Chinese are also worried about the inflow of Western goods and technology into the Soviet Union and the extent to which this helps to build up the country's industrial strength. They repeatedly draw attention to the large credits that have been granted by Western bankers to the socialist bloc and suggest that this is in effect arming their worst enemy. They point out that the Soviet Union has been able to pump large extra sums into its 'frenzied campaign of arms expansion and war preparations' because of the steady flow of loans from the West.

Any country which shows awareness of the growing threat from the Soviet Union is praised and encouraged. Yugoslavia frequently receives favourable mention, and the recent settlement in 1976 of territorial issues between Yugoslavia and Italy was welcomed by Peking with enthusiasm. Any signs that the Italian and French communist parties are prepared to assert their independence of Moscow are quickly noted and praised. France, which in de Gaulle's day was disliked and feared as the country seeking to appease the Soviet Union, is now praised for its realistic recognition of the dangers of Russian expansionism. French interest in Africa is encouraged and the presence of the French navy in the Indian Ocean is welcomed as a valuable stabilizing factor. In the *Peking Review* of 25 February 1977 France was credited with a 'new strategic concept'. It was said that in the last few years the Soviet Union had repeatedly tried to bully and intimidate France and had engaged in subversive activities against it. In response to this situation France had increased its military expenditure and had shown a greater willingness to co-operate with the other countries of Western Europe in 'front line' defence against the Warsaw Pact countries. President Giscard d'Estaing was quoted as saying that the French combat fleet in the Mediterranean had been substantially increased. The French government was also praised for declaring that France would never allow the Mediterranean 'to fall into the hands of others, especially the two super powers, which lie outside the Mediterranean'. The *Peking Review* reported, with obvious satisfaction, that France's new strategic policy had greatly irritated the Russians, who were quoted as having accused the French of wanting a return to 'brinkmanship'.

In south-east Asia France is no longer treated by the Chinese as an enemy. The development of close relations between Vietnam and France is welcomed, and French economic and technological assistance is regarded as a useful supplement to their own efforts to counter Russian influence.

Judging from their own publications the Chinese regard themselves as engaged in a desperate race against time. Chinese propagandists repeatedly accuse the Soviet Union of preparing for war at an 'early date'. In May 1977 the Vice-Chairman of the Chinese Communist Party, Yeh Chien-ying, declared that:

'The Soviet Union and the United States are locked in an increasingly fierce struggle for hegemony and some day war will break out. We must . . . be prepared for a big war. We must race against time and work as quickly as possible so that well before the outbreak of war we will have built up industry in the interior. (*Peking Review*, 20 May 1977)

To an outsider the fear of the Soviet Union seems excessive; it seems unlikely that with all the avenues of expansion now open to them the Russians would risk a direct assault on China. In the same way that the Soviet strategy is now designed to outflank Western European defences by moving into the Indian Ocean region, similarly in Asia their objective is to outflank China in the north Pacific and south-east Asia—rather than resort to direct confrontation across their land borders.

That the Chinese themselves do not seriously regard a direct Russian invasion as imminent is perhaps indicated by the somewhat anti-climactic ending of the above quotation from Yeh Chien-ying. The new leadership has repeatedly stressed Mao's dictum that in order to strengthen national defence 'we must first of all strengthen our work in economic construction'. The building up of industries 'in the interior' is seen as promoting development, as well as a sensible defence precaution. Nevertheless priority is still being given to the development of nuclear weapons, and soon after the new leadership came to power considerable publicity was given to a successful hydrogen bomb test and to the launching and recovery of satellites. This was no doubt intended to warn the Russians that China now had an effective nuclear capability. But there are no signs of increased mobilization on the borders with the Soviet Union.

It seems probable that the Chinese do not so much fear a threat to their own territory as that the Russians will deny them what they now see to be within their grasp—the opportunity to recover their position as 'the central kingdom'. The thought that one day the Russians instead of themselves might become the dominant power in Asia is intolerable to them.

In spite of the bitter memories of the Japanese occupation of China in the period 1935–45, the Chinese are turning to Japan as an ally against Russia. Since the establishment of diplomatic relations between the two countries in 1973 trade has expanded rapidly. In their drive to acquire modern technology the Chinese would clearly prefer to secure this from the Japanese than from Western countries. Japanese exports to China exceed those to any other Asian country and long-range contracts are being entered into which will result in a steady increase in the flow of fuels and raw materials to Japan. The pattern is emerging of an alliance between the vast manpower and natural resources of China and the modern technology and trade expertise of Japan.

The Chinese are becoming increasingly vocal in support of Japan in its quarrels with the Soviet Union. They give strong support to the claim of Japan for the return by Russia of the four disputed islands in the Kurile chain; and when the Soviet government declared on 1 March 1977 a two-hundred-mile exclusive fishing zone off the coasts of the U.S.S.R. this was denounced as 'blackmailing' Japan. That was said not only to exclude Japanese fishermen from important fishing grounds upon which they were traditionally dependent, but to pre-empt the future of the four islands by including them in the zone. The Japanese were urged to counter the Soviet move by declaring their own two-hundred-mile zone, which would include the islands within it. Mao is being quoted as having said that 'the Chinese people wholeheartedly support the just struggle of the Japanese people' and the Chinese people are described as rejoicing in the knowledge that the Japanese are united in combating the 'hegemonic acts' of the Soviet Union.

All this does not appear to have been particularly welcome to the Japanese. They are still uncertain as to how close they wish to be drawn to China. Earlier hopes of a profitable co-operation with the Russians in the development of Siberia and the Soviet eastern territories have diminished in the face of the immense practical difficulties and the inability of the Japanese to establish satisfactory working relations with the Russian authorities. But the Soviet Union as a whole has become a significant trading partner and the Japanese are acutely conscious of the strategic grip on the north Pacific that the Russians are gradually establishing.

If only because of its own experience as a naval power, Japan is well aware of the significance of the dramatic expansion of the Russian submarine fleet. The reports in May 1977 that the new Delta class was being deployed in the Pacific caused considerable uneasiness in Japan, especially among the commanders of the Self-Defence Forces, who know that Japan has at present no counter to such a weapon. Since they cannot themselves afford to risk a confrontation with the Soviet the Japanese are unwilling to be associated with China's persistent bellicosity. Sooner or later the Japanese may have to decide whether or not they should throw in their lot with the Chinese, but for the present they are anxious to avoid any irreversible entanglements. The negotiations for the Japan-China Treaty of Peace and Friendship have been stalled for several years because of the unwillingness of the Japanese to accept a denunciation of 'hegemony', since this would be taken to be directed against the Russians.

Another possible ally for the Chinese in their struggle with the Soviet Union is Korea, but there is a marked ambivalence in their attitude towards this country. They have refused to commit themselves to military support for Kim Il Sung's régime and they are careful in their propaganda to make it clear that they favour the 'peaceful reunification' of Korea. This cautious attitude may reflect their estimation that Kim's prospects are declining. There seems little prospect now that the North Korean armies could take over the south, even after the prospective withdrawal of American troops. South Korea has undergone rapid economic expansion in recent years and has a rate of growth which exceeds Japan's. In the event of another war it is possible that the south would win. The present situation might therefore be regarded as in China's best interests. A united and independent Korea might disturb the delicate balance in north Asia, and in any case could not be expected to be compliant with China's wishes. The Chinese are no doubt also concerned that, for some years at any rate, the Russians would be in a stronger position to influence a united Korea than they would themselves. In short, the pragmatists in Peking might well see South Korea as a useful impediment to the extension of Soviet power on their northern flank.

Since the Russians have maintained strong opposition to ASEAN, it follows as a matter of course that China should support this organization, and its meetings are always favourably reported in the Chinese foreign language media. An enthusiastic welcome was in particular given to the agreement on the Strait of Malacca signed at the Special Meeting of the Foreign Ministers of ASEAN on 24 February 1977 by the ministers of Malaysia, Singapore and Indonesia. This agreement re-affirmed the declaration issued in 1971 opposing internationalization of the straits and foreshadowing arrangements for joint management by the three countries. The new agreement promulgated a series of additional measures to ensure the safety of navigation in the Strait of Malacca and the Strait of Singapore.

The signing of the 1977 agreement was described by the *Peking Review* of 25 March 1977 as a 'telling blow to the Soviet scheme to internationalize the straits and to Soviet maritime hegemony'. It went on to say that in recent years 'Soviet social imperialism has been hard at work trying to establish hegemony over a vast expanse from the Black Sea, Mediterranean Sea, Red Sea, Indian Ocean and West Pacific Ocean to the Sea of Japan'. It added:

Since the Soviet Union built up in 1968 a squadron in the Indian Ocean, its warships have frequently been going back and forth between the Indian and Pacific Oceans by passing through the Strait of Malacca. In November 1973, a Soviet cruiser and a missile destroyer pushed their way into the strait without permission of the nations concerned. Facts show that the social–imperialist country is trying to control the strait and make this strategically important body of water a passage for expansion into the Indian Ocean.

The rapid increase in recent years of the Russian merchant navy is a matter of concern to the Chinese, who see it as a further means of promoting 'social imperialism'. They are particularly worried about the penetration of south-east Asian waters by Russian shipping lines. They allege that this has been achieved by offering freight rates which are twenty to forty per cent lower than ruling international rates. Statistics are quoted to the effect that in 1975 Malaysian ports berthed 250 Soviet ships, which was five times the number a decade earlier, and that a similar expansion had occurred in Singapore, Bangkok and Manila.

The Chinese warn that the Russians are expanding their shipping services not just for economic gain but to achieve 'maritime supremacy that fits in with its global strategy for world hegemony'. Soviet naval personnel and KGB agents are said to operate in the area under the cover of merchant seamen, and their tasks are alleged to be not only to gather intelligence but also to engage in subversion and sabotage in south-east Asian ports. The Russians are also accused of sending espionage ships into south-east Asia under the pretext of engaging in sea lane surveys and meteorological and scientific research.

Allowing for a certain exaggeration it is clear that the picture described by the Chinese is substantially accurate. The south-east Asian countries have themselves expressed concern at the damage which Russian competition is doing to their own shipping lines, and in April 1977 ASEAN decided to set up a Shipping Council designed to protect regional shipping interests. Official concern at improper activities by Soviet ships and personnel have also been expressed in Thailand, Indonesia and the Philippines.

Although observing their customary reticence, there is no doubt that the Japanese are also concerned at the increasing proportion of sea-freight in the Indian and Pacific Oceans that is falling into Russian hands. The number of Soviet ships that now visits Japanese ports has in recent years increased severalfold and this means that a growing proportion of Japan's own overseas trade is carried in Russian vessels. This is seen as a possible additional constraint on their free access to overseas supplies and markets.

The overall growth of Soviet power is being watched very closely from Tokyo. The official attitude still is that this does not present any danger to Japan and confidence is expressed in the protection afforded by the alliance with the United States. But the declaration in 1977 by the Russians of a two-hundred-mile exclusive fishing zone was an example of how little use the American alliance was in protecting important Japanese interests. The declaration of this zone increased the difficulties that Japan has faced in recent years in obtaining from the Soviet Union satisfactory agreements for the operation of her fishing fleets—which make a significant contribution to the diet of the Japanese people and to the overall economy. The United States was in no position to give them support because of its own declaration of a two-hundred-mile zone, and it was evident that in any clash between Japanese fishing fleets and the Soviet navy the Japanese would have been on their own. They declared their own two-hundred-mile zone, but otherwise confined themselves to diplomatic protests. They eventually accepted an agreement with the Russians which in 1977 drastically reduced their salmon catch.

This episode has strengthened the feeling of some Japanese that the United States-Japan security treaty is really only likely to be applicable in circumstances of global war, and that Japan's essential freedoms could be progressively eroded long before any such war occurred. They point to the fact that Russian control of the Sea of Okhotsk and the Sea of Japan is already a fact; and that if similar control were established over the South China Sea and the Strait of Malacca the Soviet Union would be in a position to blockade almost all Japanese overseas trade.

Public debate on these possibilities is usually avoided in Japan, but it is unlikely that they are far from the minds of its leaders. It is easy to imagine that their thoughts are turning back to the great debate which occurred behind the scenes during the 1930s: whether the Japanese could safely undertake the move into China and south-east Asia without first having driven the Russians out of north-east Asia. The Imperial Japanese army is credited with having supported the 'strike north first' policy and, according to David Bergamini (author of *Japan's Imperial Conspiracy*, Heinemann, 1971) their opposition to the 'strike south first' policy was only overcome by the personal intervention of Emperor Hirohito. There may be some in Japan today who regret this decision. With hindsight it might seem that a war against Russia could have been won, especially after Hitler's onslaught in the west, whereas the 'strike south' was doomed to failure. The danger which fifty years ago the Japanese army had hoped to remove must now seem more pressing than ever.

For the present the only policy open to the Japanese is one of non-provocation. They might hope that in the long run the Chinese might become strong enough to outweigh the Soviet Union, but they can have little expectation that this is likely to happen in the next quarter of a century. They would, therefore, have little to gain by throwing themselves prematurely into the arms of the Chinese.

It is conceivable that the Japanese might allow themselves to be progressively drawn into the Russian orbit. This might not be entirely to their disadvantage. The potential wealth of the eastern territories of the Soviet Union is great, and the Japanese could gain substantial economic advantages from participating in its development. But they have no reason to hope that the Russians would allow them to do so on favourable terms. The difficulties which they have already faced in making acceptable arrangements for joint ventures in Siberia are a sufficient warning of what the Russian attitude is likely to be as their confidence grows in their own power. Moreover, the Japanese would expect that the Russians have not forgotten—as they would not themselves have forgotten—the humiliating defeat the Russian navy suffered at the hands of the Japanese at the beginning of the century. They cannot, therefore, look forward with any pleasure to the prospect of being dependent for their livelihood on the Soviet Union.

In south-east Asia it is possible that the Japanese will try to use their economic strength to counter Russian expansion. Their active interest in Vietnam has already been described and it can be assumed that if they could exert any influence to discourage the Vietnamese from allowing the establishment of Soviet bases in Vietnam they would do so.

They are also moving forward slowly and cautiously elsewhere in the region. The Japanese government is conscious that anti-Japanese feeling is still strong in some quarters and that the activities of Japanese businessmen have not always served to dissipate this. Moreover, Japanese trade with the area has not grown as much as might have been expected. Before World War II the resources of south-east Asia were believed by the Japanese and by outside observers to be vital to their economy. Japan has, however, become a trading nation on a global scale and draws her supplies from all over the world. Nevertheless the area is significant both as a source of raw materials and as a market, and its importance is likely to increase. The economies of several countries in the area are now growing rapidly, especially Singapore and Malaysia, and the Japanese are already major participants in this expansion. Their policy in regard to providing aid and credits has been liberalized and Japanese businessmen are being encouraged to show more sensitivity towards local feelings. They are the largest contributor of funds to the Asian Development Bank, the main purpose of which is to provide credit to the south-east Asian countries. They also adopt a helpful attitude towards the economic activities developed by the Association of South-east Asian Nations and now hold regular twice-yearly meetings with the group. Although discreetly avoiding any overt political activity, they clearly regard ASEAN as a potentially important factor in enabling the countries of the area to resist pressure from both the Soviet Union and China. In 1977 the Japanese Prime Minister promised continuing support for the efforts of the ASEAN countries towards regional cohesion and development.

The problem which causes greatest anxiety to Japan is freedom of navigation through the Malacca Strait, the South China Sea, and the sea lanes between Japan and Australia. Almost all Japanese commerce, except with North and South America, passes through these waters. Any interference with shipping in the area would have an immediate effect upon the Japanese economy. Like the Chinese, therefore, they strongly support the efforts of the ASEAN countries to regulate these waterways and are most anxious that control should not pass to any outside power, least of all to the Soviet Union.

What happens in the Malacca Strait will depend to a critical extent on Indonesia and for this reason alone it must be expected that there will be strong great power competition for influence in that country. In recent times this has been fairly muted but it will undoubtedly develop steadily in the coming decades.

Indonesia has the potential to be a great power in its own right. It already has a population larger than Japan's, and by the end of the century it will reach 200 million. At present it produces a significant percentage of the world's oil and although the prospect of the discovery of large new reserves is not regarded as good it is likely that Indonesia will for some time remain an important world supplier. The country also has substantial reserves of minerals. In agriculture it still has vast unused productive capacity and if this were fully utilized it is possible that, in spite of its own rapid population growth, it could by the end of the century produce food for export.

In the government's economic planning an attempt is being made to shift the emphasis away from excessive industrialization and urbanization towards agriculture. Australian aid, although tiny compared with Indonesia's needs, is wisely being given primarily to projects which will promote development in the rural areas. Assistance is being given in developing a large-scale livestock industry with export potential. (This type of industry is always difficult to establish in a tropical peasant economy, but it can be valuable in making use of lands which would otherwise be unproductive.) Australia is participating in a small way in international projects for the development of irrigation systems and road networks, and also in rural health and animal disease control.

Indonesia's greatest problem is that its population will almost double by the end of the century, and whether it will be able to develop its vast economic potential soon enough to avert disaster will depend primarily on its own efforts. The country is enormously diverse—ethnically, linguistically and religiously—and few outsiders, least of all the Australians, have any real perception of the difficulties of maintaining political unity. To criticize Indonesia for not having a Western-style democracy is absurd: experience has shown that this works, if at all, only in societies with a homogeneous cultural background and with widely shared social and economic aims. In a country as diverse as Indonesia strong central authority is indispensable in balancing the needs and aspirations of the different communities.

Underlying the diversity is a growing sense of nationhood—drawing its inspiration not only from the period of revolt against Dutch rule but also from the kingdoms of the past. One characteristic common to all Indonesians—and from which Australians could take example—is tolerance. There have been outbreaks of communal violence, but on the whole Hinduism, Buddhism, Islam and Christianity live peacefully side by side, all having become imbued with ancient Indonesian ideals and rituals. Their wrath is usually stirred only when there is an attempt to deny the basic tenets of religion, and this seems to be why the reaction against communism in 1965 was so violent and widespread. Unlike in Western countries the Indonesians look to their rulers not only for government but also for religious leadership. The nation is founded on the five principles of Panh Sila: belief in one Supreme God, Just and Civilized Humanity, the Unity of Indonesia, Democracy and Social Justice for all. These principles are regarded as 'inseparable and mutually qualifying'.

The Indonesian masses still hope for the emergence of the great leader who will restore Indonesian greatness under the rule of 'Justice', as prophesied by King Jayabhaya in the twelfth century, and this aspiration has a more powerful influence over their minds than any desire for representative government. Nevertheless it would be wrong to regard Indonesian society as entirely un-democratic. The village has been the basic social unit throughout Indonesian history and its affairs have traditionally been managed by consensus. The work of the village is run on a communal basis and village leaders, if not always elected, are obliged to be responsive to the wishes of the villagers. The principle of *gotong royong*, or mutual help, still applies in the countryside. Rulers at the regional level and at the centre have traditionally respected the self-reliance and independent spirit of the villages and although the villages have been subjected to many exactions their communal autonomy has almost always been recognized. President Suharto, who came to power in 1968, is the son of Javanese peasants and it is unlikely that he has forgotten the ancient tradition of the village from which he came.

Much will depend on the ability of the Indonesian people to maintain their unity in the presence of the pressures which they will face in the next twenty-five years. The shifts that are taking place in the global strategic balance will mean that Indonesia and the waters surrounding it will have in the future the kind of importance that the Mediterranean had in the past. Access to this region will be vital to the ambitions of three of the four greatest powers: Russia, China and Japan.

The Russians began their efforts to establish their influence in Indonesia as far back as the early days of Sukarno. At first they disliked him, because they regarded him as principally responsible for preventing a communist take-over after the Japanese withdrawal in 1945. But by 1955 they had overcome their ideological objections. In that year they allowed the Peoples' Republic of Germany (East Germany) to provide a loan of nearly ten million dollars (US) and during the following period the Soviet Union provided non-military aid in excess of that given by the United States. In 1959 Mr Kruschev visited Djakarta and this was followed by an even stronger flow of aid. In the early 1960s credits were provided by the Soviet Union for the purchase of a billion dollars' worth of arms and military equipment. By 1963 the Soviet Union was Indonesia's largest creditor.

During the period of Sukarno's 'confrontation' with Malaysia the only strong supporters of Indonesia were the Soviet bloc, and this increased suspicions that the Indonesians were planning to establish domination over south-east Asia with Soviet help. After Sukarno's downfall 'confrontation' was abandoned and the new régime drew away from the Soviet Union, turning for assistance to the United States and other Western countries. But Russia remains Indonesia's largest creditor and since the armed forces are still largely equipped with Soviet weapons, ships and aircraft, Indonesia is dependent upon a flow of Russian spares and replacements.

A natural counterweight to Russian influence in Indonesia might seem to be China. But relations between the two countries are severely complicated by the racial friction between the Chinese communities in Indonesia and the local people. Outbreaks of hostility against the Chinese have repeatedly occurred since the first immigrants arrived from southern China several centuries ago. In recent times the Chinese in Indonesia have suffered more violence than any other group of overseas Chinese.

The reasons the Chinese problem has been more severe in Indonesia than elsewhere in south-east Asia are complex. As in most other countries, the relative wealth and economic power of the Chinese have been resented and their conspicuously different cultural and social attitudes have attracted the animosity of the nationalist groups. But in recent years the most important cause of their misfortunes has been their involvement in Indonesian politics in a way that gave rise to the suspicion that they were acting in the interests of Communist China.

Australian commentators discount this suspicion and declare it to be an example of Indonesian 'paranoia'. But the conspiratorial nature of Asian politics—and indeed of present-day Western politics —should not be overlooked. All across the political spectrum—from left to right—the public manifestations of political activity are only a thin cover for intense behind-the-scene intrigue. That Chinese and Russian agents were active among the left-wing Indonesian parties can no more be doubted than that Western agents (pre-eminently the C.I.A.) were active in support of the right.

It was understandable that the Chinese should give their support to the left-wing parties. Most of the hostility to them came from the conservative classes: from the Indonesian entrepreneurs, who resented Chinese competition, and from the strict Moslems, who regarded the Chinese as pork-eating infidels. Since the communists were anti-capitalist and non-religious it was natural that the Chinese would hope that if they came to power their community would receive better treatment than from the right-wing parties. This feeling was reinforced in 1963 when the Indonesian communists broke with the Soviet Union and allied themselves firmly with China.

It would of course be an over-simplification to say that

anti-Chinese feeling existed only among the Indonesian upper classes: it was present in varying degrees throughout society. It was, therefore, not possible for the communists to accept overt support from the Chinese community, because this would have diminished their popular appeal. They sometimes spoke out against anti-Chinese excesses, on the grounds that they were the work of counter-revolutionaries who were opposed to Marxist principles of racial equality, but this was itself sufficient to attract accusations that they were the tools of the Chinese and of Communist China. This was no doubt the reason why there were no Chinese among the principal leaders of the party and few at any other level.

It seems certain, however, that substantial covert support was given to the communists by the Chinese, including large financial contributions; and this may well be one of the reasons for the extraordinary growth of the party in the period from 1950, when it was a demoralized remnant, to 1960, when it had become the third largest in the world after China and Russia.

Such successes as the communists had among the armed forces might also have been partly due to Chinese money: there is good reason to believe that financial inducements were of considerable importance in attracting the support of both officers and rank and file. In the case of the armed forces it is likely that the Chinese government was itself involved. There is a widespread conviction in Indonesia that the Air Force, and in particular its chief, Omar Dhani, received substantial support from Peking.

If this picture is the correct one, the coup of 1965 and its aftermath, and also the continuing suspicion shown by the present régime towards Communist China, become more explicable. It must be remembered that although to outsiders there might be no evidence of the involvement of the Chinese community, or of Peking, in the affairs of the Indonesian Communist Party, to Indonesians wise in the ways of their own conspiratorial politics, the truth would have been obvious. It is a matter of settled conviction among many Indonesians, including important members of the present régime, that the Communist Party of Indonesia instigated the coup of 1965; that it was encouraged and supported in so doing by both the Chinese in Indonesia and by Peking; and that the Chief of Air Force, Omar Dhani, who was the only military leader to support the coup, did so because of the assistance he had received, and had been promised for the future, from Peking. They are similarly convinced that the Chinese communists are the instigators and supporters of the Fretilin movement in East Timor.

Although its influence in Indonesia is at present minimal, the

Peking government is working to rebuild its contacts. It continues
its support for the Indonesian Communist Party (P.K.I.), although
the party was officially banned in 1967. Both Peking and the P.K.I.
accuse the Soviet 'revisionists' of trying to sabotage the Indonesian
revolution and their objective is to spread fear and suspicion of
Russian expansionism. A principal aim of the P.K.I. is now to
promote 'a peasants' armed struggle for an anti-feudal agrarian
revolution under the leadership of the working class'. This is not
only classical Maoist doctrine, but it has the effect of separating,
or appearing to separate, the P.K.I. from the Indonesian Chinese
commercial class.

At the end of 1976 Peking became concerned at the attempt
made by pro-Russian Indonesian communists, some of whom are
in Moscow, to usurp control of the P.K.I. The 'Moscow revisionist
clique' was accused of issuing a false document in the name of the
P.K.I. aimed at creating 'confusion, panic and splits within the
ranks of the Communists and revolutionary people of Indonesia'
(*Peking Review*, 6 May 1977). Jusuf Adjitorop, the secretary of
the Central Committee of the P.K.I., is quoted as saying that the
'Soviet modern revisionists and their flunkeys . . . are traitors to
the P.K.I. and the Indonesian revolution, despised by the Indonesian
communists and the revolutionary people . . . We must wage a
consistent and merciless struggle against the Soviet revisionists and
their lackeys.'

Although the Indonesian Chinese are never mentioned in all this,
Peking can be confident that they are listening. They are China's
best hope for resistance to Russian influence in Indonesia. The
prospect that they could make this resistance effective—if this were
their wish—has increased in recent times. In the period following
the 1965 coup they were the target of numerous outbreaks of
violence and there were further sporadic attacks in 1973 and 1974.
But the Suharto régime has accepted that the co-operation of the
Chinese community is essential to the economic growth of Indonesia
and anti-Chinese disorders are now firmly discouraged. The Chinese
community has been instrumental in channelling much-needed
capital into Indonesia—often from other overseas Chinese communities—and they have provided indispensable financial and
managerial skills. They are careful to avoid any political involvement and any overt contact with Peking. But they know that their
best hope for a secure future would be if China established a strong
influence in Indonesia. The Indonesian leaders also know that this
is what the Chinese community believes, and this is why many of
them will continue to oppose any return to close relations with

Peking. But the time may not be far distant when they will either have to yield to Russian pressure, or to accept the help of China in resisting it.

Meanwhile Peking is behaving with circumspection. Although it gives propaganda support to Jusuf Adjitorop, whose position as spokesman of the P.K.I. it upholds, it is nowadays careful to avoid criticism of the Suharto régime (in marked contrast to the abuse directed against it in the period after the 1965 coup). By its encouragement of ASEAN it gives indirect support to Indonesia and to its prominent role in the organization. It has made known its readiness to resume diplomatic relations with Djakarta and it perhaps hopes that Adam Malik, who is known to have tried to prevent the breach with China in 1967, might one day be able to persuade the Suharto régime to restore relations.

In the competition for influence in Indonesia the Japanese are an increasingly important factor. They are now playing a major part in the country's economic development. Their investments in the past ten years have been more than four times that of the United States, and they are the foreign partners in several of the most important joint ventures in Indonesia. They are also Indonesia's biggest customer; in 1976 they took about half of the country's oil exports and their imports of a wide range of raw materials and manufactures is increasing. They have also been influential in supporting the kind of international financial backing which Indonesia has needed to overcome the successive economic problems which the Suharto régime has faced since it came to power.

The Japanese have been careful to avoid any appearance of seeking to exert political influence. The anti-Japanese demonstrations in Djakarta in January 1974, during the visit of Prime Minister Tanaka, were a reminder that anti-Japanese feeling still persisted, and the Japanese have followed a policy of being as inconspicuous as possible. The sheer size of their economic effort will, however, inevitably have a political impact, and the assumption is increasingly made that it will serve to counter Soviet influence. Since it is vital to Japan that Russia should not control the Malacca Strait this seems a reasonable assumption; nevertheless the ability of the Soviet Union to apply pressure upon Japan itself is likely to inhibit any strong Japanese effort to oppose the Russians in Indonesia. Japan's strategic weakness limits its political influence in Indonesia as elsewhere in south-east Asia and the Pacific region.

The obvious aim of any Indonesian government must be to maintain a careful balance in its relations with the great powers. This has been the consistent policy of President Suharto. He has also shown acute awareness of the fact that neighbouring countries in the region have a vital interest in avoiding the domination of Indonesia by any one power. His strong support of ASEAN is a reflection of this awareness and also of the hope that he will be able to draw support from the region in maintaining Indonesia's independence. His task is complicated, however, by the persistent fear among its neighbours that Indonesia itself seeks to dominate the region. This stems partly from the country's sheer size: its population of over 150 millions is almost as large as the rest of south-east Asia put together and in resources it overshadows the other countries. Indonesian leaders, including Sukarno, have in the past argued that Moslem areas which are now included in Malaysia and the Philippines should rightly belong to Indonesia, and from time to time the idea is revived of a Pan-Malayan movement under Indonesian hegemony. Under Suharto such ideas are muted but it would be difficult to persuade other countries in the area that they have been entirely set aside or that they would not be revived under a future leader. These continuing suspicions are the biggest obstacle to co-operation between Indonesia and its neighbours.

Nevertheless, substantial progress has been made in recent years. One of the most significant achievements was the conclusion of the agreements mentioned above between Indonesia, Singapore and Malaysia for the regulation of the Malacca Strait and adjacent waterways. At the summit meeting held at Bali in February 1976, a permanent ASEAN secretariat was established, and an Indonesian was appointed as secretary-general. The organization has great significance in developing a sense of regional unity, and common problems are being increasingly dealt with on the basis of common policies. By general consent political differences between the member countries are set aside and primary emphasis is given to economic co-operation. There is perceptible progress towards the lowering of tariff barriers between the member countries, although Indonesia is still reluctant to go as far as its partners in reducing protection for its new industries. A programme for joint industrial ventures is being developed, and a special ASEAN council has been created to enable consultation and co-operation in the development of oil resources in the area, and also in meeting the energy needs of members in the event of another crisis in oil supplies.

The Indonesians have moved into an active role in the United Nations' economic organizations for the region—the Economic and Social Commission for Asia and the Pacific (ESCAP, formerly ECAFE) and the executive secretary is an Indonesian. They were founding members of the Asian Development Bank, and have received substantial funds from it. They are willing participants in the growing range of co-operative undertakings in the region. This reflects a deliberate effort to dispel suspicion of Indonesian ambitions towards domination, and although the prominence of Indonesian officials in the region sometimes has a contrary effect, relations of trust and good will are undoubtedly being developed.

In the long run Indonesia's prospects of remaining substantially independent rest upon the success with which it deals with its economic problems. Nothing can now stop the doubling of the Indonesian population in the next twenty-five to thirty-five years. The density of population in Java, where sixty-four per cent of Indonesians live, is already 1500 to the square mile. It is true that the island is remarkably fertile, but Bangladesh is an example of a fertile country which can be reduced to famine by over-population. A partial solution might be to transfer people to other Indonesian islands where population density is lower, but the efforts already made in this direction have produced a modest result and it is unlikely that they will bring substantial relief. The only effective solution will be to increase food production throughout Indonesia to keep pace with the population growth.

Compared with most other Asian countries Indonesia is in a fairly favourable position to do this. Its foreign exchange earnings from oil are considerable, and although these may diminish in the future there are good prospects of substantial earnings from nickel and other minerals. If priority is given—as the Indonesian authorities declare that it will be given—to investing these earnings in agriculture there is no physical reason why food production cannot be raised to the necessary levels. This prospect is all the better since Indonesia will be self-sufficient in energy resources.

Success will, however, depend upon the maintenance of political stability, and upon skilful management of the economy. Indonesia has suffered greatly in recent years from mismanagement and misdirection of resources. If major mistakes are made in the future Indonesia could again find itself dependent upon foreign economic support. This might provide the Russians with an opportunity which they would be quick to take. Western countries, including the United States, are likely in the coming decades to be faced themselves with declining real standards of living, and be unready to give high priority to assistance to Indonesia, which is already regarded as a country which has sufficient wealth to provide for itself. Japan would no doubt wish to do its best, but its own resources might be fully stretched. The Soviet Union would, on the other hand, have so much to gain from establishing its influence in Indonesia that it would probably be prepared to devote large resources to bringing the country into its own economic orbit.

Another circumstance which would present opportunities for the Russians would be if the Indonesians again came into conflict with their neighbours. It is not conceivable that the present régime would revive the 'confrontation' policy of Sukarno, but there are causes of friction with both the Philippines and Malaysia over territorial issues and considerable political wisdom on the part of all three countries will be required if they are to be resolved without disrupting the unity of the region.

Australia's interest in all this is plain: it is vital to us that Indonesia should remain an independent country, free of any controlling influence by Russia or China. Indonesian rulers will be engaged, in the coming decades, in the difficult task of balancing one great power against another. Great skill will be required to ensure that the balance is not tipped in favour of any one of them. The outcome will depend largely on Indonesia's own efforts, but Australia's policies could ease or intensify Indonesia's problems. We could help to lessen the danger of economic dependence by lowering our tariff barriers against Indonesian products, by providing technical training and technology (especially of the kinds applicable to agriculture) and by close co-operation in defence. We should do all in our power to encourage the further development of co-operation between Indonesia and its neighbours, bearing in mind that our influence can only be effective if we show ourselves capable of a sympathetic understanding of the internal and external problems of the countries in the area.

We will have our own problems in resisting Russian pressure. If the Soviet Union is able to control the oil resources of the Middle East and the sea lanes of the Indian Ocean—as it is clearly its ambition to do—we will have to be careful to avoid actions which would attract Russian hostility, and this in particular is likely to inhibit our freedom of action in regard to the vast areas of continental shelf and the two-hundred mile resources zone which we are now intent upon claiming. Provided, however, that we do not rashly confront the Russians, there is a reasonable chance that they will avoid any hostile action against us. Their primary objective will be the control of Indonesia and the nexus of straits that join the Indian and Pacific Oceans. If and when they achieve this Australia would have no option but to join the Soviet orbit and we would be wise to do so without a struggle.

4

Papua New Guinea's Uncertain Future

When Papua New Guinea became independent on 16 September 1975 its prospects as a viable national State were much better than might have been expected a few years previously. Exports of copper from Bougainville have put its balance of payments in a healthy state and prospects for the discovery of further mineral resources are good. Exports of agricultural products are also increasing and newly developed industries like cattle-raising and fishing are making important contributions to the national income. The pessimistic view formerly held by Australian administrators that the territory could never have a viable economy has been swept away, and there is now growing confidence that the people of Papua New Guinea can look forward to steadily rising standards of living.

The country is fortunate in the political leadership which emerged during the period leading to independence. It has shown itself adept at operating the modified Westminster-type system of government that was installed. There is a single house of parliament elected by universal suffrage, but each elector has in effect two representatives—one from each of the eighty-nine electoral divisions into which the whole country is divided and one from the province in which he resides.

The transition from self-government to independence was made under a coalition government led by Michael Somare. He has shown qualities of mature leadership which other more advanced countries might envy. He is the son of a former sergeant in the New Guinea police force and was a small boy when the Japanese occupied the Sepik district in which he lived. He went to a Catholic mission school and later trained as a teacher. He was chosen in 1965 to attend a course at the Administration College in Port Moresby, and became a member of the group of students who later helped to form the Pangu Party, of which he is now leader. He uses the English language confidently and vividly—having benefited in this respect from a period as a journalist and radio broadcaster. He is a quiet but persuasive public speaker. The Sepik people from whom he comes are unusual in New Guinea in their artistic development and capacity for community organization and these qualities may have helped to form his own ability to give firm and imaginative leadership. Perhaps because he comes from one of the more remote communities he is trusted by the other major groups and has earned the respect even of the radical separatist leaders.

It must be expected, however, that his problems will worsen. The 1977 elections—the first after independence—ended the post-independence honeymoon. Somare was re-elected Prime Minister by a substantial majority of the new parliament but several experienced ministers lost their seats and he now has a rather diverse team. Difficult decisions have to be faced in all aspects of government and it must be expected that political turbulence will increase. The numbers of the governing group in the country are tiny, and since political consciousness among the people is still at a primitive level none of them can be regarded as having a mass following. They are an élite, operating in a political vacuum, and there is a danger that competition among them will degenerate into faction. If this happens the prospects for a united and prosperous country will sharply diminish.

As of 1978, however, the outlook seems promising. The way in which Michael Somare's government has managed the economy has received the commendation of the World Bank (whose interest in Papua New Guinea's economic development goes back to the early 1960s). In a report released in 1977 the Bank forecast that it would be twenty years before Papua New Guinea would be financially self-reliant, and that during this period continuing Australian grant aid would be indispensable; but that if the performance of the past five years were maintained the prospects of establishing a sound and progressive economy by the end of that period were good.

The government has drawn up a national development strategy which is based firmly on the World Bank's advice and which should, with luck, avoid the worst errors committed in other developing countries. Priority is rightly given to production in the rural areas, with emphasis on subsistence and locally grown cash crops and, where appropriate, the establishment of local light industries. Unfortunately Papua New Guinea suffers already from one of the evils found in other developing countries—excessive urbanization. This carryover from the days of the Australian administration has led to the creation of slums and unemployment in the principal towns. It is rather despairingly estimated that urban populations will continue to grow at a rate of up to twelve per cent over the next few years. Such concentrations of under-privileged people are the breeding grounds for social and political disorder, and if they are allowed to grow at this rate present expectations of peaceful progress could be nullified. In the long term the planned development of the countryside could be expected to check the flow of people to the cities but meanwhile the government would be wise to deal vigorously with the problems that already exist.

Another threat to orderly progress is separatism. If Bougainville, with its huge copper reserves, became an independent State the foreign exchange earnings of Papua New Guinea would be halved, and the hope of attaining economic self-reliance in the next twenty years would disappear. There are undoubtedly mineral deposits in the other islands, possibly including some as rich as on Bougainville, but these would take several years to bring into production and meanwhile the developmental plans for the rest of the country would be seriously delayed.

The pressure for Bougainville independence seems likely to continue. There is inherently no reason why the province should not become a separate State. With a population of 100 000 and an annual income from copper of over 250 million dollars (Aust.) it would be more viable than most other mini-states in the Pacific region. The people are markedly distinct from ethnic groups in the other New Guinea islands, many of them exhibiting a striking combination of deep black skin with fine features and slender physique. (They also have their own language, but since there are 700 different languages in Papua New Guinea this is not a matter that especially distinguishes them from other groups.)

If Bougainville, which has been re-named the Northern Solomons, were joined with the British Solomon Islands (which are due to become independent in 1978) it would constitute a coherent geographical and ethnic entity. The racial make up of the southern Solomon Islanders is similar and they have many cultural traits in common with the northerners. There has been considerable Australian influence in the British Solomons in recent years and administrative arrangements have been increasingly based upon practice in Australia and Papua New Guinea. The currency used is the Australian dollar. There is a significant Australian aid programme and Australian capital has been invested in mining and cattle industry. There would probably be sufficient administrative compatibility between the two territories to make union a fairly simple process. The best course for both might, in fact, be for them to join together, and then remain in Papua New Guinea as a substantially autonomous province.

In the period of self-government prior to independence there was strong pressure in Bougainville for the holding of a referendum to decide whether Bougainville should be a separate State, but this was refused by both the Australian and Papua New Guinea governments. The Australians and the local leaders equally wished to avoid any break-up of the Territory before independence, fearing that this might result in general fragmentation. The refusal to meet the wishes of the Bougainvilleans led to some violence in Kieta, the provincial capital, and at the copper mines, but this subsided as the time for independence approached. In 1976 an agreement was reached between the national government and the Bougain-villeans, giving the latter a measure of autonomy within a united Papua New Guinea. In regard to the critical question of resources it was agreed that control of development and exploitation would remain with the national government. Royalties would be handed over to the provincial governments but the national government would collect all corporate and personal income taxes and customs duties. The agreement will require complex constitutional arrange-ments and its success in practice will depend upon a large measure of good will and co-operation between the centre and the provincial government. Only time will tell whether this will be forthcoming.

The concessions to the Bougainvilleans naturally led to pressure from other groups, and the national government agreed to the setting up of provincial governments in areas where they were desired by the local communities. The Tolais of East New Britain have always had a strong sense of separate identity and a provincial government was inaugurated in that region in 1976. Other provin-cial governments are planned for the Central, East Sepik and the Eastern Highlands districts. Pressure in other areas for such arrangements is so far not strong, but is expected to increase as political sophistication develops in the outlying regions.

All the arrangements for provincial governments so far made apply only to the former territory of New Guinea. The problem of separatism in Papua is still unresolved. Before independence Papua had a different juridical status from New Guinea: it was an old-style colony and not a Trust Territory; and its people were Australian citizens rather than 'Australian protected persons'. This led many Papuans to believe that they deserved more of Australia than the New Guineans—including if they wished the right to become part of Australia. Successive Australian governments sought to disabuse the Papuans of any such hopes: one of the rights of Australian citizenship which was always denied them was the right to domicile in Australia. As the time of independence approached most Papuan leaders felt that they had no alternative but to join with New Guinea in the new State. Separatist feeling has not, however, disappeared and could again become a serious issue in a period of economic or political disturbance. As it happens, western Papua, at Ok Tedi, is the area where the prospects are at present most promising for finding new mineral reserves. If important discoveries are made it can be expected that, as in Bougainville, local leaders will argue that the wealth should belong to the Papuans and not to the national State. One of the sanctions against separatism is that the Australian government has made it clear that it would give no aid to any territory that withdrew from the new State, but this would have diminished force if Papua was to discover wealth of its own.

That such ideas are in the minds of many Papuans was demonstrated at the elections of July 1977 when Papua Besena (the party pledged to separatism) won substantially increased support. The party's leader, Josephine Abaijah, in a deliberate test of strength, stood for the same electorate as Sir Maori Kiki, who was at the time Deputy Prime Minister, Minister for Defence, and Minister for Foreign Affairs and Trade. He was the most senior Papuan leader in the country, but he was defeated by Josephine Abaijah by a considerable majority. After her victory she declared that she would continue to work for a separate Papua state.

Following the 1977 election Somare appointed as Minister for Decentralisation Father Momis, who was leader of the Bougainville separatist movement and who was elected to parliament for the first time in 1977. This was a shrewd and courageous political move and has increased confidence in the government's sincerity in regard to the devolvement of powers to the provinces. But in a country as diverse as Papua New Guinea there is a thin line between decentralization and disintegration and great political skill will be needed to ensure that this is not crossed.

In short, in spite of a promising beginning, the internal stability of Papua New Guinea cannot yet be regarded as assured. The same, unfortunately, must be said of its external security.

Independence was pressed strenuously on Papua New Guinea by the Whitlam government and when it was proclaimed in May 1975 the reaction of both the government and the Australian people was one of relief. This was based on the feeling that Australians would no longer have to worry about the possibility that the 'White Australia' policy might be undermined by migration from Papua New Guinea; and also that it would no longer have any responsibility for the defence of those indefensible islands. In return for this relief the Australians were quite happy to set aside a small annual sum to assist the economy of the new State. (At the time of independence it was announced that this aid would be tied to particular projects, which would in effect have meant continuing interference by Australia in the country's internal economic management. Fortunately this policy was reversed in 1976 by the Fraser government, which pledged a basic minimum of $180 million of un-tied aid for each year over a period of five years.)

When the Australian Prime Minister, Malcolm Fraser, visited Papua New Guinea in February 1977, it was agreed that neither country wished to enter into a mutual security treaty. Instead they would consult as need arose about common security interests and 'other aspects of their defence relationship'. These other aspects included the attachment of a few Australian servicemen to the Papua New Guinea Defence Force and arrangements for military training on a small scale in Australia. No term was set to these arrangements and it was accepted that they could be ended at any time by either government.

Michael Somare has shown himself to be realistically aware both of his country's own defencelessness and of Australia's inability to give it protection. He has, in particular, recognized the need for good relations with the Indonesians and has shown better sense in dealing with them than some Australian politicians. Shortly after independence he visited Djakarta and, in contrast to abusive statements being made in Australia at the time, he assured President Suharto that he appreciated the Indonesian government's position on East Timor and regarded it 'entirely as a domestic matter of Indonesia'.

He sought accord with the Indonesian authorities concerning the border between Papua New Guinea and Irian Jaya and agreement was reached that 'measures had to be taken to ensure that their respective territories should not be misused in whatever manner by elements contrary to the other to conduct subversive or negative actions against the other'. This accord stood both governments in good stead when disorders broke out on the Irian Jaya side of the border in June 1977 and 1978, which led to some violent incidents on the Papua New Guinea side. The Australian media, as is their custom, sought to dramatize the incidents and to create the impression of serious friction between Papua New Guinea and Indonesia, but Somare handled the matter soberly and sensibly, thereby preventing undue alarm in his own country and any significant damage to his relations with the Indonesians. It seems likely that there will be further disorders along the border—which runs for much of its length through difficult country and is virtually impossible to patrol—but Somare is patently determined to deal with the problem in his own sensible and pragmatic way. He would, no doubt, be grateful if Australian commentators and politicians kept out of the business.

Michael Somare has also sought common ground with the Indonesians on the law of the sea. It is in the interests of both countries, consisting as they do of chains of islands, that a new 'archipelagic state' concept should be accepted by the international community. This would give them more assured control over the waters between their islands and the continental shelves by which they are mostly linked. It would also give them a more advantageous basis for a two-hundred-mile exclusive fishing zone (which it must be expected that in due course both countries will declare).

It might be too early to assume that this conciliatory attitude towards Indonesia, which is very much a personal policy of Michael Somare's, will be a permanent Papua New Guinea attitude. The long drawn out dispute in the 1950s over the future of Netherlands New Guinea (now Irian Jaya) had a marked effect on the generation which has now come to leadership in Papua New Guinea. Many of them were persuaded that the Irianese were the same kind of people as themselves and were uneasy when they passed under what is regarded as Asian rule. Australia's inability to prevent this transfer made a marked impact: being in effect the first lesson for the people of Papua New Guinea that there was little Australia could do to advance their external interests.

Sukarno's campaign of confrontation of Malaysia in the years 1963–65 strengthened the fear and suspicion of Indonesia, and there are many Papuans and New Guineans who are prepared to believe that Indonesia's ultimate ambition is to take over their country. The opposition parties have not been above exploiting these fears and suspicions and Somare has been accused of appeasement towards the Indonesians in his attitude regarding the border problems and also because of his acceptance of the takeover of East Timor. This hostile attitude is shared by the nascent student movement in Port Moresby, which in February 1976 held a demonstration outside the Indonesian Embassy against the 'aggression' in Timor.

Somare himself seems to feel that one way of diminishing the possibilities of conflict between Indonesia and Papua New Guinea is to develop the relationship in the context of a wider association. He has shown considerable interest in ASEAN and although he believes that Papua New Guinea membership would at present be premature, he has made known his desire to keep in touch with its activities. He is attracted by the idea that Papua New Guinea might serve as a bridge between south-east Asia and the southwest Pacific and has suggested to the Indonesians that contacts should be established between ASEAN and the South Pacific Forum. He has expressed support both for ZOPFAN (the ASEAN proposal for a Zone of Peace Freedom and Neutrality in southeast Asia) and for a nuclear-free zone in the South Pacific. He has not been deterred by the current Australian and New Zealand indifference to these two proposals and it is conceivable that he might have in due course a role to play in bringing them closer to realization.

Another of Michael Somare's early overseas visits was to China. He said that the visit was designed to further Papua New Guinea's 'universalist' foreign policy: relations had already been established with the United States and the Soviet Union and by seeking relations with China he wished to demonstrate his country's evenhanded approach to the great powers.

He arrived in Peking shortly after the death of Mao Tse–tung, but he was nevertheless cordially received by Hua Kuo–feng, who in the following week was officially proclaimed Mao's successor as Chairman of the Communist Party of China. During the same month a Chinese trade fair was held in Port Moresby and there are signs that China sees both economic and political value in establishing trade links with the country.

In the past the Chinese who migrated to New Guinea were not popular and it remains to be seen whether the development of trade with mainland China will revive this hostility. For the present the Papua New Guinea government is resisting the establishment of a Chinese diplomatic mission in Port Moresby on the grounds that it is not yet in a position to provide facilities for a large number of diplomatic missions.

There is a lingering dislike of the Japanese among the Papuans and New Guineans but this has not prevented the rapid development of trade relations. After Australia, Japan is the country's most important economic partner. It takes a large proportion of the copper mined in Bougainville and also draws imports from the timber and fishing industries (in which the Japanese have made substantial investments). A number of important joint ventures are being developed in manufacturing, power generation and mining.

The growing Japanese economic presence has caused uneasiness and the government is under pressure to apply strict controls. Nevertheless, in view of the country's need for both Japanese investment and expertise it must be expected that Japan's economic influence will continue to grow.

Michael Somare's efforts to build up good relations with Asian governments do not obscure the fact that there is in Papua New Guinea a deep dislike of Asians. This comes partly from the New Guineans' lack of self-confidence in dealing with them. They are afraid of being exploited by people whom they regard as more sophisticated than themselves. They are, in truth, more comfortable in dealing with their Pacific island neighbours and it would seem logical and natural that it would be in this direction that they would most actively develop their external relations.

In the Pacific, Papua New Guinea is a large fish in a large pool full of small fish. Its population, rising towards three million, is almost double the total population of the rest of the Pacific islands, and its potential resources overshadow all the others. Many of its social and economic problems are, however, similar to theirs. Most of its people still live at the subsistence level and face an abrupt transition into a modern technological society. In some of the islands this transition is more advanced than in Papua New Guinea, and in others less so, but there would be much mutual benefit in the interchange of ideas and assistance. If Papua New Guinea maintains its own political stability it could give valuable leadership to the whole region, especially in finding solutions which might be better adapted to local problems than those proffered by Western countries.

A promising context for the exercise of Papua New Guinea leadership is the South Pacific Forum (see p. 113). In August 1977 the eighth meeting of the Forum was held in Port Moresby, and Michael Somare played an active role. He proposed that the Forum should maintain contact with ASEAN on problems of common interest and this was endorsed. He also took the lead in discussions on protecting the environment of the South Pacific and the Forum adopted his proposal for an environmental 'management programme'.

Under Michael Somare Papua New Guinea has thus moved fairly

positively towards an independent foreign policy, but for the next twenty years or so it is likely to remain economically dependent upon Australia. This is not only because it is expected to require economic aid for that time, but because by its own choice it will remain part of the Australian economic area. Under the Trade and Commercial Relations Agreement which came into force on 1 February 1977 duty-free entry into Australia will be allowed on all but a few items. For its part, Papua New Guinea will not discriminate against Australian trade and investment, although Australia will receive no preferential treatment in the Papua New Guinea market above other countries. This will mean that production will develop along the lines of least resistance—in providing goods for the Australian market. Whether this will be for the ultimate good of the country only time will tell: it could mean that such commodities as coffee, cocoa and tea will be grown for the Australian market at the expense of crops which might have a steadier international demand. But since the first priority of the government is to develop the rural economy it probably has no alternative but to put heavy reliance upon the Australian market for the disposal of the cash crops on which the rural areas will have mainly to rely. The best hope for eventual economic independence will be in the development of the country's mineral and timber resources, and perhaps in the discovery of significant oil and gas deposits.

For many years before independence, successive Australian governments were warned by their officials that if the boundary between Papua and the State of Queensland were not rectified it would be a source of serious friction between Australia and Papua New Guinea. These warnings were unheeded and the prediction has come true.

In 1879, before Papua was declared a British colony, Queensland extended its control over the Torres Strait islands to within sight of the coast of Papua. This action was taken because it was believed that the strait would become an important waterway and also because the Queenslanders wished to control the lucrative pearling industry then operating in the area. When the British annexed Papua in 1884 (after having disallowed an attempt by the colony of Queensland to do so in the previous year) the need for such an arrangement disappeared: since there were British colonies on both sides of the straits there could be no doubt that the waterway was firmly in British hands. But because of the commercial advantages the Queenslanders were deriving from the existing arrangement they blocked all attempts to divide control over the islands on a more rational basis.

The Queenslanders are still doing so. Their reasons have changed. There is no longer a Torres Strait pearling industry and although the waterway is important to shipping plying to the east coast of Australia it is never likely to become a major international sea lane. The argument now is that the Torres Strait Islanders are Australians (although they have never been accorded by the Queensland authorities the full rights of white Queenslanders) and that therefore they should not be forced to join Papua New Guinea. For economic reasons the Torres Strait Islanders agree with this. They are to a considerable extent dependent upon welfare payments and they would lose these if their islands ceased to be part of Queensland. In any case, to change territorial sovereignty over the islands would now be politically very difficult: it would require not only the agreement of the governments of Australia, Queensland and Papua New Guinea but, perhaps, also an Australian referendum.

In negotiations between the Australian governments and the government of Papua New Guinea which have taken place since independence it has been accepted by both sides that there should be no transfer of sovereignty and that all Torres Strait Islanders should remain Australian citizens. It has been agreed, however, that the maritime boundary between the two countries (which had never been settled and which constitutes a separate issue from the question of territorial sovereignty) should be drawn in accordance with customary international law. This boundary would apply not only to the sea but also to the continental shelf lying between the two countries. Substantial agreement was reached between the Australian government and Papua New Guinea as to where this boundary should be drawn, but the Queensland government continued to withhold agreement.

Sir Maori Kiki, who had the main responsibility for the negotiations, lost his seat to parliament in the 1977 elections, partly as a result of charges of appeasement towards the Australians, and the government formed by Michael Somare after the elections has taken a harsher line. It has made it clear that unless there is an early settlement of the issue it will take its case to the International Court of Justice. If it does, it will propose a boundary in accord with the traditional principles of international law, but without regard to Australia's constitutional and political preoccupations. The Papua New Guinea government claims that its case would attract widespread international sympathy and it is easy to see that this might well be true. The opportunity to reach a settlement on the equitable basis that the Papua New Guinea government has already shown itself ready to accept would in any case pass. Whether the Australian people should be grateful to Queensland for pursuing its historic attitude to this conclusion and causing continuing friction with Papua New Guinea is questionable.

Papua New Guinea has made a promising beginning as an independent State, but its future will depend largely on developments which it will have little power to influence. It is an integral part of the nexus of islands and waterways which connect the Indian and Pacific Oceans and if this were to fall under the domination of one power Papua New Guinea would inevitably be part of its dominion. Like Australia its best hope for independence—in fact its only hope—is that the countries of south-east Asia will be able by their collective efforts to prevent such domination.

5

The Changing South Pacific

New Zealand and the islands of the south-west Pacific have the good fortune to be strategically unimportant and if their leaders behave with good sense they should be able to avoid direct involvement in future conflicts. They will be affected by the outcome of the struggle for control of the Pacific region and will have to come to terms with the power that wins it; but since they cannot directly influence the outcome they would be wise to avoid dissipating their energies in trying to do so. As in the case of Australia, they have little to gain from dependence upon any of the great powers, but much to suffer from attracting their hostility.

Like the Australians, the New Zealanders have not in the past acted on this simple premise. They sent forces to Europe in the first and second world wars, and most New Zealanders are still proud of having done so. They also made a contribution to the Korean war which on a per capita basis was second only to that of the United States—believing, as the Australians did, that this was a price worth paying for the ANZUS pact. They also accepted that the Korean war was being fought to combat global communism and to uphold the United Nations—not realizing, again like the Australians, that neither of these reasons was valid.

It was not until New Zealand was drawn into the Vietnam war that questions were seriously asked, for the first time in the country's history, as to whether its involvement in distant conflicts was in its best interests. New Zealand's contribution was this time more grudging than Australia's—the New Zealand combat unit being no more than 500 men—but the government justified its action on the same lines as the Australian government. Keith Holyoake, who was Prime Minister at the time the decision was made (and who was once characterized by R. G. Menzies as a man who always discovered the obvious with 'immense surprise') defended New Zealand participation on the basis of a crude version of the 'domino theory'. The North Vietnamese were regarded as fighting in the cause of global communism, and Holyoake declared that if South Vietnam was defeated 'the entire free world's position in south-east Asia would be jeopardised'. He rebuked his critics for their 'glib dismissal' of the domino theory and said that it had been amply demonstrated that 'to allow a state to fall before aggression tends to increase rather than reduce the chances that its neighbours will face the same fate against even more difficult odds'. Believing that the North Vietnamese were acting as agents for China he was impervious to suggestions that a united Vietnam could be a buffer protecting the other 'dominoes'—if, indeed, he ever grasped what the argument was about.

From the beginning there were people in New Zealand who questioned both the wisdom and the morality of this approach. There were some who believed that the conflict in Vietnam was a civil war and should be left to the Vietnamese to settle; that the introduction of white troops would only worsen the conflict; and that the use by Western forces of destructive modern weapons was inhumane and immoral. While Holyoake remained Prime Minister these arguments had little effect on government policies. He was, however, shaken by President Nixon's decision in 1969 to begin the withdrawal of United States forces, and in the following years the New Zealand forces were trickled out of Vietnam.

The New Zealand Labour Party came to power in December 1972. It announced some new approaches to foreign policy with a clearer voice than the Australian Labor Party (which won the election held at about the same time in Australia). An attempt was made to remind New Zealanders of the facts of geography and to encourage them to realize that their future did not depend on relations with distant countries but on co-operation with their neighbours in Asia and the Pacific. The new government was not given time to consolidate its new policies, but some changes of direction were made. In a review in February 1975 of the policy of the Labour Government, W. E. Rowling said that New Zealand had 'become engaged more fully, more vigorously and more constructively in the affairs of our region than ever before'. He added that it was fundamental to New Zealand's new approach that 'an independent and self-reliant policy would find its most rewarding expression in co-operation within the region'. He made the acute and realistic observation that the superpowers had 'become almost totally pre-occupied with the cross-currents of their own relationships' at the expense of their long-standing ties with other countries. The implication was clear that the time had come for the smaller countries to look to their own interests.

Rowling said that America's military disengagement from mainland Asia was a 'good and welcome development'; and that any direct re-involvement militarily by outside powers would be 'not only misguided and futile but dangerous'. He added, no doubt as a sop to public opinion, that the ANZUS Treaty had 'continuing validity', but stated flatly that the likelihood of its security provisions ever being invoked was remote.

New Zealand has traditionally seen the South Pacific as its main sphere of interest. The Labour government accepted that links with Polynesia must continue, but it cast its ambitions somewhat further. It saw a particular value in developing a close association with Australia, Papua New Guinea and Indonesia, and as a long-term goal looked forward to the creation of a forum that would encompass all the countries of Asia and the Pacific.

An initiative taken by the New Zealand Labour government which attracted a good deal of international attention was its proposal to the United Nations that the south Pacific should be declared a nuclear-free zone. This idea was inspired principally by the concern among the New Zealand people at the testing in their Pacific territories by the French of nuclear weapons, but it was also linked with the desire to prevent the deployment in the area by the superpowers of nuclear-armed ships or aircraft. These concerns were shared by Fiji, Papua New Guinea and the other countries of the south Pacific and a resolution was put to the General Assembly calling for the establishment of a nuclear weapons free zone. The resolution was adopted by 110 votes in favour, with twenty abstentions. The United States and the Soviet Union, not surprisingly, abstained, in the company of most of their respective allies.

There was a widespread feeling, shared even by the New Zealanders themselves, that although worthy, the objective of establishing a nuclear-free zone in the south Pacific was unrealistic. This was also the view of the Whitlam government, but since it gave its support to the idea of a 'zone of peace and freedom and neutrality' for the Indian Ocean it seems that the real reason for lack of enthusiasm was a disinclination to offend the United States. It must be admitted that in so far as it was purely hortatory the United Nations resolution *was* unrealistic. The preamble to the resolution acknowledged that the co-operation of the existing nuclear powers would be necessary for the establishment of the zone, but its operative section did no more than 'express the hope' that these States would so co-operate.

The New Zealand approach was itself ambivalent. In his speech to the General Assembly in support of the resolution, Rowling said that the creation of the zone 'should not disturb necessary security arrangements'. He presumably meant that New Zealand's relations with the United States should not be disturbed. But this was the rub. An exclusive alliance with one superpower is incompatible with the kind of neutrality which would be the indispensable basis for a nuclear-free zone.

Rowling declared that provision must be made for 'adequate verification', but the New Zealanders' own draft included no such provision. Indeed no effective verification would be possible until the countries in the zone had agreed to establish a neutral system to which they were all committed; to accept responsibility themselves for supervision and control; and to treat the activities of all non-zone powers on a basis of equality and non-discrimination. Because of their own confusion of thought as to their objective, the New Zealanders' initiative has proved abortive and the United Nations resolution, in spite of some half-hearted attempts at further consultations, is a dead letter. The conservative government which succeeded the Rowling administration in New Zealand has little sympathy with it and no interest in following it up.

After the elections in 1975 New Zealand, like Australia, reverted to the policies of the past. This was resoundingly affirmed in 1976 by Allan McCready, the Minister for Defence in the Muldoon government:

> The keystone of our defence policy is the ANZUS treaty, under which we have the assurance of support, if necessary, not only from our closest neighbour (Australia) but also from one of the world's two great powers—a consideration which grows more important with the expansion of Soviet military power in general and sea-power in particular.

He added that the idea of a nuclear-free zone in the South Pacific was not only impracticable in today's world, but unrealistic, in so far as it could hinder the provision of the defence assistance on which New Zealand would depend in an emergency. He rejected the possibility of armed neutrality on the grounds of cost. He said that New Zealand devoted only 4·1 per cent of its budget to defence, whereas neutral states like Sweden and Switzerland spent 10·5 per cent and 19·5 per cent respectively. He also concluded that unarmed neutrality would not offer any real prospect of security to a country so small, isolated, and dependent on overseas trade as New Zealand.

Some New Zealand commentators have pointed out that with a total armed forces strength of only 12 000 regular personnel the country was in any case virtually unarmed. The largest army formations that can be effectively manned are battalions, of which there are four. The Navy consists of four frigate-type vessels, and the air force has a total of about seventy planes, mostly obsolescent. These forces could not be expected to offer serious resistance to a determined attack either on New Zealand's sea communications or its territory. They are, in fact, not designed to operate alone but, like the Australian, must depend on the co-operation of allies.

New Zealanders are increasingly doubtful whether such allies would be forthcoming in time of need. They recognize that Australia does not have the means to defend itself, much less New Zealand; and their confidence in the readiness of the United States to give protection is waning. The new government's policy did not, therefore, go unchallenged. Shortly after it came to power the Prime Minister, R. D. Muldoon, decided that visits to New Zealand by nuclear-powered United States warships should be permitted. Such permission had been refused in the previous ten years and the reversal was regarded as a rejection by New Zealand of the concept of a nuclear-free zone. The Labour Party leader, W. E. Rowling, argued that New Zealand's best hope lay in its strategic unimportance, and that to encourage visits by nuclear warships gave it unnecessary importance. The Prime Minister brushed this argument aside. He said that New Zealand would be totally vulnerable if it did not retain the freedom of sea lanes, and that the first consideration in foreign and defence policies was the preservation of the country's 'lifelines by sea'. He drew attention to the expansion of Soviet strength in the Indian Ocean, and to the development of Russian long-range missile capability in the Pacific; and declared that 'the only power capable of providing a balance against the Soviet Union' was the United States. Like the Prime Minister of Australia (at this time Malcolm Fraser) Muldoon carefully avoided the issue of whether the United States still had the will and the ability to maintain this balance.

Muldoon seemed, however, to share with Fraser the belief that China could be a valuable counterweight to the extension of

Russian influence. In expressing opposition to 'hegemony' in the region during his visit to Peking he adopted China's anti-Russian jargon, and said he was convinced that China had no 'offensive global designs'. What effective help he expected from China in return for this surprising warmth was not disclosed.

A more realistic assessment of New Zealand's position than that offered by government leaders was contained in the report of a task force on economic and social planning issued in December 1976. This was headed by Sir Frank Holmes, and included representatives of the main government departments. The report took only six months to complete and its lucidity and realism is in striking contrast to the many reports produced in Australia after prolonged and confused hearings, often presided over by judges who have little understanding of government. The report, which is entitled *New Zealand at the Turning Point*, deals mainly with internal problems, but it includes a cogent chapter on the country's relations with the outside world.

Commenting that New Zealanders' understanding of their position in the world is still dominated by ideas from the past, it says:

> Much of the public discussion in this area still confuses the issue by implying that we have some big-nation role handed down to us. The facts of life are however different. Our size and isolation, our dependence and vulnerability, particularly in economic terms, and the fact that in world terms we belong to a minority—the Western-type affluent society—all these factors point up the simple fact that we are expendable as far as the power centres of the outside world are concerned . . . It is clear that our pre-occupations do not weigh heavily with other countries. In very few capitals of the world can New Zealand enjoy real influence on political decisions.

It says much for the good sense of New Zealanders that this baldly realistic statement could be made by a group consisting largely of public servants; in Australia they would probably have lost their jobs.

The report went on to say that the lesson was not that New Zealand should 'go it alone'; its broad interests lay increasingly in forming constructive partnerships with the developing countries, especially those in south-east Asia and the Pacific. On defence, the report declared that New Zealand's forces would never again have a role in other people's wars; and that they should be organized to meet present requirements rather than to fight past battles. Present requirements are described as 'maintaining security around New Zealand's strategic perimeter'.

Unfortunately this concept is not defined and, indeed, it would be difficult to do so. Clearly it means more than New Zealand territory and territorial waters, because enemy forces could blockade New Zealand without approaching her coasts. New Zealand is in a similar position to Australia: its security depends not so much on the defence of its own territory as on the safety of its communications through the Pacific and Indian oceans—the 'sea lanes' about which Prime Minister Muldoon spoke.

There is one respect in which New Zealand's communications seem less vulnerable than Australia's: it is not so dependent upon the straits and waterways passing through the Indonesian islands. Much of the country's exports and imports could be carried along routes to the south of Australia and eastward across the Pacific. Nevertheless, it seems likely that in circumstances in which the flow of trade through the Indonesian straits was interdicted, this interdiction would eventually be extended to other available routes. New Zealand's minimal armed forces would clearly be unable to prevent this. The question therefore arises whether they are worth keeping.

The same question arises for Australia, and the answer is probably the same. Neither country can afford defence forces sufficient to defend their overseas communications or their home territory. Nor can they any longer rely on the United States to defend them. The only realistic concept is that of co-operation with the countries of south-east Asia to try to insure the freedom of the nexus of waterways between the Indian and Pacific oceans and, by extension, of New Zealand's sea lanes.

Before arrangements of this kind could be made, relations of confidence and trust would have to be built up with the other countries of the region. Because of its past behaviour and present policies Australia is greatly handicapped in developing such relations. It is possible that New Zealand is in a better position to do so. It is not as actively disliked as Australia. It does not carry the stigma of the 'White Australia' policy, and its treatment of the Maoris is acknowledged to be more humane than Australia's treatment of the Aboriginals. Its attitude in international economic relations has been visibly less grasping than Australia's and its tariff restrictions have been less harmful to the developing countries. Because it is smaller and less assertive than Australia its influence is less feared, and it has a reputation for genuine concern for the maintenance of the rules of international law. It is possible, therefore, that it could make a strong diplomatic effort to encourage the development of defence co-operation in south-east Asia without provoking the suspicion and hostility that Australian efforts would arouse.

It is unlikely that a move could be made by New Zealand under the present ruggedly conservative government, but the mature and realistic thinking which underlies the report of the Holmes Task Force encourages hope that such an initiative is not beyond the bounds of possibility.

The report emphasized that New Zealand should give first priority to its relations with Australia, and this is sensible in that New Zealand has nowhere else to go; but it would be unfortunate if this encouraged the tendency simply to follow Australia's lead. Unless its policies change markedly Australia is likely to drift into a situation in the coming years of being unable either to cope adequately with its own problems or to give help to its neighbours. The structural distortions in its economy make it impossible to establish satisfactory trading relations with its south-east Asian neighbours and immigration policies remain substantially unreformed. Any hopes that New Zealanders might entertain that Australia will give a lead towards the creation of a stable economic and strategic balance in south-east Asia and the south-west Pacific are likely to be disappointed. New Zealanders should not, therefore, neglect their responsibility to work independently towards this objective.

This would mean that they would have to look beyond their traditional sphere of interest. They are proud of the contribution they have made to social, economic and political development in the islands of the south-west Pacific and rightly so; but, no less than New Zealand itself, their problems cannot be solved except in a much wider context.

The natural resources of the Pacific islands are very limited and in most cases the high birth-rate continues to overwhelm the developmental efforts that have so far been made. Compared with Australia, New Zealand has adopted a liberal attitude towards the immigration of Pacific Islanders (it has accepted 80 000 since the end of World War II), but it is clearly impossible for sufficient numbers to be admitted to make a significant difference to the rapidly growing population in the islands. The prospects for the development of agriculture, heavy industry or mining are generally poor, and the only hope lies in the growth of commerce with nations outside the region. The Japanese, Russians and Chinese are all showing increased interest in the area, and although some of their activities are causing concern, there seems to be no alternative but to accept and even encourage such interest. Because of their experience in the area and their relations of trust with many of the island governments, New Zealanders are in a good position to advise them on how to deal with the great powers in a way which would safeguard their own essential interests.

Australia is, meanwhile, likely to come under increasing pressure to accept its own responsibilities towards the islands of the South Pacific. It has in the past derived substantial economic benefit from its trade relations with the region, but has given little in return. It has given rhetorical support to international assistance programmes to the area, but until recently its own aid has been derisory. Its balance of trade with most of the islands has also been heavily in its own favour.

But it is in the migration field that Australia's policies have been most discreditable. Immigration into Australia has been virtually prohibited for most of the century, notwithstanding that its ability to absorb the island peoples is far greater than New Zealand's. In the main islands the birth-rate is over three per cent and the population will double by the year 2000. In most other parts of the world there are no physical bars to increasing food production to keep pace with population growth but in the Pacific islands the soil and climatic conditions make it very difficult to do so. The prospects are also poor of increasing the production of the traditional export crops—sugar, copra and bananas—to the extent sufficient to pay for imports of food. There are few opportunities for industrial development (although manufacturing activities may increase in relation to the deep-sea fishing operations of outside powers). Overall resources are unlikely to be sufficient to provide minimum standards of sustenance in many of the islands. (The French colony of New Caledonia is an exception because of its large reserves of nickel. Another exception is Nauru: because of its phosphate deposits it is one of the richest communities in the world.)

In most circumstances where population overwhelms resources, transfers of people are no solution, if only because it is impracticable to carry them out on a scale sufficient to relieve the pressure. There are difficult social problems in getting people to move, in finding countries to receive them and in settling them into their new homes; and the costs of the actual transfer are usually high. For the Pacific islanders, however, these problems would be manageable. Their overall numbers are not great: leaving aside the French and American territories the total population of the islands at present is a little more than one million and can by the end of the century be expected to grow to more than two million. If Australia and New Zealand were between them to absorb about 25 000 migrants a year the economic future of the region would be transformed. The pressure of numbers would be usefully reduced, and the island economies would be greatly benefited by remittances from the migrants. Many of the island migrants would be literate in English, so that they could be readily assimilated into Australian industry and society—more readily, say, than the migrants from the rural areas of Turkey (of whom nearly 25 000 have been brought to Australia in the past ten years). It is inevitable that when Australia's economy resumes normal growth we will again suffer a labour shortage. The countries of southern Europe cannot be expected in future to be able to provide us with the necessary manpower and it would be beneficial to ourselves as well as the Pacific islanders to bring them into our work force. It need hardly be added that it would also help to ameliorate our racist image.

We would have to treat the islanders better than we treated those who were recruited into Australia as indentured labourers in the last century. They would have to be accepted on a basis of full equality with European migrants: they would have to be brought in as families, ensured opportunities of employment and provided with decent housing. Special measures would be needed to prevent the creation of ghetto communities. Above all, the Australian people would have to be educated to treat them with fairness and humanity.

The South Pacific country which is likely to face the worst problems is Fiji. It is also the country towards which Australia has the clearest obligations. The Australian-owned Colonial Sugar Refining Company has dominated the Fijian economy since the beginning of the century and throughout this period it has repatriated substantial profits to Australia. Its operations have been the direct cause of the country's racial problem. Labour was brought in from India (first under the notorious indenture system and later as 'free' migrants) to grow the sugar for the C.S.R. mills. The Indian community is now larger than the Fijian: of a population of 550 000 slightly more than half are Indian, and because the Indian birth-rate is higher than the Fijian the Indian majority will increase. The Fijians naturally fear that they are, or will be, disinherited in their own lands, and as population pressure grows the hostility between the two communities is likely to worsen. The mainstay of the economy is still sugar, but in recent years the balance of visible trade has been heavily adverse. Fortunately the gap has been filled by income from tourism, and Fiji's position at the crossroads of trans-Pacific sea and air traffic has been of great economic benefit. Tourism is a tender plant, however, and can easily be killed by internal disorder, or by changes of fashion in international travel. It is, in any case, an industry which tends to benefit the urban Indian communities rather than the rural Fijians.

Although Australia has made large profits from Fijian sugar production, it has refused to import it into its own territory, because of the need to protect the Queensland sugar industry. Its immigration prohibitions have extended alike to Fijians, Indians and part-Europeans; and if any who have found their way to Australia have sought to stay permanently they have been expelled with customary inhumanity.

Those in Australia who become indignant about South Africa's apartheid policy, or about Indonesia's treatment of the Timorese, might well give some of their attention to persuading the Australian people to fulfil their heavy moral obligation to the people of Fiji and the other Pacific Islands.

To the east of Fiji lie Samoa and Tonga. These are more fortunate, in that their racial composition has remained predominantly Polynesian. American Samoa is still a dependency of the United States, but Western Samoa and Tonga are independent States. The Samoans and Tongans are self-reliant people and have shown themselves to be capable of self-government. They are increasingly suffering from over-population, however, and in recent years they have emigrated in growing numbers to New Zealand. Since their education is based on English-speaking systems, and since they are of the same racial stock as the Maoris of New Zealand they have assimilated relatively easily into the New Zealand community. But the economic and social problems of absorbing them are becoming increasingly onerous and New Zealand is unlikely on its own to be able to provide a sufficient outlet for the islands' surplus population.

Apart from our clear moral obligations, we may be impelled by self-interest to give more serious attention to the problems of the South Pacific. The measures so far taken have been of little value. The South Pacific Commission, in which Australia has for many years had a leading role, is run on an annual budget which would barely pay for the Colonial Sugar Refining Company's stationery. The Australian government has pledged increased aid funds, but the problems of the islanders cannot be solved by permanent subventions. As economic and social distress among them increases they are likely to turn for help to those powers now developing their interests in the area: Japan, China and the Soviet Union. These powers are not likely to have any tenderness towards Australian interests, and in so far as the islanders fall under their influence, the profitable relationship which Australia has hitherto enjoyed could come to an end. This could happen not only in regard to trade but also in communications: Fiji is, for example, important in air and sea traffic between Australia and the United States and any interference with this traffic could do significant damage to the Australian economy. We therefore have an important interest in giving the islanders an outlet in Australia and thus enabling them to withstand the developing pressure from other outside powers.

Russian shipping lines now ply throughout the region and the Soviet Union has established diplomatic and consular posts in several islands. Japanese fishing activities are of growing economic importance to the South Pacific and their trade with the area is expanding. It was inevitable that the Chinese would also move into the region; they have shown particular interest in the Fiji–Samoa–Tonga group and have established embassies in Suva and Apia. At the end of 1976 an agreement was signed between Western Samoa and China for economic and technical co-operation. Under the agreement China has undertaken to assist with construction projects, including the provision of loan funds and engineering and technical personnel. These arrangements were entered into a few months after the Soviet Union had established diplomatic relations with Western Samoa and sent a fisheries mission.

Although the economic difficulties of the islands are severe, they are small scale: the cost of providing them with assistance is tiny compared with the needs of other developing regions. This means that countries like Russia, China and Japan can secure economic and political influence in the region in return for very modest outlays.

The French territories in the Pacific—New Caledonia and French Polynesia (Tahiti, Papeete and the Marquesas, and related islands) —have long been regarded in Australia as firmly attached to France, and therefore primarily the responsibility of the French government. In spite of some progress towards self-government close links with France are likely to persist, at least for some time to come. New Caledonia is firmly tied to the French economy because of its nickel production (of which it is the world's second largest supplier); while French Polynesia remains important as a testing ground for the development of France's nuclear weapons.

A new Statute for New Caledonia which gave local representatives more say in territorial affairs was inaugurated in September 1977. The French High Commissioner, as the agent of the French government, retained full control of such critical areas as finance and mining, and also of foreign affairs, defence and immigration.

Most of the local representatives are in any case French in origin, and are usually amenable to the French government's wishes.

In spite of the Territory's mineral wealth (which includes iron ore and large reserves of chrome) native New Caledonians remain relatively impoverished. The mining industry is mostly manned by Europeans and part-Europeans and by Asians. The indigenous population, numbering about 60 000 out of a total of 140 000, are engaged mainly in the production of copra and coffee and, like other Pacific islanders who are dependent on these crops, suffer a good deal from fluctuations in world prices. As the population increases, so will the pressure on arable land, and it is possible that in future the native New Caledonians will be less quiescent than in the past.

In French Polynesia there was formerly a vigorous native independence movement. In the years after World War II this was led by a Tahitian, Pouvanna a Oopa, but in 1958 he was arrested and deported to France and the movement declined. In a referendum in the same year French Polynesia voted by 63·7 per cent to remain in the French Community. The French nuclear tests brought considerable prosperity to the islanders and agitation for independence subsided. Demands nevertheless continued for more local autonomy and this was to some extent met by a new Statute for French Polynesia which was promulgated in 1977. The Polynesians were given more control over their own economy than the New Caledonians and an elective Council of Government was given considerable powers of internal self-management.

The Tahitian population is one of the most mixed in the Pacific. Pure-blood Polynesians are in a minority. There is a large Chinese community—estimated at about 10 000—and there are numerous part-Europeans. So far the different races have lived in harmony —partly, no doubt, because the French authorities are there to hold the ring, and partly because of the relative prosperity of the islanders. Tourism, based on an unmatched combination of beautiful scenery and beautiful women (a felicitous result, perhaps, of the racial blend) accounts for half the territory's foreign earnings.

The islands of the New Hebrides are one of the world's political oddities. Their government is divided between Great Britain and France; and they have two educational systems and two currencies (one of which is the Australian dollar). In the early part of the century there was an active Australian interest in the Territory and suggestions were several times made that Australia should replace Great Britain as partner to the French. No Australian government was prepared to undertake such a responsibility and in recent times the Territory has almost disappeared from Australian consciousness. It does not have the mineral wealth of neighbouring New Caledonia and its economy depends mainly on the export of copra, cocoa and coffee. It has derived some benefit from deep-sea fishing by foreign powers in the South Pacific and a fish-freezing and packaging plant has been built on the main island, most of the product being exported to Japan.

A strong movement towards independence, led mainly by Europeans and part-Europeans, has developed in the New Hebrides in recent years. The governing powers allowed the creation in 1975 of a Representative Assembly, and a dominant position in this body was won by the New Hebrides National Party. In 1977 this party (renamed the Vanuaaku, or 'Our Land' party) called for immediate independence. It demanded the creation of a ministerial system of government within the Representative Assembly and refused any longer to recognize the jurisdiction in rural areas of the British and French district agents. The governing powers' response was to agree to a larger measure of self-government, with a 'Governing Council' and an Assembly based on universal suffrage. They have conceded that these measures could 'lead to independence' but have so far refused to set a date for its achievement.

Although Australia nowadays shows little interest in the group of islands comprising the territories of New Caledonia and the New Hebrides they have a considerable strategic importance to us. They constitute the eastern rim of the Coral Sea—of which the Solomon Islands and Papua New Guinea form the northern rim. In World War II the Japanese developed plans to seize New Caledonia as part of an overall scheme to capture Fiji and Samoa and cut Australia off from the United States. Another objective was to bring the Queensland coast within the range of Japanese bombers. The minerals of New Caledonia were also regarded as an important prize.

These plans were aborted by the failure of the Japanese to secure control of the Coral Sea. The naval battle fought in these waters on 8 May 1942 was a draw, but it meant that for the time being both New Caledonia and Port Moresby were safe from invasion. The Japanese did not have a second opportunity, because in the following month their main aircraft carrier fleet was heavily damaged by the United States Navy at the battle of Midway Island.

Australia's lucky escape in the last war should not be allowed to obscure the fact that if a hostile power were installed in New Caledonia and the New Hebrides it could control the approaches to the whole of eastern Australia. It is unlikely that the group could be seized in isolation (the Japanese experience showed the difficulty of doing this) but it is the natural extension of the whole chain of islands running from Sumatra in the Indian Ocean to the Solomons in the Pacific, and any power that secured strategic control of this chain would have no difficulty in establishing itself in the New Hebrides and New Caledonia.

With the exception of the small territory of American Samoa (about 30 000 people) the United States' possessions lie north of the equator. Nevertheless they have in the past had considerable strategic importance for the South Pacific. Guam, which is the southernmost island of the Mariana group, is the piece of American territory most remote from mainland United States. It was captured by the Japanese in December 1941 a few days after the attack on Pearl Harbor, and later became an important point on the last ring of defence of the Japanese islands. It was re-taken by the Americans in August 1944, and since the war it has been built up into an important United States air and naval base. Since it is American territory, with only a small native population, it is politically more secure than the American bases in the Philippines and Japan. It lies virtually at the centre of an arc which would pass through Tokyo, Manila and Port Moresby, and is important for the support of American forces in the western Pacific. Nevertheless its strategic value is limited: it is tiny in area—less than a quarter of the size of the Australian Capital Territory—and although it has strong defences it is likely to become increasingly vulnerable to long-range missile attack. It is in a similar case to the Nimitz class aircraft carriers, without their manoeuvrability.

The possibility has sometimes been discussed of developing the island of Palau, which is the closest of the whole group to the Philippines, as a major American naval and air base in the event of the closure of the Philippines bases. It has a relatively large unused land area and is surrounded with high coral reefs, within which it would be practicable to construct a large port. This would have unpredictable environmental consequences, however, and might interfere with the important maritime research which is carried out from the island because of its position at the confluence of important Pacific Ocean currents. Its development as a major base would, therefore, attract opposition both in the United States and abroad.

Palau has potential importance also as a commercial port. If the necessary facilities were developed it could serve as an alternative to Singapore and enable shipping bound for the north Pacific to avoid, in case of need, passage through the Malacca Strait. But such a development would encounter the same environmental problems as in the case of a major naval base.

There is, in any case, little prospect of developing either a naval base or a commercial port until the political future of Palau is resolved. The people object to being thrown in with the rest of Micronesia and in 1976 a majority voted for separation from the United States. They would prefer the island to become a commercial shipping entrepot rather than an American base, and even if they maintained some relationship with the United States it is doubtful whether the political climate would be conducive to the maintenance of large American military, naval and air installations.

Other alternatives for the Americans are the Saipan and Tinian Islands in the Marianas. Tinian is the island from which the American aircraft took off in 1945 to drop the atomic bomb on Hiroshima, and under agreements recently reached with the local authorities the Americans will continue to have the use of more than half the island. They will also have rights on Saipan, which is the main island of the group. These islands have sought 'commonwealth' status with the United States (similar to Puerto Rico) and if this is accepted by the U.N. Security Council (which has the final say on the future of this whole Trust Territory) the political situation would presumably be favourable to the development of a full-scale base. In view of the isolation and vulnerability of the islands there must, however, be considerable doubt whether the United States would wish to commit large resources to its development.

Other islands in this region made famous by the American defence forces are the Bikini and Kwajalein atolls in the Marshall Islands. Bikini was the site of early nuclear testing and is still uninhabited because of continuing radioactivity. Most of the population of Kwajalein was removed to make room for a missile-testing site for the United States army. This is still in use, but it is not certain that it will be needed for much longer. Because of fears that the Russians were developing armed satellites a battery of nuclear missiles was established on the island with the role of countering such satellites, but this was regarded as ineffective and the missiles were withdrawn in 1975.

Australians were at the beginning of this century greatly concerned about the strategic importance of the islands north of the equator: the Marianas, the Carolines and the Marshalls. They regarded their takeover by the Germans in the 1880s as inimical to their security and tried to get the British to oppose it, who in turn sought to prod the Americans into doing so. But the latter raised no effective objections to Germany's activities and contented themselves with taking Guam (at the same time as they occupied the Philippines) from the Spanish.

During World War I it was intended that Australian forces should occupy the German possessions in the Pacific, but the Japanese anticipated them; and at the Versailles Conference it was agreed that Japan should be given a League of Nations mandate over all the former German Pacific island territories except Nauru and New Guinea. This was strenuously opposed by the Australian Prime Minister, W. M. Hughes, but to no effect. He prophesied that the Americans would one day regret their compliance in this arrangement, and lived to see his prophecy come true in World War II. Since the end of the war they have been in American hands as a United Nations Strategic Trust Territory and although there is now considerable development towards autonomy, they are likely to remain closely associated with America. But their strategic importance has diminished; it is doubtful whether in the wars of the future they would serve an important military purpose. Although they consist of 2141 atolls and islands, they total only 700 square miles of land in 3 million square miles of ocean. They do not have the resources to attract a future aggressor, and even if additional American bases are developed in the region it is unlikely that they would be more than expendable outposts of United States power.

The phosphate-producing islands of the South Pacific—Nauru and Ocean Island (in the Gilbert and Ellice Group)—have been of substantial economic importance to Australia in the past. The great expansion of the Australian wheat and wool industries since the beginning of the century would hardly have been possible without the cheap fertilizer made from the phosphates of these territories. Nauru was taken over from the Germans jointly by Britain, Australia and New Zealand as a League of Nations mandated territory, and this was converted into a United Nations Trusteeship after World War II—which was terminated in 1968 when the island became independent. For a half century Australia controlled the territory on behalf of the three Trustee powers and during that period it was able to obtain virtually unlimited supplies of phosphates at low cost. Since Nauruan independence this cost has risen markedly, and in any case the deposits are likely to be exhausted before the end of the century; but Australia has been lucky in finding extensive deposits on its own territory. Meanwhile the Nauruan population of less than 4000 has become one of the richest communities in the world, with a national income averaging $13 000 per head. What its future will be when the phosphate is exhausted—the island has no other resource—is uncertain.

Australia also drew large supplies of phosphate from the British colony of Ocean Island, although at a somewhat higher price (because the British met administrative costs for the whole Gilbert and Ellice Group out of the proceeds).

When the Japanese occupied Ocean Island and Nauru during World War II, for obscure reasons they removed the native populations to other islands. The Nauruans were later returned to their homeland, but the Ocean Islanders, otherwise known as the Banabans, were settled on Rabi Island in the Fiji group. This was purchased out of phosphate royalties and the Banabans have since lived there on a proportion of the profits from the phosphate exports from Ocean Island. Two developments have, however, disturbed this seemingly comfortable arrangement. The phosphate deposits are at the point of exhaustion, and the Gilbert and Ellice Islands are expected to become independent next year. The Banabans cannot hope to secure independence on Rabi Island, since it is part of Fiji, and they want Ocean Island to be given independent status and to be restored to a livable state by the reclamation of the phosphate workings. The Banabans obtained a judgment from a British court in 1977 that they should receive damages for the failure to replant the worked out lands, and in June 1977 they received a payment of 10 million dollars (Australian). Whether this will settle the matter is not clear, but the Australian government's attitude is that it is no longer its business.

The Pacific islands have received some benefits in recent years from a revival of European interest. The European Economic Community under the Lomé convention gave special access to goods from the independent States in the region, many items of which are free of customs duties or quotas—although not of course including those which would compete with products protected by the Community's Common Agricultural Policy. Under the Lomé convention the islands are also eligible for financial and technical assistance from the Community.

The Fijian Prime Minister, Ratu Mara, has been active in seeking common cause with the other beneficiaries of the Lomé convention: the former colonial territories in Africa and the Caribbean (known collectively as the A.C.P. States). In April 1977, the 'Suva Declaration' was issued, largely as a result of Ratu Mara's efforts, which laid down a programme for trade co-operation between the

A.C.P. countries, the development of joint enterprises and co-operation in transport and communities. It is not clear how effective co-operation can be between countries scattered so widely across the face of the globe but the agreement was significant in that it reflected the growing desire of the Pacific islanders to co-operate with countries facing the same problems as themselves.

This desire was also reflected in the establishment of the South Pacific Forum. This was set up by the former British, Australian and New Zealand territories to supplement, and perhaps ultimately to replace, the South Pacific Commission. This Commission was the creation of the colonial powers—Britain, France, the United States, Australia and New Zealand, and although island represent-atives attend the meetings their status is subordinate to the delegates of the colonial powers. The Commission's principal function is to channel into the region the aid provided by the metropolitan governments and, at the insistence in particular of France, it was not allowed to concern itself with political issues. In recent years a South Pacific Conference was established in association with the Commission, in which representation was allowed on a more equal basis and it continues to provide a useful meeting ground for representatives of the independent States in the area and the remaining colonial territories. Its functions, however, remain largely restricted to the co-ordination of social and economic aid and technical assistance.

In the South Pacific Forum the leaders of the independent States in the region have felt themselves to be less under the shadow of the colonial powers. Its members comprise at present only British Commonwealth countries and territories, including Australia and New Zealand, but the island leaders hope that it will eventually be joined by the United States and French territories. It set up its own Bureau for Economic Co-operation, located in Suva, and has initiated a number of ambitious co-operative ventures. At the seventh meeting of the Forum, held in Nauru in 1976, it was decided to establish a shipping line to be known as the Pacific Forum line, and it is working on proposals to develop better air services in the region. It has decided on a common policy in regard to the current international discussions on the Law of the Sea: the members expect considerable benefit from the creation of two-hundred-mile resources-zones, believing that they will obtain a larger share in the profits from deep-sea fishing. They realize, however, that they will be involved in increased responsibilities for surveillance and control over the new zones, which can only be met by joint action. They also hope by concerted action to strengthen their capacity to deal with the countries that send large fishing fleets from outside the region; and the establishment is planned of a South Pacific Fisheries Agency to deal with their problems.

All such evidences of self-help on the part of the Pacific islanders are welcomed by Australia, and small amounts of money and technical assistance have been proffered to help the process along. Unfortunately there is little prospect that a solution will be found by these means to the fundamental problem of too many people being dependent upon too few resources.

In 1936 Australia laid claim to more than three-sevenths of the Antarctic continent—an area larger than Australia itself. The claim was based on exploration activity by British and Australian explorers over the previous century but it has been recognized by only a few other countries. In particular, it is not accepted by either the Americans or the Russians, who since the last war have developed extensive scientific and exploration activities in the area —far beyond anything that the Australians have undertaken or could afford.

Traditionally, international acceptance of territorial claims have depended not only on discovery and exploration but also on occupation. The Australian claim is, therefore, unlikely to gain general recognition, if only because none of our activities could be regarded as constituting occupation of the eight million square kilometres claimed. All claims were in any case put on ice by a treaty drawn up in Washington in 1959 and signed by all the countries with interests in the Antarctic—the United States, Soviet Union, Great Britain, France, Japan, Norway, Belgium, Argentina, Chile, South Africa, New Zealand and Australia. (Later signatories were Poland, Czechoslovakia and Denmark.)

The inspiration for the treaty was mainly the desire to provide an international framework for the continuance of scientific work in the Antarctic, but it proved innovative in a number of important respects. While none of the existing claimants were called upon to renounce their claims, these were in effect frozen for the duration of the treaty—a period of thirty years. Article IV of the treaty stated that:

No acts or activities taking place while the present treaty is in force shall constitute a basis for asserting, supporting or denying a claim to territorial sovereignty in Antarctica or create any rights of sovereignty in Antarctica. No new claim, or enlargement of an existing claim, to territorial sovereignty in Antarctica shall be asserted while the present Treaty is in force.

The treaty broke new ground in declaring Antarctica to be a demilitarized and nuclear-free zone. Article I prohibited 'any measures of a military nature, such as the establishment of military bases and fortifications, the carrying out of military manoeuvres, as well as the testing of any type of weapon'; and this was reinforced by Article V, which declared that 'any nuclear explosions in Antarctica and the disposal of radioactive waste material shall be prohibited'.

These enlightened provisions were accepted largely because at the time the region was not regarded as having, or likely to have, strategic or economic importance. The treaty did not include any provisions for inspection or enforcement of Articles I and V, although it was the hope of several of the signatories, including Australia, that Article III would help to ensure that no country broke the rules in secret. This article laid down that information, and more importantly, personnel should be exchanged between the expeditions and stations of all countries. The results of scientific observations were to be made freely available to all parties and to the world.

As far as is known, the signatories have kept the rules, although of course it would be possible for the superpowers in particular to conceal any breaches that they have made. The scientists of other countries have been allowed to visit American and Russian bases, but it is perhaps unlikely that they would have been told all that was going on. Since the treaty was signed, a thorough evaluation has, no doubt, been made for their own purposes by both countries of the strategic possibilities of the continent. In view of its remoteness from their own centres of power it is improbable that either give it high strategic priority, although the oceans surrounding it may have some importance as lurking grounds for nuclear armed submarines.

From Australia's point of view the Antarctic has little direct strategic relevance. One of the arguments used in asserting the Australian territorial claim was that it was important that the sector facing the Australian continent should not be allowed to fall into hostile hands; but there are far more convenient places from which to attack Australia than the Antarctic continent.

The possibility that the area contains exploitable living and mineral resources appears to have increased since the treaty was signed. The presence of oil has been established, and it is reasonable to assume that other minerals lie beneath the ice. A special committee was set up under the treaty in 1975 to study these possibilities and its recommendations were considered at the full conference of the treaty partners in September 1977. It was agreed at the conference that a special consultative meeting should be held in Canberra in 1978 to prepare a draft convention on conserving Antarctic marine living resources. There was less unanimity in regard to the exploitation of minerals. No agreement was reached as to whether there should be voluntary restraint in exploration and exploitation, or whether a special régime should be set up before exploitation began. These questions were to be discussed at a meeting in London at the end of 1978.

It has been argued in Australia that in order to maintain its territorial claim the Commonwealth government should increase its activities in the area. These have indeed been minimal. Australia's main base for Antarctic operations is, moreover, not on the continent itself, but on Macquarie Island, which is a dependency of the state of Tasmania, and is well north of the 60° parallel which is the limit of the Antarctic zone as defined under the treaty. It has established three bases on the coast of the continent but the activities at these are sporadic.

There is a strong case for a more serious Australian effort in Antarctica: its relationship with the environment and ecology of the whole southern hemisphere is close and delicate, and it is a major Australian interest that nothing should be done to upset the balance. It would, however, be futile to maintain our grandiose territorial claims. Expanding our scientific effort—desirable as this might be in itself—would not strengthen these claims, because the treaty expressly states that no such activities can be used as a basis for any assertion of national sovereignty. In any case exploration and scientific research conducted by other countries in the so-called Australian sector has been, and will undoubtedly continue to be, much more extensive than Australia's own.

Claims based upon British and Australian exploration before the inception of the treaty are insubstantial. Although these were exciting and dangerous adventures, they give no more support to a territorial claim than the explorations of other nations.

Australia's best course—and indeed its only hope of maintaining effective influence in the region—would be to give a strong lead towards the internationalization of the whole continent. This would be the best way to preserve the most valuable aspects of the present treaty—demilitarization and the sharing by the world community in the results of scientific research—and to prevent a struggle for territorial control in which Australia could only be a loser.

The present treaty expires in 1991 and it has been suggested that the simplest course would be to seek its renewal. The situation since the treaty was signed has, however, changed, and by the time of its expiry will have changed much more. No regulatory body was set up under the treaty and although provision was made for consultatory conferences these were given no collective authority. By 1991, when the world energy crisis is likely to be at its peak, there may well be fierce international competition for the fossil fuel resources of the Antarctic and unless some regulatory body is established the ecological consequences could be disastrous for the southern hemisphere and especially for Australia.

The countries other than Australia who have asserted territorial claims are Argentina and Chile (whose claims are in part mutually conflicting); Great Britain (whose claims conflict with Argentina and Chile); France; Norway and New Zealand. Neither the Soviet Union nor the United States have made claims, but reserve the right to do so.

It will not be easy to gain the agreement of all these countries for internationalization. Argentina and Chile are closest to the Antarctic continent—separated from it only by the Drake Passage —and these countries have in the past insisted that the areas they claim are national territory rather than colonial possessions. They are not likely to be easily shifted from this view. But Great Britain and New Zealand have in the past been ready to agree to internationalization and it is not too soon for Australia to seek their co-operation in working towards general acceptance of an international régime.

Such a régime would be compatible with an arrangement for a neutral non-nuclear zone in the Indian Ocean and the South Pacific, and could be organically related to it. An Australian government which was committed to the latter could speak with enhanced authority in regard to the former.

Internationalization would mean that the benefit of any resources in the area would not accrue to any individual country, but to the international community. The Antarctic was the scene of the first major experiment in demilitarization and it would be fitting not only that this experiment should be confirmed and consolidated but that it should also be the base for the world's first resource-sharing arrangement. Attempts to redistribute existing wealth for the benefit of the poorer nations have so far failed and are likely to continue to do so; but it should not be beyond the ability of man to devise an equitable way of sharing *new* resources. This possibility might well arise in connection with the potential wealth of the deep ocean bed (it seems too late to prevent the exclusive exploitation of the continental shelves by individual nations) and the internationalization of the Antarctic might provide not only for the distribution of the resources of the continent but serve as a model for arrangements for the deep-sea bed. Australia already has more than its due share of natural resources, and now that it has laid claim to the vast continental shelves that extend from its coastline it will have much more than it will by its own efforts be able to exploit. Since it can neither develop the resources of the Antarctic nor exert national control over them, it would lose nothing by proposing internationalization; and it would earn the good will of less well-endowed nations if it could help to persuade its partners in the Antarctic Treaty to accept a resource-sharing régime.

An Australian initiative in this direction could draw on hitherto unused provisions of the United Nations Charter in relation to the creation of Trust Territories. As well as providing that territories can be administered by individual States the Charter envisages that such responsibilities can be assumed by the United Nations Organization itself. There is also a provision that where a Territory is designated a strategic area, authority over the Trusteeship should reside in the Security Council rather than in the Trusteeship Council (which is in any case nowadays moribund, since all the territories previously under its care have become independent). It would, therefore, be possible (under Articles 81, 82 and 83 of the Charter) to establish the Antarctic zone as a strategic Trust Territory under the authority of the Security Council. This would be appropriate in view of the need to maintain the demilitarization of the zone; and the proposal might be the more acceptable in that four of the powers actively interested in the Antarctic (France, Great Britain, the Soviet Union and the United States) are permanent members of the Security Council.

A procedure which could be adopted would be for a trusteeship agreement to be drawn up and accepted by both the General Assembly and the Security Council which would provide that:

(1) All nations with actual or potential claims to Antarctic territory would permanently renounce these in favour of the United Nations Organization.
(2) The whole zone within the 60° parallel, including the oceans, would be permanently demilitarized.
(3) Ownership of all resources in the zone, on land or under the sea, including fish and marine organisms, would be vested in the United Nations Organization.
(4) Individual countries would be licensed by the United Nations Organization to exploit the resources of the zone, on terms

which would allow due recompense for the cost of such exploitation, but which would distribute the remaining increment among those members of the United Nations most in need of economic help (the distribution being made by the Economic and Social Council or by a body specially set up under this Council).

(5) An Antarctic Commission would be set up, responsible to the Security Council, which would have the following powers:

   (a) Inspection and control to ensure observance of the demilitarization provisions;

   (b) Issuance of licences for operations in the Antarctic and authority to deny or withdraw them from any nation in breach of the provisions of the Trust Agreement.

   (c) Co-ordination and regulation of all activities in the zone, including exploration, scientific research, land, sea and air communications, and the exploitation of resources, with particular concern to preserve the environmental and ecological stability of the zone and of the southern hemisphere.

The inclusion of the oceans would mean that this arrangement would go a good deal further than the present Antarctic treaty, which specifically excludes the high seas from its provisions. But the time is coming when the traditional laissez-faire attitude towards the high seas will have to be replaced by some form of international regulation of the exploitation of its pelagic resources (as well as of the sea-bed) and the Antarctic would be a good place to start. (The demilitarization provisions would be greatly weakened if they applied only to the land, and if the waters surrounding the continent could still be used, say, for the deployment of vessels armed with long-range nuclear missiles.)

It might seem far-fetched to hope that these arrangements could be set up in the present-day world. But who knows? Common sense might one day reappear in the conduct of affairs between nations, and what could be more sensible than the internationalization of the Antarctic?

6

Japan in Danger

The most urgent external problem which the United States will face in the next ten years will be its relationship with Japan. Existing policies are rapidly losing their relevance and the likelihood is that by the end of the next decade Japan will once again be outside the strategic umbrella of the United States.

The confusion among Americans as to what should be done is nowhere better exemplified than in the currently fashionable concept of 'trilateralism'. This was sponsored by Jimmy Carter and his associates before he became President but it is now given bipartisan support. It is a difficult concept to render into clear language. Its original intention was to co-ordinate economic policy between the United States, Western Europe and Japan, but it now appears to be regarded as a means of creating an enduring 'partnership' between the North Atlantic powers and Japan. The concept had its origin in recognition by the Americans of the fact that they could no longer exert economic or strategic dominance in the world. In place of their own previous hegemony they wished to construct 'a community of developed nations' which would still be able to command predominant global influence.

A Trilateral Commission was established, consisting of representatives of Western Europe, Japan and the United States. Zbigniew Brzezinski, who is now National Security Adviser to President Carter, was appointed Director. From his statements it is clear that the basis of collaboration was to be ideological: a shared interest in capitalist democracy and opposition to socialism. Although the language of the cold war is avoided it is possible to discern behind the rhetoric of 'trilateralism' the continuing American concern to counter the expansion of the communist bloc. Also apparent is the Americans' recognition that because of their own loss of global strategic control the only way to do this is to construct a balance of power favourable to the advanced capitalist countries.

The whole concept seems unrealistic. For it to succeed it would require the west Europeans and the Japanese to subordinate their immediate national interests to the wider good. This was difficult enough when the United States was sufficiently strong, economically and strategically, to impose some degree of discipline; it would be wishful thinking to expect that it could be achieved when the United States must rely largely on persuasion.

The concept of 'trilateralism' is intrinsically asymmetric. Japan has an advanced capitalist economy and a political structure which exhibits some aspects of Western parliamentary democracy. But it would be an exaggeration to say that it shares the same values and political objectives as Western countries. The motives of the Japanese people derive not only from the past century of rapid Westernization but from their own long history. In facing the acute dangers of the coming decades they will not act in accordance with any sentimental notions of obligations to the West (why indeed should they feel any?) but in the way which in their judgement will be most likely to ensure the survival of their nation and their own social and political values.

There is also an economic asymmetry in the triangle. There are strong and close-knit economic relations between the United States and Europe on the one hand and between the United States and Japan on the other; but Japanese trade with Western Europe is only about ten per cent of their overall trade. In global trade Japan is a strong competitor of most European countries and in view of her open and covert protectionism is not highly regarded as a trading partner. The community of interest between Japan and Europe, on which the concept of 'trilateralism' depends, is thus highly imperfect.

In economic relations the United States can still exert powerful influence over Japan. It is by far Japan's biggest single market (taking about twenty per cent of her exports). But this influence can only be exerted effectively in bilateral matters: in persuading, for example, the Japanese to limit particular exports to the United States when they damage American producers. On wider issues American pressure has usually been met with resistance—for example, in regard to lowering overall protection barriers, or adjusting exchange rates. United States pressure is, in fact, limited by its own self-interest. Punitive economic action against Japan would damage its own economy and America is not likely to expose itself to such damage in the interests of others.

Once Carter and Brzezinski reached the seats of power, 'trilateralism' quickly yielded to reality. The first important policy initiative taken by the new president was in the field of energy and this strikingly illustrated the limits of America's power of persuasion in regard to both Europe and Japan. An important element in his plan was that all three sides of the United States–Europe–Japan triangle should indefinitely forgo the development of the fast-breeder nuclear reactor, because of its capacity to produce dangerous quantities of weapons-grade plutonium. Unfortunately for Carter both Europe and Japan see this reactor as a means of reducing their dependence on outside sources of energy. The fast-breeder reactor produces fifty to sixty times more energy from a given amount of uranium than the conventional reactor and some believe that by the beginning of next century it could make Western Europe and Japan virtually independent of outside supplies of fuel for the production of energy. Since their present dependence is increasingly regarded in both Europe and Japan as a greater threat to their survival than nuclear proliferation, they are unlikely to be deflected from their plans to develop fast-breeder reactors—either by American pressure or by internal opposition.

The Americans also sought to dissuade the Japanese from setting up plants for the enrichment of uranium and for the reprocessing of spent nuclear fuel. The United States supplies Japan with enriched uranium for its nuclear reactors, on condition that the spent fuel is returned after use, the reason being that if such fuel is reprocessed it produces weapons-grade material. The Japanese insist, however, that they need a reprocessing plant in order to be able to re-use the spent fuel and economize on the import of uranium. They entered into arrangements with a European consortium to construct such a plant and requested the United States to waive its ban. When the Japanese Prime Minister, Takeo Fukuda, visited Washington in March 1977 he pressed strongly for this, and in the communiqué at the end of the visit it was stated that President Carter had agreed 'to give full consideration to Japan's energy needs' in the formulation of the new American nuclear policy. When this was announced a few weeks later it appeared at first that Fukuda's plea had been in vain. Carter called for the indefinite deferment of commerical enrichment and reprocessing of nuclear fuel and asked both the European countries and Japan to continue to rely on the United States for enriched fuel, which Carter undertook to guarantee to supply. Those European countries which already have their own reprocessing plants and an alternative source of supplies of enriched fuel in the Soviet Union quickly made it clear that they would not abandon their own planned developments for enrichment and reprocessing plants. The Japanese have been more cautious, but it is certain that they will eventually insist on developing both enrichment and reprocessing plants. In September 1977 the United States agreed that the Japanese should be allowed to run a reprocessing plant on the understanding that the plutonium would be left in a mixture which could not be converted directly into explosives. It must also be accepted that they will ultimately develop fast-breeder reactors.

They will do these things not only because of their need for energy but because such facilities are essential to their maintaining a nuclear weapons option. A picture is emerging in Japan of a balanced development in all the technologies which would be needed for an indigenous nuclear capability. In the field of electronics Japan has for some years been in the front rank, and in recent times rapid advances have been made in rocketry and satellite-launching technology. In July 1977 the Space Activities Commission announced a programme of space exploration which provided for manned orbital flights and planetary probes during the 1980s. None of this expenditure is charged against the defence budget (which is limited to one per cent of the gross national product) but it is clear that it will provide the basis within the next decade for the acquirement of full nuclear weapons capability within a short time of any decision to do so.

That there has been American technological involvement in these developments can hardly be doubted, and this leads to the conclusion that in some quarters in the United States the thought that Japan would become a nuclear weapons power is accepted with equanimity. Relations between Japan and America have in recent times been good: even the opposition parties in Japan are no longer calling for the abrogation of the United States–Japan Security Treaty, and many Americans no doubt feel that a fully armed Japan would be a reliable ally of the United States.

This might be another miscalculation. Apart from the difficulties that Japan would have, even with nuclear armaments, in making itself secure, it is not likely that once they were fully armed the Japanese would give priority to American interests over their own.

Americans may believe that the Japanese are bound to them by ties of gratitude for what they have received since the end of World War II, but it is not certain that the Japanese see the relationship in the same light. History did not begin for them in 1945: their memories go back to 1853, when Commodore Perry forced open their doors and plunged them into a period of domestic turbulence and external danger. They also remember the racial antipathy shown to Japanese settlers in Hawaii and California and the connivance of Woodrow Wilson with the Australian Prime Minister, W. M. Hughes, in blocking the inclusion of a racial equality clause in the League of Nations Charter. They recall the sustained efforts made by the Americans to stifle Japanese naval expansion—from the time of the Treaty of Portsmouth (signed after the Japanese defeat of the Russians in 1905) to the Washington Naval Agreements of 1921–22. Present-day leaders of Japan had direct experience of the embargo placed by the United States on trade with Japan in 1941 and, above all, of the atomic attack in 1945 on Hiroshima and Nagasaki.

Although they are now rich, the Japanese will not have forgotten that it is because of the Americans that they have no present means of protecting those riches or ensuring the survival of their sacred nation. To acquire these means will be their over-riding concern in the future, as in the past. They see, more clearly than most others, the danger in which they stand and it is not conceivable that they will allow consideration of American interests to add one iota to the risks they already run.

It is not, of course, certain that Japan will choose the nuclear option. It may prefer to accept partnership with either Russia or China, in the hope that in so doing it might nevertheless maintain its own national integrity. The question would then arise for the United States as to which alternative would serve its interests best. Again, there are many Americans who have already made up their minds: because of their fear of the Soviet Union and their desire to build up the countervailing strength of China, many would prefer a China–Japan alliance to a Russia–Japan one. Whether this would be in their long-term interests is questionable but it now seems unlikely that the issue will be seriously debated in the United States. In the same way that there is a continuing drift in American opinion towards accepting a re-armed Japan there is also a growing, if unexamined, assumption that an alliance between Japan and China would be natural and desirable.

If Taiwan will be the test of the United States policy towards China (as suggested in Chapter 7), it seems that Korea will be the test in regard to Japan. The Japanese have for many centuries regarded Korea as the strategic periphery of their own islands, and since the end of World War II the Americans have repeatedly assured them that they recognize that it is essential that South Korea should not fall into communist hands. General MacArthur's campaign in Korea was justified on the grounds that it was essential to Japan's safety that Kim Il Sung should not be allowed to overrun the south. I have suggested elsewhere that this was a false assumption: that Japan's security would have been better served by an independent, united Korea, even if it called itself communist. It is doubtful whether the Japanese themselves believed in the myth of global communism, but they did accept the idea that they would be safer if the Americans controlled South Korea. This control is now in question. During the 1976 presidential election campaign Jimmy Carter promised that the American forces would be withdrawn from Korea if he were elected, and when he assumed office he confirmed that this promise would be carried out. The problem seemed less simple once he came to power, and the withdrawal is to be phased over a five-year period. Nevertheless the American commitment to withdrawal has already had a potent effect on the delicate balance in north Asia and has provoked much reflection in Seoul, Pyongyang and, above all, in Tokyo.

In spite of rapid economic development in South Korea, a central element in the present situation is that North Korea still has the preponderance of military strength, if the American forces are left out of account. The North Korean army has more armour and artillery than the south, and more missiles and combat aircraft. The manpower in the southern forces is somewhat greater and they have modern American equipment. But the north has the additional advantage that its military industries are more advanced than in the south.

While the Americans remain, these factors are not decisive, because of the superiority in equipment and weaponry of the United States divisions: they have plentiful armour and fire-power, and a strong anti-tank capability. Moreover, they are backed by a full air wing, equipped with modern fighter aircraft.

The Americans have let it be known that they will continue to deploy an air wing in South Korea after the withdrawal of ground forces, and that in the period during which their own forces will be phased out they will re-equip the South Korean forces. It would be optimistic to assume, however, that this would ensure military stability in the Korean peninsula. Because the south lacks developed military industries it would be heavily dependent upon American support facilities—at least until the promised American assistance in developing these industries has had time to take effect. If, meanwhile, the north launched a new attack, the Americans might for the second time have to return to rescue the southerners—in circumstances a good deal less favourable than in 1951, when the North Korean forces were relatively poorly armed.

There is a longer term possibility that is as disturbing. The South Korean economy is growing rapidly and given time it undoubtedly has the capacity to develop its own military support industry to a level which would outmatch the north. The South Koreans would then have an independent military capability markedly superior to that of the north. The temptation to re-unify the country by force would no doubt be strongly felt in Seoul, all the more so since the restraining influence of the Americans would no longer be present.

The danger that this would offer to the strategic stability of north Asia is obvious. Neither the Russians nor the Chinese seem ready to disturb the present equilibrium and they have been careful to avoid any military commitments to Kim Il Sung. But if it appeared likely that the south would overrun the north, one or the other— or perhaps both—would be obliged to intervene. In fact, the Chinese could be expected to move very quickly, since they would regard it as essential for their own security to pre-empt Russian military control of the Korean peninsula—reaching down as it does into seas of vital strategic importance to China. For their part the Russians might by this time—say five years from now—be ready for a forward move in the area. The well-developed ports of South Korea would be a valuable prize and would greatly increase the strategic mobility of the Soviet navy. An attack by South Korea could thus precipitate a conflict between Russia and China which could have dangerous consequences for the rest of the world.

If the United States' pledge to maintain the safety of Japan were to remain credible it could hardly stand by while the Russians overran the peninsula; but if it intervened it would find itself in a major confrontation with the Soviet Union, in circumstances in which it would be at a severe strategic disadvantage. If the Americans decided to send reinforcements they would face a much greater problem than in 1951. The North Koreans now have sufficient naval forces and missile capability to complicate and delay the American operations; but the main danger would be that the Russians would establish a blockade which could only be broken by the Americans at great risk—both of local tactical defeat and of escalation of the war.

It might, indeed, be unrealistic to expect that the Americans would attempt reinforcement. President Carter's decision to withdraw the ground forces was based on a determination to avoid American involvement in another land war in Asia. From the financial point of view it would have been cheaper to keep the American division in Korea than it will be to station it at home, and for both officers and men there were training advantages in deploying it overseas. With the example before him of another democratic president, Truman, who withdrew the American forces from Korea and then sent them back, Carter is unlikely on this occasion to have decided to take them out with any other intention than to keep them out.

Fortunately there is hope that the present régime in South Korea will avoid adventurous policies. President Park Chung Hee has been much criticized in Western media, but he probably has the support of the majority of South Koreans. He has been more successful in meeting the aspirations of the people than his predecessors. The rapid economic gains of recent years—which were substantially maintained during the world recession which began in 1973—have been shared among all classes. Unlike in many other developing countries there are no great disparities between country and city, and the real incomes of both peasants and workers have risen significantly. Park has sometimes dealt ruthlessly with his opponents, but there is nowadays more social justice in South Korea than ever before in its history—much more, for example, than in India, despite the ostensibly democratic form of the latter's government.

While prosperity lasts, it is unlikely that there will be a challenge to Park's leadership. Nor will there be any disposition to put economic gains at risk by undertaking military action against the north. The country may, however, face increasing difficulty in finding markets for its rising manufacturing output and it may not be possible to maintain the recent rates of progress. If resources are diverted to military industry and to the purchase of modern armaments this could also cause a sharp drop in prosperity. In such circumstances the régime might see the forcible reunification of the country as a way out of its difficulties.

The best hope for Korea and for its neighbours is that a peaceful reconciliation will be achieved between the two halves of the country while there is still time. Because of the hostilities of the past, and the development of wide divergencies in social and ideological attitudes, this will not be easy. On the other hand, both northerners and southerners are dedicated to maintaining the independence of the Korean people and ultimately their leaders may accept the necessity of combining to ensure this.

An abiding problem is the political isolation of North Korea. Its main diplomatic contacts are with the communist countries, and although some members of the non-aligned group have tried to draw it into contact, its relationship with the outside world remains tenuous. The Whitlam government sought to help in bringing it into the world community by establishing diplomatic relations between Canberra and Pyongyang. Unfortunately the North Koreans were not happy with the treatment they received in Canberra and withdrew their representatives after about a year. They also asked the Australian mission to leave Pyongyang. Formal diplomatic relations continue to exist, but Mr Whitlam's successor made no efforts to revive active contact.

From the Japanese point of view the worst case in regard to Korea would be if the Russians occupied the whole of the Korean peninsula—either in spite of American intervention or because there was none. At the least the Russians would be in a position to apply greatly increased economic pressure on Japan. Trade with both Koreas already represents a significant proportion of the total overseas trade of Japan; and if the Russians controlled the whole of the two-hundred-mile resources zone on the western side of the Sea of Japan the fishing resources on which the Japanese are heavily dependent could be seriously curtailed. With strategic control of this sea the Russians could exert considerable psychological pressure on the Japanese—as they have already shown themselves prepared to do through their control of the seas to the north of Japan.

What could the Americans do to protect the Japanese from this pressure? Clearly they could do little unless they were able to give a convincing impression that they were prepared to go to war with the Soviet Union on Japan's behalf.

The United States forces which were maintained in Japan and Okinawa were formidable. The structure and capability of the forces were described by the United States government (in hearings before the House of Representatives Committee on International Relations, 23 March 1976) as follows:

Army: The United States Army in Japan was essentially one of logistic support and was well-situated geographically to support operations in Korea and throughout the western Pacific.

Air Force: This consisted principally of a tactical fighter wing, a tactical airlift squadron, a strategic refuelling squadron, and a reconnaissance squadron. The role of these units was defined as 'support for deployed forces'.

Navy: The role of the Navy was similarly defined and stress was laid on the importance of the availability of advanced naval bases in Japan and Okinawa. The ships present in Japanese waters varied widely from time to time but the bases were regarded as essential to the effective deployment of the United States Navy in the western Pacific.

Marines: A marine amphibious force was maintained including combat forces and an air component.

Communications: A communications network was developed in Japan and Okinawa which was described as vital to a rapid response by the American forces to an enemy threat.

In 1968 the number of American military personnel in Japan was 40 000 men and in Okinawa 39 000. Ten years later these forces had been reduced to about one half. It is a significant indication of American strategic priorities that during the same period the deployment of United States forces in Europe remained constant at about 300 000 active personnel.

When President Carter announced the decision to withdraw the American forces from Korea he said that the United States would continue to honour its obligations under the 1954 Mutual Defence Treaty with South Korea. As in the case of similar treaties with Japan and Taiwan, the Korean treaty contains the provision that in the event of an armed attack each party 'would act to meet the common danger in accordance with its constitutional processes', and is, therefore, not binding on the United States government. Like all the other American security treaties, its credibility rests largely upon the presence of American forces in positions where they would inevitably be involved in any hostile attack and in sufficient strength to ensure that the enemy would be held.

By these tests the credibility of the United States' guarantee to South Korea and, indeed, to Japan was by 1978 already much reduced, and as the remaining ground forces are withdrawn from South Korea it will be diminished further.

The Japanese are also concerned that their prospects of resisting Soviet pressure in the north Pacific would be greatly diminished if the Russians were able to gain a dominant position in south-east Asia. One reflection of this apprehension is the active economic role which Japan has been pursuing in Vietnam since the end of the war. She is hopeful that this activity will enable her to counter Russian influence, but it is also becoming apparent that she is trying to encourage reconciliation and co-operation between the Indo-China States and the other countries of south-east Asia. During the discussion with ASEAN leaders at Kuala Lumpur in

August 1977 the Japanese Prime Minister, Takeo Fukuda, was reported to have told them that Japan was most anxious to see peace maintained in the area and, therefore, wished to do all it could to avoid a confrontation between communist States and the ASEAN countries. At a press conference after the meeting he made the significant remark that if Japan wanted to do so it could equip itself with one of the strongest armed forces in the world. He added that the Japanese were determined not to do this, but would use the resources which would otherwise be spent on defence to help developing countries. At the same conference he pledged Japan to provide US$1000 million of aid for five industrial projects to be developed jointly by the ASEAN countries.

Japan's influence in the region is handicapped by the memory of her past military power and fear of her present economic strength. She is, nevertheless, making a strong effort to develop a position in the region from which she might counter the spread of Russian influence and, if need be, of the Chinese. Whether she can do this with economic power alone must be regarded as doubtful.

One thing is clear: the withdrawal of American power from Asia initiated by President Nixon and confirmed and extended by President Carter has led to a basic strategic shift in the western Pacific. The period of unchallengeable American control of the area has passed, and the security of the non-communist countries rests increasingly in their own hands. This applies to Japan no less than to the smaller countries. The area is likely to undergo a period of acute strategic instability, as a result of which a very different power structure is likely to emerge. The transition will inevitably be dangerous and difficult and the world will be lucky if it is accomplished without a major disaster.

7

West Pacific Triangle

In spite of its apparent abandonment by the world Taiwan has built up a position of quite remarkable economic and political strength. It is the critical factor in relations between China and the United States; it is an increasingly important element in Sino–Soviet competition; and its future will have a significant, and perhaps decisive, effect on Japan's prospects for independent survival.

It would be easier to forecast the future relationships between all these countries if it were possible to penetrate the minds of the government and people of Taiwan. They must now regard the withdrawal of American forces as inevitable and both the Kuomintang rulers and the Taiwanese people are doubtless giving careful thought as to what their future course should be. The difficulties in forecasting what they will decide are discussed in Chapter 8; in this chapter Taiwan's relationship with other powers will be considered.

Richard Nixon has claimed that he realized the necessity for a settlement with Communist China as early as October 1967, when he wrote the famous article in the American journal *Foreign Affairs* foreshadowing what later became known as the Nixon doctrine; and that he began secret approaches to Peking soon after he was elected president. He has also indicated that he authorized the then Secretary of State, William P. Rogers, to hint at his intentions in a speech he made in Canberra in August 1969, in which he said that the United States looked forward to a time when it could enter into a useful dialogue and a reduction of tension with Communist China. Little notice was taken of this hint by either the Australian government or the media—the news of Henry Kissinger's visit to Peking in 1971 was received with shocked surprise.

That visit prepared the way for Nixon's own to China in February 1972. Before leaving he explained, in his report to Congress of 9 February 1972, what his attitude would be to the question of Taiwan. He said categorically that with the Republic of China (that is, with the Kuomintang régime on Taiwan) 'we shall maintain our friendship, our diplomatic ties, and our defence commitment', adding that 'the ultimate relationship between Taiwan and the mainland is not a matter for the United States to decide'.

He apparently thought, no doubt on the advice of Henry Kissinger, that this formulation would satisfy the Communist Chinese. When he arrived in Peking he was disabused. In the communiqué issued in Shanghai at the end of prolonged and strenuous meetings, the Chinese position was stated as follows:

> The Taiwan question is the crucial question obstructing the normalisation of relations between China and the United States; the government of the People's Republic is the sole legal government of China; Taiwan is a province of China which has long been returned to the motherland; the liberation of Taiwan is China's internal affair in which no other country has the right to interfere; and all United States forces must be withdrawn from Taiwan. The Chinese government firmly opposes any activities which aim at the creation of 'one China, one Taiwan', 'one China, two governments', 'two Chinas', and 'independent Taiwan' or advocate that 'the status of Taiwan remains undetermined'.

In reply Nixon abandoned the stand he had taken two weeks previously. The United States' side declared that:

> The United States acknowledges that all Chinese on either side of the Taiwan Strait maintain there is but one China and that Taiwan is part of China. The United States government does not challenge that position. It reaffirms its interest in a peaceful settlement of the Taiwan question by the Chinese themselves. With this prospect in mind, it affirms the ultimate objective of the withdrawal of United States forces and military installations from Taiwan. In the meantime it will progressively reduce its forces and military installations on Taiwan as the tension in the area diminishes.

An attempt was subsequently made by Kissinger and Nixon to suggest that this was not a material change in the American position, emphasizing in particular that an American withdrawal from Taiwan would only take place if tension in the area 'diminished'. But the truth was that on 9 February Nixon had declared that the United States defence commitment would be maintained, while on 27 February he pledged himself not only to the 'ultimate' withdrawal of United States forces and military installations from Taiwan, but to reduce them progressively in the meantime.

It could be argued, and was so argued in comment inspired by the Nixon administration, that the word 'commitment' used by the president on 9 February should be taken to refer to the United States security treaty with the Republic of China and that Nixon had given no undertaking that this would be abrogated. But this was a semantic deception: since the United States expressly did not challenge the position that Taiwan was part of China it undermined the juridical status of its own treaty. In any case, it was the presence of American forces which gave substance to the treaty, and their withdrawal would, at any rate in the eyes of the people of Taiwan, render it a dead letter. The treaty contains the usual phrase that each party would act 'in accordance with its constitutional processes' and it is in substance no more binding on the United States than the SEATO and ANZUS treaties. The likelihood that the United States forces, once withdrawn, would ever return is remote.

Throughout its association with Taiwan the United States has always avoided giving cognizance to any distinction between the Kuomintang government of the island and the Taiwanese people. It has accepted the claims of both the Communist Chinese and the Kuomintang that the Taiwanese are Chinese and, therefore, that they have no right to independence or even to self determination. This attitude was confirmed by the United States in the Shanghai communiqué and any possibility that the Taiwanese would be consulted was in effect foreclosed. Whether they might ultimately insist on being heard is discussed in Chapter 8.

Normalization of relations between the United States and China did not proceed as rapidly after the Shanghai communiqué as might have been expected. The Nixon administration became embroiled in the Watergate scandals and the Vietnam war dragged on for another three years. Nixon was disabled from taking further serious foreign policy initiatives and his successor, Gerald Ford, did not have the self-confidence to undertake any. The presidential election then intervened and the newly elected president, Jimmy Carter, assumed the task in 1977, as during the election campaign he said he would, of seeking an 'early movement toward normalising diplomatic relations in the context of a peaceful resolution of the future of Taiwan'. His Secretary of State, Cyrus Vance, visited China in August 1976 and although no visible progress towards agreement was made the run-down of forces on Taiwan was continued.

The six years that have passed since the Shanghai communiqué have been a useful breathing space for Taiwan. It has become one of the most affluent countries in Asia, and in spite of the lack of diplomatic recognition it has extended its commercial influence throughout the world. Its armed forces are well-equipped and well-trained and after the American withdrawal it will be able to afford to keep them at a high level of efficiency. If China sought to take over the island by military means it would be faced with great difficulties and, in fact, it is unlikely that it will have the necessary forces for a considerable time to come. By the time it was ready to do so it might find itself faced with a greatly changed strategic situation.

If it is true, as I have suggested in Chapter 3, that the Russians are actively seeking bases in the South China Sea, they must be looking with great interest at the harbours of Taiwan. In the south of the island is Kao–hsiung, with handy access to the South China Sea and the open Pacific. It has been developed into a major international port, has a spacious and well-protected harbour and maintenance and refuelling facilities. In the north, at the lower end of the East China Sea, is Keelung, which is Taiwan's second largest port and which has facilities almost equal to Kao–hsiung. On the east coast of the island there is the smaller but useful port of Hualien. Russian commercial ships already make regular use of these ports and the Soviet naval authorities are familiar with the facilities they have to offer. It seems likely, therefore, that an arrangement with the Taiwanese authorities whereby Soviet submarines and surface vessels had assured access to these ports would be very attractive to the Russians. If their hopes of obtaining full and secure use of Cam Ranh Bay in Vietnam (see p. 55) are not realized, the ports in Taiwan would be all the more valuable to them. That there have been discussions between the Russians and the government of Taiwan cannot be doubted; the president of the Kuomintang régime, Chiang Ching–kuo, has already warned the Americans that if pressed too hard he will turn to the Soviet Union for help.

If there is concern in Washington that the Russians might take the Americans' place in Taiwan there are no signs of it; but the Americans must be aware that Soviet forces based on Keelung and

Kao–hsiung could drive a wedge between the American bases in the Philippines and Okinawa and undermine the ability of the United States to maintain control of the western Pacific.

The Carter administration acceptance of a policy which could lead to the establishment of Soviet bases in Taiwan is another indication that the American defence authorities take it as inevitable that they will have to yield strategic control of this part of the world. It is, therefore, understandable that American thinking is turning increasingly towards helping the Chinese to overcome their technological and military inferiority, in the hope, presumably, that they will themselves be able to restrain the Soviet Union.

Until 1971 the Americans had insisted on tight restrictions on the supply to China, either by American firms or its allies, of militarily useful supplies and equipment. After Nixon's visit to China the American administration turned a blind eye to the sale by Western European countries of military equipment and technology, and have themselves supplied such militarily significant items as inertial guidance systems for aircraft and ground equipment for controlling earth satellites. Since the Vance visit in August 1977 sales have taken place in computers, communications equipment and nuclear-reactor components. Such sales will no doubt increase in scope and volume and will significantly assist China in modernizing her armed forces. But even with this equipment it would take many years for the Chinese to provide themselves with arms that would match the Russians. The only way they could do this in the next few years would be to buy ready-made weapons systems from Western Europe or the United States.

If China sought to buy armaments on a large scale, the United States would be placed in an acute dilemma. The Russians have warned the Americans that if they help China to arm with modern weapons they will create a Frankenstein monster who would be able to attack Japan and other neighbouring countries. The Russians have a clear interest in exaggerating the aggressive intentions of the Chinese and their warnings need not be taken too seriously. Nevertheless, it must be assumed that once China had the military means to do so it would certainly wish to seize Taiwan. This is not only because of its claim that Taiwan is part of China, but also because Taiwan is a vital element in the balance of power in the region. China would certainly wish to deny its use to the Russians or to, say, a re-armed Japan; and in China's own hands Taiwan could be used to prevent the closing of the Russian pincers in the Pacific.

Taiwan would also be very useful in extending China's economic

and political influence in Asia. It has become an important focus
of overseas Chinese economic activity, which is interlocked with
overseas Chinese interests in Hongkong and Singapore. The economic role of the overseas Chinese is becoming increasingly
important to the development of the whole region and is, in fact,
indispensable to it. China can take over Hongkong any time it
wishes; if it also seized Taiwan it would have strong leverage over
the economy of south-east Asia—an objective which the Chinese
would no doubt see as having advantages for them as great as, or
even greater than, any attempt at military takeover of the region
would bring.

In his report to Congress on 9 February 1972 Richard Nixon
proclaimed 'the end of an undisputed United States superiority in
strategic strength and its replacement by a strategic balance'. This
has meant that the security of the United States depends not on
its own military capacity alone but on the world balance of power
in the classic sense. If the United States is not to be faced eventually
with an overwhelmingly powerful coalition it must try to prevent
the domination of the rest of the world by any one power: but this
means, in effect, that it must rely on others to resist Russian
expansion.

It is for this reason that there are now many in the United States
who see an advantage in helping China to arm itself with modern
weapons, and who would not object to a Chinese seizure of Taiwan.
But there is another vital element in the balance which cannot be
ignored: what would be the reaction of Japan?

Taiwan itself is important to the Japanese economy—providing
over thirty per cent of its imports and taking fifteen per cent of
its exports. But its main significance lies in its relationship with
south-east Asia. Competition in the long run in this area between
China and Japan is likely to be severe, and the Japanese would
be at a serious disadvantage if the powerful economic influence of
Taiwan and, through it, of the overseas Chinese, were at the disposal
of Peking.

This is another illustration of the fact that the long-term
prospects of Japan are not good. It can expect increasing pressure
from Russia in the north and from China in the south, and strong
competition from both in south-east Asia. It cannot hope that its
problems would be solved by the maintenance of a balance between
Russia and China. Russia already has the means to apply severe
pressure on the Japanese economy, and China in the coming decades
is likely to be able to do likewise. Because of America's loss of
strategic superiority it is increasingly unlikely that it would be able

to save the Japanese from economic strangulation. Japan might, therefore, be faced—well before the end of the century—with having to accept the embrace of one of its powerful neighbours to save it from the other. From America's point this would undoubtedly be a dangerous shift in the balance of power. Whichever country obtained control of Japan would gain enormous economic strength and perhaps a decisive advantage in the struggle for world power.

Faced with the inevitable, the Americans might prefer to see the advantage go to China. They might consider that the combined strength of Japan and China would be no more than sufficient to offset the power of the Soviet Union. But this might be a miscalculation. There seems little doubt that a bloc comprised of China and Japan would in the long run be much more efficient economically than the Soviet bloc. The combined drive and organizing ability of the Chinese and Japanese could produce a burst of economic growth greater than the world has so far seen, and if south-east Asia were added, as it certainly would be, the bloc would command vast manpower and material resources. The century of the Asians would indeed have arrived; and the Americans might find themselves looking back with nostalgia to the simple days of American–Russian competition.

It might appear that there is another possible alternative—namely that the Japanese might decide to provide themselves with the means to defend their economic interests. Whether they should be encouraged to re-arm will no doubt become a matter of sharp debate in the United States. But time is again the critical element. For Japan to have any hope of creating a secure strategic zone for itself the best time for it to move would be now. The objective would be the same as in the 1935–45 period: to gain defensive depth on the mainland by seizing north China, Manchuria and the Russian Far Eastern region, and to secure access to resources by taking over south-east Asia and the South Pacific (this time making sure of Australia). If Japan possessed nuclear weapons, an antiballistic missile defence system, a fleet of nuclear-powered submarines, and missile-firing ships and aircraft it might be able to do it.

Ten years from now Japan could have all these things. Rapid progress is being made in the development of the nuclear industry and in missile-launching systems. Given the political will, there is no doubt that the Japanese could by 1988 provide themselves with a full nuclear armoury. But by then the Russians can be expected to have an unbreakable grip on the north Pacific. To have a credible counter-strike capability Japan would need missiles which could strike at the main centres in western Russia. Because of Japan's geographical location the Russians would have a good chance of intercepting missiles launched from its territory and the Japanese would need a large fleet of nuclear-powered submarines equipped with nuclear-armed missiles of longer range than any which exist at present. That they could produce such a fleet is undoubted, but the cost would be enormous and its effectiveness would be at the mercy of technological change—for example in the efficiency of Soviet defensive systems. It is unlikely, therefore, that the Japanese would ever dare use—or even threaten to use—nuclear weapons. So an armed Japan would eventually have to face the same choice as an unarmed one—which side to join. The only difference would be that an armed Japan would increase the military as well as the economic strength of its masters.

For a people as proud and resolute as the Japanese this is a harsh dilemma, and it would be rash to predict the road they will take.

From all this it will be seen that in the coming period the United States will be faced with some very difficult decisions—all the more difficult since whatever they decide the result will be unpredictable. Because of their fear of Russia they will undoubtedly lean towards assisting the Chinese, but even in the short run this will have its dangers. It must be taken for granted that there are still those in the Kremlin who believe that Chinese power should be broken before it is too late. It cannot, therefore, be ruled out that a rapid increase in Chinese armaments might provoke a direct attack across the border. The best time for this would be soon: not only because of the weakness of China, but also because the Soviet Union is stronger at present in the military resource most needed for such an enterprise — manpower—than it will be in future years. Following World War II there was a strong surge in the Russian birth-rate and this has meant a plentiful supply of conscripts for the armed forces during the present period. But the surge was temporary and Russia will have increasing difficulty in maintaining large forces on both the Chinese border and in Eastern Europe and at the same time meeting the manpower requirements of its industries.

There is little doubt that present Russian forces could over run Manchuria and north China (including Peking) with relative ease. Presumably they have been deterred from this by the realization that it might not solve the problem. To take over central and south China would require more forces than even they could muster, and they would in any case be faced, in the territories they occupied, by guerrilla warfare conducted with all the skill and tenacity which the Chinese exhibited during the revolutionary period. Nevertheless, there are some circumstances in which the Russians might consider that the risks would be justified.

The test might well be Taiwan. The Russian strategists would have to assume that once China controlled Taiwan the possibility of an ultimate Chinese challenge to Soviet power in the Pacific would be substantially increased. If it seemed likely that the Chinese were preparing to seize the island, the Russians might decide to pre-empt this by attacking China in the rear.

An important related factor is the vulnerability of Russia's far eastern ports. Vladivostok is the only base that is ice-free during the whole year, and it is dangerously close to the Manchurian border. China already has the capability to mount either a nuclear or a conventional attack across the Manchurian border; and it must be assumed that the immediate Chinese response to a Russian invasion would be to try to eliminate Vladivostok. The newly developed Soviet bases on the Gulf of Tartary and the Kamchatka peninsula would also be attacked. It seems unlikely, therefore, that the Soviet Union would risk a major clash with China until it was certain that it had alternative bases in the Pacific from which it could operate its naval and air forces. Taiwan would seem to offer an ideal solution to this problem; but a takeover of Taiwan by the Chinese would pre-empt that solution.

That a confrontation between China and the Soviet Union is ultimately inevitable is taken for granted in both Moscow and Peking, and Western governments would be unwise to assume that they know better. They would also be unwise to continue to regard the fate of Taiwan as of marginal importance, or to view with indifference the possibility of such a clash.

The United States has already committed itself to the principle that Taiwan should be part of China and unfortunately Australia has done likewise. It is to be hoped, however, that a better sense of strategic realities will be exhibited by other countries and that there will be a concerted effort to encourage and support the separate existence of Taiwan.

The outcome of the current debate in the United States as to whether China should be sold, or even given, American weapons and technology to assist it to overcome its military inferiority to the Soviet Union is likely to have an important bearing on the future of Taiwan. At its present level of military strength it is most unlikely that China would attack Taiwan, even if all American forces were withdrawn and the mutual security treaty abrogated. To have any chance of success they would have to mobilize on the coast facing the Taiwan Straits—the part of China most remote from the

Russian border—all their effective air and naval strength and their best armoured divisions. The Russians might then decide that this was their opportunity to move into Manchuria, and to take out the missile-testing sites and nuclear installations in Sinkiang. They would be largely unopposed, and the Chinese would have little hope of re-deploying their forces in time to prevent a major Russian breakthrough.

It is inconceivable that in present circumstances the Chinese would take the risk of uncovering their borders with the Soviet Union. If, however, they acquired sufficient armaments to maintain a defensive position on the Russian border, and at the same time mobilize the forces necessary for the capture of Taiwan, they might decide that the attempt was worth making.

Few people in America would suggest that China should be supplied with advanced offensive weapons but there is a fairly large group which believes that there would be no harm in letting them have defensive weapons. It is not easy to distinguish between offensive and defensive weapons, but to protect its borders against Russia China would at least need attack aircraft and tanks. If she had sufficient of these to be reasonably sure of holding a Russian attack she would then be able to mount an invasion of Taiwan. This is why the Russians are so vehemently opposed to any Western military help to China: whatever its nature it increases the possibility that China will seize Taiwan before Russia has had the time to consolidate its own position in the western Pacific.

There can be no doubt that for the countries in the region the best thing would be for Taiwan to remain free of either China or Russia for as long as possible. Apart from postponing the time when Japan will be faced with its fateful choice, it would give the countries of south-east Asia an opportunity to develop their individual and collective strength against the day when they will have to face the winner of the contest for supremacy. If Washington, out of negligence, allows Taiwan to pass to China they will increase the danger to south-east Asia—and Japan—and will also bring closer the day when they will be faced with a change in the global balance of power which will be highly dangerous to themselves.

As far as Australia is concerned neither the present government nor the Labor opposition seems aware that the problem of Taiwan exists. This is unfortunate, because we are one of the few countries whose national interests would not be damaged if we spoke up strongly in favour of its independence. Other countries are reluctant to do so, for ideological reasons or because of political sensitivities caused by the presence in their midst of large overseas Chinese communities. Japan, for its part, is inhibited because of its own previous role as the colonial power in Taiwan and its anxiety not to challenge China's claim to sovereignty.

The price that Australia might have to pay for championing Taiwan's independence would be no more than the severance of diplomatic relations with Peking. As past history shows, China would still continue to trade with us, and Peking is no longer such a closed capital that it is essential to have separate representation there. (Hongkong is in any case a better place than Peking to find out what is going on in China.) Other countries in the area would be grateful if we took such a lead, although they might be reluctant to acknowledge it. The prospects for the Vietnamese to maintain their independence would be diminished if either the Chinese or the Russians took over Taiwan, and this is undoubtedly recognized by the realists in Hanoi; and the same is true of the ASEAN nations. One of the most useful things Australia could do to help its neighbours, therefore, would be to seek international support for maintaining the independence of Taiwan.

Before the Nixon visit to China in 1972 a number of possibilities existed for achieving this. The Australian government had for many years asserted that the people of Taiwan were as much entitled to self-determination as any other community and it is probable that if the issue had been put to the test a majority of the members of the United Nations would have agreed. At the end of World War II a sensible and logical course would have been to put Taiwan —like the other Japanese Pacific colonies—under a United Nations Trusteeship. This was rendered impossible by the uncritical acceptance by the great powers of the claim by both the Communists and the Kuomintang that Taiwan was part of China. Nevertheless, an act of self-determination would still have been possible at the time of the admission of Peking to the United Nations. Any move in this direction was again prevented by collusion among the great powers, and by the total intransigence of Chiang Kai–shek (who lived long enough to see his own government reduced to an international nonentity). With the passing of the wartime leaders of both communist and Kuomintang China the voice of the people of Taiwan might yet be heard. This could only happen if the world community came to realize that the future of this small but vigorous country is vital to the stability of Asia and therefore to the peace of the world.

Much remains mysterious about the struggle for leadership in China after the deaths of Chou En–lai and Mao Tse–tung but the outline of future national policy is now clear: development will be given priority over social equality; self-sufficiency will be diluted in favour of economic co-operation with the rest of the world; and in defence the emphasis will be shifted from mass but lightly-armed forces to sophisticated modern weaponry.

It is misleading to suggest that the central argument among the contenders for power in China was concerned with friendship and co-operation with the Soviet Union: rather the differences related to the means by which the threat from Russia could best be met. In spite of their brave talk the Chinese leaders have an acute sense of China's vulnerability, and they have been greatly concerned to avoid provoking a Russian attack before they have the means to meet it. It is said that Teng Hsiao–ping, whose return to power was formally acknowledged in July 1977, was opposed to undue reliance on the West and wished to redress the balance in favour of the Soviet Union. His whole background makes this unlikely: he has been as resolute as any in opposing Russian influence; but it is probable that he saw danger in highly publicized swings towards the West—such as the Nixon visit in 1972, or the purchase of Rolls Royce aircraft engines in 1975. Teng Hsiao–ping, like the other rulers of China, can be expected to continue to abide by the precepts of Sun Tzu, the Chinese strategist of the fourth century B.C. Two of these, in particular, are likely to be very much in their minds: that all warfare is based on deception; and that he who knows when he can fight and when he cannot will be victorious. The Chinese know that they cannot fight now, but they hope to keep the enemy guessing about their present and future prepared- ness. In an age of satellite surveillance it is very difficult to hide the physical signs of military preparedness, but it can be assumed that they will do their best to confuse the world as to their real objectives and the progress they are making in achieving them. To outsiders it may continue to appear that the Chinese are following an erratic course; but it would be a mistake to believe that they do not have a clear idea where they are going and how they intend to get there.

That the post-Mao régime is now firmly installed can scarcely be doubted. Teng's formal return to power was surprisingly long delayed, but it now seems probable that he spent the time before he officially resumed the reins in consolidating support for his régime. His influence with the leaders of the armed forces has always been great and it is unlikely that he lost this when he was temporarily ousted in 1976. Mao disliked, and tried to prevent, the creation of a military and bureaucratic élite, but Teng Hsiao–ping (and before him Liu Shao–chi) saw this as the only practical means of governing China. He also believed that civil government could only function if it had the support of a united and loyal army. It was his particular role after Mao's death to restore the unity and recover the loyalty of the army leaders, and there can be little doubt that he did this by assuring them that in future their authority would be upheld and that the country's defences would be given high priority.

To a considerable degree China is still governed by a coalition of provincial military and party leaders, and the centre is dependent upon their support for the execution of its policies. In the past Shanghai has been one of the most important centres of regional power and was the source from which Mao drew much of his political strength. But the purging of the Shanghai group (now stigmatized as the 'gang of four') led by Mao's widow, Chiang Ching, suggests that Teng Hsiao–ping has been able to construct an alliance among the other provincial leaders to contain Shanghai. The chapter in Chinese history in which this city was pre-eminent in political influence and revolutionary fervour appears to have closed. As China moves into the phase of a centralized, army-backed bureaucracy, the radicals of Shanghai will have to conform.

With the settlement of China's internal difficulties it can be expected that overall development will gather speed. Mao's policy of giving preference to agriculture has ensured that the new régime has a firm basis for development on a broad front. The results of decades of preparation will soon be apparent in rapid rates of growth in the main industrial sectors. Mao's call for China to catch up with the United States by the end of the century is heavily emphasized in internal propaganda and the new régime claims to be confident that this will be realized. Highest priority is being given to 'catching up with and surpassing the world's advanced levels in science and technology', which are said to be the key to the modernization of industry, agriculture, and, above all, of national defence. It is accepted that this kind of progress will only be possible if China draws on foreign science and technology, but at the same time the Chinese people are urged 'to put stress on their own creativeness, independence and self-reliance' (*Peking Review*, 22 July 1977).

In the next quarter of a century China's main concern will be national survival. Her leaders believe that they are at last on the threshold of a 'great leap forward', but they fear that because of the country's military weakness there is a danger that all might be lost. They will require all the subtlety and flexibility of which they are capable if they are to avoid this danger. Their over-riding objective will be to hold the Russians at bay while they build up their strength. At the same time they will have to avoid attracting a pre-emptive Russian attack. In the international arena they will put their weight against the Russians wherever it seems safe to do so, and they will give open—or sometimes covert—support to Russia's opponents. But there will be limits beyond which they will be careful not to provoke the Russians and there may even be circumstances in which they will deem it wise to seek—or appear to seek—reconciliation with them. But it is unlikely that any Chinese leader would ever accept the idea of submission to the Soviet Union, or a status of permanent inferiority.

If it is conceivable that China might, as a tactic for survival, seek temporary reconciliation with the Soviet Union, is it also conceivable that as an alternative tactic it might seek an alliance with the United States?

Co-operation between China and the United States will undoubtedly develop, for the reasons already given: the Americans for their part are anxious to see China become a counterweight to Russia, while the Chinese need American science and technology. It is possible that this co-operation might extend so far as to include the provision of military technology and armaments. But it is difficult to conceive of an alliance of the kind, say, which exists between Japan and the United States and which would allow the stationing of American forces in China. Even if the present leaders of China regarded this as politically acceptable—which seems unlikely—they would know that this would be the one situation above all others in which a pre-emptive Russian attack would be likely. As for the United States, it seems out of the question that any American administration would reverse the whole trend of recent policy and accept such a dangerous and costly commitment.

In their struggle for survival the Chinese will be substantially on their own. From this perspective it cannot be said that they have more than an even chance of surviving; but if by the year 2000 China is still independent it will be well on its way to becoming the world's predominant power. While there is little Australia can do to affect the outcome, it might be worth casting our minds forward to the next century and asking ourselves which result Australians would prefer—Russian or Chinese hegemony?

If our racist attitudes continue—and there is little hope that they will disappear—Australia would obviously be more comfortable under Russian hegemony. The Russians exhibit typically European racial attitudes and might not object to the maintenance of the

'White Australia' policy. Moreover, we would be a long way from the centre of the Russian empire and provided we conformed to instructions in matters of trade and external relations we might be allowed a good deal of internal autonomy. But it is difficult to believe that the Asians, who by 2000 A.D. will comprise two-thirds of the world's population, will not—sooner or later—reassert themselves. Australia's fate would not then be a pleasant one.

We might be better off if the Chinese (in an alliance perhaps with the Japanese) won the present contest. We would have then to abandon 'White Australia' but if we were reasonably co-operative we might not be ill-treated. China would find our resources and industry useful and might not see any advantage in destroying our social and political system. We might even be drawn up to levels of cultural and economic development which we have not so far achieved, and which we seem to be incapable of achieving by ourselves. We would at last become part of Asia, but it might not be far-fetched to hope that we could make a contribution towards reconciliation between the dominant Asian races and the world's white minority. Our sons and grandsons might in this way have an opportunity to redeem the racist crimes of their forbears.

8

Links in the Island Chain

In the days when American strategy in the Pacific was based upon holding the 'island chain' off the east coast of the Asian mainland, the Philippines was regarded as of great strategic importance. It was the anchor of a line which ran northward through Taiwan, Okinawa and Japan. In spite of aberrations such as the campaigns in Korea and Vietnam, the dominating element in American strategic thinking from the end of the Pacific war in 1945 until recent times was the belief that to maintain United States control of the western Pacific it was necessary—and sufficient—for it to deploy strong forces in key places in this chain.

The gradual abandonment of this concept in recent years is well exemplified in the Philippines. In 1947 the United States and Philippines governments signed an agreement which was to run for ninety-nine years, under which the Americans were granted the right to use a network of army, navy and air force bases. A mutual security treaty was entered into in 1951, on the customary United States model, and extensive American help was given in organizing and equipping the Philippines armed forces. One of the largest air bases in the world was developed at Clark Field, north of the capital Manila, and an extensive naval base was built at Subic Bay. At Sangley Point, on Manila Bay, a large naval air station was built. During the twenty years following the end of the war the American military presence was ubiquitous and conspicuous. American manpower stationed in the country reached a post-war peak in 1968 when there were about 30 000 men.

By 1978 this was down to less than 10 000. Outlying bases had been closed down and operations at Clark Field, Subic Bay and Sangley Point were on a reduced scale.

There has been over the years a good deal of internal political opposition to the presence of the American forces and the United States has from time to time yielded some of its privileges in order to conciliate this. But the withdrawals of recent times have not been in response to this pressure; in fact in the Philippines, as in Japan, the opposition has become muted as the prospect of a full American withdrawal has come closer. The decision to withdraw is based upon the American government's new strategic policy which, as its actions increasingly demonstrate, no longer calls for the maintenance of powerful forward forces on any part of the island chain.

Reconsideration of the security interests of the United States in the Philippines began with the withdrawal of American forces from Vietnam and was quickened by the collapse in 1975 of the South Vietnamese régime. The signs were correctly read by the Philippines president, Ferdinand E. Marcos, who warned, in a speech shortly after the North Vietnamese victory, of the need for the countries in the south-east Asian region to re-appraise their national interests. He said that the internal divisions in American society made it doubtful whether the United States government would in future be able to meet its commitments to other countries. Marcos said that it had become questionable 'whether the identity of interests which formed the Mutual Defence Treaty between the Philippines and the United States still exists insofar as the United States is concerned'. He added bluntly that American commitments now appeared 'to have little value except as forms of psychological reassurance'.

Marcos acknowledged that without the counterpoise of American power the growing strength of the Soviet navy in the western Pacific could prove dangerous to the security of the region and of the Philippines. On the other hand, the presence of the American bases themselves might involve the Philippines in 'animosities, suspicions and conflicts' not of their making.

Thereafter Marcos moved quickly to disengage his country from the 'cold war' posture to which it had adhered longer than most other of the United States allies. He opened diplomatic relations in 1975 with the countries of Eastern Europe, although at this time he avoided formal contacts with the Soviet Union. It became clear during the same year that Marcos regarded China as a central element in his new foreign policy. He paid a five-day visit to China in the middle of 1975 and made sure that this was highly publicized throughout his own country. The Filipino people were reminded that contacts and trade had existed between China and the Philippines for several centuries before Magellan's ships reached the Philippines. Whereas in recent decades Filipinos had been hostile to the spread of Chinese migration throughout the south-east Asian region, government statements now recalled the historic Chinese cultural and commercial role in the region. Peking's warnings about the aggressive intentions of the Soviet Union were echoed in the Philippines media. Prominence was also given to the assurance that Teng Hsiao–ping (then holding the post of vice-premier, which he afterwards lost but has again resumed) gave to Marcos at the banquet of welcome in Peking. Teng declared that his government always maintained that all countries, big or small, should be equal. He said that the Peoples' Republic of China supported 'all the oppressed peoples in their just struggles' but at the same time held that the social system of a country should be chosen and decided only by its own people. He also told Marcos, as he has told many other visitors since, that China 'consistently and firmly' believed that it was possible for countries with different social systems to develop 'State relations' on the basis of the five principles of mutual respect for sovereignty and territorial integrity, mutual non-aggression, non-interference in each other's internal affairs, equality and peaceful co-existence.

If Marcos was dubious about this assurance he did not show it. He took comfort from the fact that the Chinese offered no strong objections to the continued presence of the American bases in the Philippines. After his visit to Peking he made a series of statements which re-interpreted his government's attitude towards these bases. Although they could no longer be regarded as ensuring that the United States would take military action in defence of the Philippines, the contribution that they made to preserving the balance of power in the Pacific justified their continued existence. He called for 'new arrangements' to end the extra-territorial rights of the United States, which were not in keeping with the 'dignity of a sovereign republic' such as the Philippines, and also asked the Americans to give some economic return for their use. Subject to these conditions Marcos was prepared to 'help the United States maintain an effective presence over the air and sea lanes of the western Pacific'. Negotiations for new arrangements are continuing, but if the run-down of American forces proceeds at the current rate they are unlikely to continue to represent an 'effective presence' in the region.

Since the end of the Vietnam war President Marcos has taken increased interest in ASEAN. For some years a difficulty existed for the Philippines in regard to the declaration made at the ASEAN conference in November 1971 that south-east Asia should be 'a zone of peace, freedom and neutrality' (ZOPFAN). At one time the Soviet Union appeared to give some support to this concept, by suggesting that it was compatible with its own proposal for a collective security system for Asia, which was launched in 1969 and is periodically revived when Asian statesmen visit Moscow. The Prime Minister of Malaysia, Abdul Razak, was on such a visit in 1972 and the Soviet Prime Minister, Leonid Brezhnev, declared that his system was based on the principles of the renunciation of the use of force, respect for sovereignty and inviolability of borders, non-interference in internal affairs, and development of economic co-operation. Abdul Razak accepted that the two concepts were compatible, even though it was clearly inconsistent with the Soviet proposal that any outside power should maintain forces in the region.

(This apparent coalescence between ZOPFAN and the Russian proposal caused sharp annoyance in Peking. The Chinese praised ASEAN but denounced the Russian collective security proposal as a strategem to advance Soviet 'hegemony'. Although they did not say so explicitly, it was widely believed that the Chinese feared that acceptance of the Soviet concept could lead to further American withdrawals.)

Marcos for some time sought to maintain that there was no contradiction between the ASEAN proposal for a zone of neutrality and the continued existence of the American bases in the Philippines. He argued that the interests of the region would be best served by a quadrilateral equilibrium of power in the Indian and the Pacific Oceans between the United States, the Soviet Union, the Peoples' Republic of China, and Japan. But in August 1975 he moved closer to the other members of ASEAN by accepting the proposition, embodied in the communiqué issued during a visit by the Thai Prime Minister to Manila, that 'foreign military bases in the region were temporary in character'.

Another move made by Marcos to improve relations with the Philippines' neighbours was to withdraw from the confrontation, which he had himself initiated, in regard to sovereignty over the Moslem areas lying in the south between the Philippines, Malaysia and Indonesia.

This confrontation had its origin in the difficulties that the Philippines government has met since independence in combating the Moslem secessionist movement based on Mindanao and the Sulu islands. The Moro National Liberation Front sought the creation of an independent Moslem State, which would include Mindanao, Sulu, Basilan and Palawan. The Filipinos believed that Sabah (a territory on the island of Borneo which had become part of the Federation of Malaysia) was the source of military and financial support for the Moro rebels and—partly in the belief that control of the territory would enable them to suppress the National Liberation Front—the Philippines government in 1962 laid claim to the territory. The claim was based on the fact that Sabah had once belonged to the Sultan of Sulu, whose territory was now part of the Philippines, but had in 1878 been handed over by him to the British North Borneo Company.

The Filipinos were doubtless correct in believing that the Moros were receiving aid from Sabah, and they became even more incensed when they realized that the rebels were also receiving assistance from Moslem countries as far afield as Libya. This intrusion was not welcome to the Malaysians and the Indonesians and, at a meeting of the Foreign Ministers of Islamic countries held in Kuala Lumpur in June 1974, agreement was obtained for a responsible attempt to find a peaceful solution to the problem. It was accepted that any such solution would have to be found within a framework which maintained 'the national sovereignty and territorial integrity of the Republic of the Philippines'.

Marcos agreed to send a delegation in January 1977 to a meeting with rebel representatives in Saudi Arabia. The talks broke down because of the rebels' demand for political autonomy for a Moro state. The position of the Philippines was strengthened, however, when the King of Saudi Arabia promised that he would not support any solution that would divide the territory of the Republic of the Philippines.

Despite the disapproval of the Malaysia government, the Prime Minister of Sabah, Tun Mustapha Harun, continued to give open support to the Moros, and this obstructed further progress towards a settlement. In 1975 Tun Mustapha met with considerable internal political difficulties, and the central government was able to insist that the Moro training camps in Sabah should be closed down. Tun Mustapha lost political power in the territory in 1976 and this has eased progress towards a settlement.

An aggravating factor has been the persistence of piracy, smuggling and drug trafficking between the island territories of all three countries in the area—Indonesia, Malaysia and the Philippines. Indonesia and the Philippines reached an agreement for joint border controls to reduce this illegal activity, and a similar agreement applied between Malaysia and Indonesia. Because of the Sabah dispute, however, no agreement had been possible between the Philippines and Malaysia.

At the ASEAN summit meeting in August 1977 Marcos made a gesture which gave some promise of solving both the Sabah dispute and the border control problem. He announced that his government was taking 'definite steps' to eliminate its claim to Sabah. He stopped short of saying categorically that the claim would be withdrawn, but said that it would be the subject of 'consultations with the people'. An unspoken assumption was that, if the claim were withdrawn, the Malaysians should agree to a border patrol arrangement which would both prevent aid going to the Moro rebels and check the endemic piracy and smuggling.

The Philippines has sought active co-operation with its neighbours in regard to the Law of the Sea. The Philippines shares a common interest with Indonesia in securing international acceptance of the archipelagic doctrine, under which the boundaries of a country consisting of a chain of islands would be measured by straight base lines connecting the outermost points of its farthest islands. Both countries have campaigned actively for the proposal at successive conferences on the Law of the Sea and so far have gained considerable support.

The Philippines is also a vigorous supporter of the proposals to extend the limits of territorial seas from three to twelve nautical miles and to provide for a two-hundred-mile exclusive economic zone. These proposals are endorsed by all ASEAN countries.

The importance of the Philippines is not confined to its relations with south-east Asian countries. Because of the Australian media's habit of reporting disparagingly on neighbouring countries the Philippines does not have a good image in Australia. It is, in fact, a dynamic country, with an educated and gifted people and with a cultural richness that contrasts markedly with Australia. If any country could be said to form a bridge between East and West it is the Philippines. Ethnically they are a blend of Asian and Pacific races, but as a result of over three hundred years of Spanish rule they have a predominantly European religion and culture. This Western orientation was strengthened by half a century of American rule (from 1898 to 1946). English is the language of instruction throughout the country, although the national language, Pilipino, is now being fostered. The great majority of the population are

Roman Catholics, although there are nearly four million Moslems, mostly in the southern islands. There are substantial Chinese communities in the main cities.

It is often said that the struggle for control of the western Pacific will be decided in the South China Sea, and if this is true the strategic importance of the Philippines is obvious. Its islands constitute the eastern perimeter of the sea and its superb harbours face towards it. When the Japanese forces landed at Lingayen Gulf in December 1941 and shortly after captured Manila, their control of the South China Sea was assured, and the way was open for their forces to spread all through south-east Asia. Any power which in future wished to control this sea could only do so if it also took control of the Philippines. The independence of this country is, therefore, vital to the independence of the whole region—including Australia.

What chance does it have of maintaining its independence? On its own, very little. Consisting, as it does, of over 7000 islands, it is virtually indefensible against direct invasion. Its only hope would be to maintain control over its sea approaches from all points of the compass. Clearly it does not have the resources for this.

The present Philippines navy can hardly be regarded as an effective combat force. It consists mainly of obsolescent patrol vessels and inshore craft. The air force is better equipped but its numbers are far below what would be required to defend the country in time of war. The army is one of the largest in the area and some of its units are battle-trained in campaigns against the insurgents in Luzon and the Moslem areas in the south; but it lacks both modern equipment and mobility.

There are signs that with the prospect of continuing American withdrawal the Philippines government is giving increasing thought to developing a defence structure better adapted to the country's needs. Plans are being developed to acquire missile-firing ships, submarines and anti-submarine chasers. There is also increasing interest in providing the air force with a missile capability. Such forces could make a valuable contribution to a collective defence system for the region, and the Filipinos would be wise to extract as much as possible of this class of equipment from the Americans before they leave.

Whether the Philippines will be able to preserve its own independence, or contribute to the security of the region, will also depend on whether it can overcome its serious internal problems. Ferdinand Marcos has established an authoritarian régime which is much criticized overseas, but the post-war history of the country has demonstrated that it cannot be ruled by an Anglo-Saxon form of representative government. Marcos still faces many problems and his continued survival cannot be regarded as assured, but he has established a degree of order in the country which it has not known for many years. Progress has been made towards a settlement of Moslem secessionist problems, and insurgency and lawlessness in the country's main island, Luzon, have been reduced to a manageable level. But as Marcos has emphasized repeatedly, the reconciliation of dissident groups and the creation of a genuinely united nation of the Philippines depends ultimately on overcoming the country's economic problems.

The Philippines' greatest handicap is its high birth-rate. It is still over three per cent and the present population of forty-five million will double by the end of the century unless the birth-rate is reduced. The total land area of the islands is only 300 000 square kilometres (compared with nearly eight million for Australia) and the population density is among the highest in the world. Malnutrition is already a serious problem: it is estimated that three and a half million of the country's eleven million children are malnourished. Half the annual registered deaths are of children under five years old, and of these half are attributable to malnutrition.

As in other Asian countries with high rates of population growth, catastrophe will only be avoided in the coming decades if there are massive increases in food production. The government now recognizes this, but the economy is suffering severe distortions because of the undue emphasis given in the past, as a result largely of the advice of Western experts, to industrialization. From 1950 to 1972 industrial production increased 5·3 times compared with 2·5 times for agriculture. There was an excessive transfer of population to the towns: the present level of urbanization is now twice that before the war. Owing to the low productivity of agriculture, inflation has been endemic, and the standards of living of both peasant and working classes have visibly declined.

At the beginning of the 1970s food production met with a series of disasters. In 1971 there were twenty-eight typhoons in four months, as a result of which rice production fell drastically. In the following year there was a widespread disease infestation, and in July 1972 the worst flood in the country's history occurred in Central Luzon, the biggest rice-producing area. The floods were succeeded by severe drought.

In the midst of this catastrophic situation President Marcos launched a food production programme known as Masagana 99.

The basic objects were to provide adequate credit to farmers, introduce modern methods, encourage the use of fertilizers, and cultivate new crop strains. The programme, which began on 21 May 1973, was concentrated in high-yielding areas. There was initially a dramatic improvement. In the first year rice production rose thirteen per cent above the average of the good seasons 1969 to 1971. The principal objective of the scheme, which was to raise crop yields, appeared to have been achieved, in that in many areas yields were doubled.

Unfortunately these achievements were not sustained. The relative failure of the second year strikingly demonstrated the close link that exists in a developing country between food production and cheap energy. Because of the international oil crisis of 1973–74 fertilizer prices rose 300 per cent in the period from May 1973 to November 1974. Other farm costs were also driven up because of the high cost of oil and petrol. Farmers' incomes again declined sharply and the government's new credit schemes were overwhelmed.

Nevertheless the Masagana 99 and related schemes have demonstrated what can be achieved, and the Philippines government continues to give high priority to agriculture. It is recognized that overall progress will only be possible if the deficiencies in the food-producing industries can be overcome. It is in the interest not only of the Philippines but of their neighbours, that they should succeed in raising their rural population above the present abject levels of poverty and thus provide a basis for social and political stability.

The northernmost islands of the Philippines are almost within sight of Taiwan, but there are sharp contrasts between the two countries. Taiwan has attained one of the highest levels of economic growth in the world. This has encompassed high productivity in the agricultural sector as well as remarkable industrial expansion. A successful land reform was carried out in the 1950s which released manpower for industry and enabled the introduction of improved farming methods. The birth-rate, which after the war was as high as in the Philippines, was by 1977 down to the manageable level of two per cent.

Much of Taiwan's economic growth has been based on trade with the United States, which absorbs forty per cent of its exports. It has benefited from large capital investments from the Americans, the overseas Chinese, and the Japanese (in that order). Political stability and a relatively high degree of literacy are two other important factors in fostering a high rate of growth.

The separate existence of Taiwan is now threatened. It is widely assumed, especially in Australia, that it is inevitable that it will be absorbed into China and it is also generally believed that it is proper that this should happen. These assumptions deserve examination.

There are two parts to the question: does Peking have legal sovereignty over the island; and in any case do the people have the right to self-determination?

Peking's claim that Taiwan has always been a province of China has no substance. The indigenous people came mostly from mainland Asia, but belong to the same southern mongoloid stock to which the Malaysians, Indonesians and Filipinos basically belong. The earliest historical contact between China and Taiwan was in A.D. 605, when a Chinese navigator landed on the island and claimed it in the name of the Chinese Empire. Owing to the hostility of the local people the contact was quickly abandoned. Almost exactly 600 years later a further landing was made and the island was proclaimed a 'protectorate of the Empire'. There were at this time a sprinkling of settlers on Taiwan and also on the Pescadores, the group of small islands lying between the Chinese coast and Taiwan. In 1367 the Pescadores were administered as part of the province of Fukien, but this arrangement was not extended to Taiwan. There was during the succeeding centuries no direct imperial rule of the island. Chinese emigration overseas was prohibited by the Ming dynasty and this prohibition applied to Taiwan. In 1387 all Chinese settlers on the island were ordered to return to the mainland.

In the following century the attitude of the imperial government again changed and the first serious movement began towards the colonization of the island. Developments in the fifteenth and sixteenth centuries had curious resemblances to the colonization of other territories in Asia at this period, except that the colonizers of Taiwan were the Japanese and Chinese, not Europeans. The first to arrive were the Japanese. A colony was established by them at Keelung, the harbour in the north of the island which is still its most important port. The colonizers were refugees who had fled from Japan during the disorders of the Ashikaga dynasty (1336–1443) and, like their European and Arab counterparts by now operating in the Indian Ocean, their principal occupations were piracy and trade in the Taiwan Strait and the East China Sea. Pirates from the Chinese mainland joined in a little later and established their own bases on the island. At the end of the sixteenth century there was a surge of migrants from the Chinese provinces of Fukien and Kwantung and their numbers became much larger than the Japanese.

In 1615 the Japanese made their first attempt to capture the island. An expedition was sent by the Tokugawa Shogunate, but it proved too small to be effective. It was repelled by a combination of the Chinese and local inhabitants. A Japanese adventurer, Hamada Yahei, organized another expedition a few years later, but by this time the Dutch had arrived and they in turn drove him off.

In 1624 the numbers of Chinese were estimated at 30 000. This was the year that the Dutch occupied the island. They had previously established themselves in the Pescadores, to the great annoyance of the Fukien authorities, and they were persuaded to leave these islands on the understanding that the Chinese would offer no objection to their taking over Taiwan. It is noteworthy that the Chinese at this time claimed no legal right to the island and the agreement reached with the Fukien authorities did not purport to transfer ownership of the island to the Dutch. In the dispute which later developed between them and the Japanese, the Dutch claimed that the land had been given to them by the Emperor of China, but this was refuted by the Japanese, who insisted that as they were the first to arrive they were entitled to possession of the island.

The Dutch established trading stations, built fortresses and churches, and imposed taxes on the inhabitants and on exports. They encouraged Chinese immigration and relied heavily on them in developing the colony. Because of its geographical location Taiwan became an important commercial centre for the region and proved a valuable prize for the Dutch. The Spaniards also sought to share in the profits and established themselves at Keelung, from which the Japanese were by this time withdrawing. They were driven out by the Dutch in 1641.

The Dutch themselves did not rule for long. They were expelled in 1661 by Cheng Cheng–kung, known in the west as Koxinga, who established an independent kingdom, with its capital at Anping on the south-western coast of the island.

This invasion by Cheng Cheng–kung is important in connection with China's present-day claims to sovereignty. He was of mixed Chinese–Japanese parentage, but he had become one of the leaders of the patriotic Chinese resistance against the Manchu invaders who had usurped the imperial throne in 1644. He was driven from the mainland by the Manchu forces, first retreating to the island of Amoy, and then to the Pescadores. In 1662 he invaded Taiwan with his remaining forces—with the same objective as Chiang Kai–shek nearly three hundred years later: that of building up a base from which to liberate mainland China from an illegitimate new régime. Like Chiang Kai–shek, he died before achieving his objective. His grandson, who came to the throne at the age of twelve, was overthrown by Manchu forces and in 1683 the island was declared to be a prefecture of Fukien.

This event is sometimes regarded as settling the question of Chinese sovereignty, but in fact in the following two centuries little was done to establish Chinese rule. Administration by the Fukien authorities was ineffective and many of the people of Chinese stock remained loyal to the Ming dynasty. There was no attempt to extend control over the indigenous tribes of the eastern and southern parts of the island and when European traders complained about the hostility of these people the Chinese authorities explicitly disclaimed responsibility.

Western commercial interests in the island developed substantially during the eighteenth and nineteenth centuries concurrently with their interests in mainland China. The harbours on the western coast of Taiwan became involved in the negotiations with the Chinese Emperor for special access for the Western powers to Chinese ports. Under the Treaties of Tientsin (1858), imposed on the Emperor by the forces of Britain and France, these two countries were given rights to the port of Taiwan-fu (near modern Tainan). By separate treaties both the Russians and the Americans were also given access to this port. The French, in addition, gained the use of Tamsui. During these negotiations the United States representative explicitly made the point that the eastern part of the island of Taiwan could not be regarded as under Chinese sovereignty.

By the middle of the nineteenth century the hostile behaviour of the native inhabitants had become an increasingly serious embarrassment to trade based on the island and, when in 1874 about fifty Japanese traders were massacred, the Japanese government decided to send a punitive expedition. The Chinese were at first unconcerned, but Peking later intervened and declared categorically that all Taiwan was under Chinese jurisdiction. The Japanese refused to recognize this claim, although they signed an agreement with the Chinese under which it was agreed that the Japanese force would be withdrawn, and that henceforth it would be 'the duty of the Chinese government to take such steps for the due control of the savage tribes in the region' as would prevent further atrocities on their part.

In the following years the Chinese for the first time made serious efforts to establish their control over the eastern and southern parts of the island, and in 1885 it was elevated to the status of a province of China. It enjoyed this status for a brief ten years. The Japanese defeated the Chinese in the war of 1894 and as part of the peace settlement (embodied in the Treaty of Shimonoseki) Taiwan and the Pescadores were ceded to Japan.

At the end of World War II the question of sovereignty over Taiwan was very confused. In the Cairo Declaration of November 1943, the United States, China and Britain had declared that Formosa should be 'restored' to the Republic of China. This was in effect endorsed by the Russians, who, when they entered the war against Japan, accepted the terms of the Cairo Declaration. On this basis Chiang Kai–shek always claimed that Chinese sovereignty over Taiwan had been regained when the Japanese surrendered on 2 September 1945. Most international lawyers considered, however, that Japanese sovereignty continued over the island until it renounced jurisdiction in the peace treaty signed in 1952.

The position until 1973 was that both the Communist régime on the mainland and the Nationalist régime on Taiwan insisted that the island was part of China, and this was supported by the Soviet Union, France and India. The United States, Britain, Japan and the Philippines held that sovereignty over the island, following the Japanese renunciation, remained undetermined. Australian governments were careful to avoid any positive statement until 1973, but in that year the newly elected Labor Prime Minister, Gough Whitlam, declared that Australia accepted that the People's Republic of China had sovereignty over Taiwan.

Meanwhile the United States had also changed its position. In the Shanghai communiqué of 27 February 1972 it was stated that the United States government did not challenge the position maintained by Chinese 'on either side of the Taiwan Strait' that Taiwan was part of China. The Japanese and others who have since entered into diplomatic relations with Peking have by their actions, including the severance of diplomatic relations with the government of the Republic of China on Taiwan, implied recognition of Peking's sovereignty, but have not explicitly stated their acceptance of it.

In the light of this history it is clear that at no time was Taiwan anything more than a loose dependency of China's and that, at the most, Chinese sovereignty over the whole island existed only for the brief period between its assertion by the government of China in 1874 and the cession of the territory to Japan in 1895 under the Treaty of Shimonoseki. (The international recognition of this treaty was regarded as involving the recognition of China's sovereignty over the territory and therefore its right to cede it, and also the transfer of this sovereignty to Japan.) The territory was never more than a colonial possession—in the same sense that other territories in the area were the colonial possessions of European powers. It was, to use the distinctions at one time fashionable among historians, a *colonie du peuplement* rather than a *colonie d'exploitation* but, except fleetingly between 1885 and 1895, it was not an integral part of the Chinese State. After the period of King Koxinga the Chinese brought Chinese culture and customs to the island, in the same way and during the same period that the Spaniards brought theirs to the neighbouring Philippines, but Taiwan was never integrated into the political, administrative and educational structure of the Manchu Empire. Its culture is predominantly Chinese; but so is the culture of Singapore. Its economic and social structure are in any case markedly different from the mainland, especially in its level of affluence. If the people wished to be an independent nation they would have as much right to become one as any other former colonial territory of an imperial power—certainly as much right as Singapore, or indeed as Australia.

The unanswered question is whether they wish to become an independent nation. The present president is the son of Chiang Kai–chek and continues to maintain the principle that Taiwan is a province of China. It cannot be taken for certain that Chiang Ching–kuo, or his successors, will not one day reach agreement with Peking for the incorporation of Taiwan into the People's Republic of China. Alternatively they may turn to the Russians for assistance in resisting Peking's pressure for incorporation. It has often been rumoured that Chiang Ching–kuo has been in regular contact with Moscow, and the story is recalled that he lived in Russia for several years and has a Russian wife. It would indeed be interesting to know the contents of the messages which are undoubtedly passing between Taipei and Moscow. It is possible that they canvass such matters as the port facilities which might be made available to the Soviet Navy (perhaps the Russians would like to return to their old ports in Taiwan) and the airfields which might be used by the Soviet Air Force. An agreement which protected Taiwan from Chinese invasion and which gave the Soviet Union what it so badly needs—bases in the China Sea—might seem attractive to both sides. For the present, however, the Kuomintang régime continues to assert that the Soviet Union has always been its enemy, and that it would not seek the help of one enemy against the other.

The other enigma is the attitude of the people of Taiwan—as distinct from their ageing Kuomintang rulers. Would they wish to become a Russian colony, after having been a Japanese and a Chinese one? Or would they prefer to be a sovereign nation, employing their resources and their great energy in their own national interests?

That they have the capacity to be a viable national State is not in doubt. Their average national income per head is one of the highest in Asia, and rising rapidly. They are expanding into sophisticated electronic and metallurgical manufactures and in some ways their industry is more modern than Australia's. They are at present heavily dependent on trade with the United States and Japan, but their commercial relations with the rest of the world, including Western Europe, are being vigorously developed. They have substantial foreign exchange reserves, their currency is strong and their internal price level steady. The distribution of wealth among the classes and as between city and country is relatively equitable, and levels of social well-being are much higher than in the neighbouring Philippines.

Taiwan is also moving quickly into the nuclear age. Its first atomic power plant began operation in 1977 and two others are under construction. In 1972 an agreement was signed with the United States for the supply of enriched uranium for a period of thirty years. The country's ability to develop its own nuclear weapons is now not doubted, and given time it could also produce its own delivery systems. It has the capacity to produce sophisticated modern aircraft: under a co-production agreement with the United States a modern jet fighter—the F5E—is now built in Taiwan.

The country therefore has the wealth, the industrial base, and the potential military capability to be an important independent power. For the present the people of Taiwan are silent about their hopes for their future. What they eventually decide will be of great importance to the other small nations in the area. If they were to establish their independence they could be the keystone in a structure of collective security for the whole region. If they fall under the domination of a great power, that power will win a critical advantage in extending its strategic control over the region.

If the people of Taiwan ultimately commit themselves to a struggle for independence they would deserve the utmost support of the peoples of south-east Asia and of Australia and New Zealand. They would be fighting our battle no less than their own.

9

The Struggle for Resources

In his studies on population growth Malthus calculated that, in the worst case, population could double in twenty-five years. This will happen in the last quarter of this century in countries of south-east Asia and the Indian sub-continent.

In Asia as a whole about one-third of the people have at present insufficient food. Each year over ten million people die from hunger-related causes. In spite of all efforts, including aid from the affluent countries, this situation is worsening.

In the United Nations document, *The Future of the World Economy*, published in 1976, it was estimated that to achieve a minimal standard of life in the underdeveloped countries by the year 2000 (US$500 per capita at 1976 prices) would require an annual growth in overall production of between 6·5 and 7·5 per cent per annum, and an increase in agricultural production of 5 per cent. In order to maintain present inadequate consumption levels an annual increase of 2·5 per cent would be necessary. This means that at the least total food production would have to be more than double by the end of the century; even a slight shortfall would mean massive starvation.

It is estimated that it is physically possible to increase the land area under cultivation in all the underdeveloped countries by about thirty per cent. But this could only be done as a result of drastic changes in social attitudes, by transfers of agricultural labour and by large investment in land reclamation and irrigation and in machinery. Moreover in the countries in Asia where population density is greatest unused cultivable land is considerably less than the average for all underdeveloped countries.

The use of new lands would not in any case be sufficient to provide the necessary food. If a five per cent increase were to be achieved —which would be necessary to eliminate present levels of malnutrition—productivity would have to be raised about two and a half times for all land under cultivation.

Again this is physically possible. In the United States agricultural output per unit of total land area under cultivation increased in the thirty years up to 1975 by eighty per cent. In the Soviet Union average rice yields have increased 2·3 times in the past twenty-five years, while in the Philippines and Thailand an increase of fifty per cent was achieved in ten years.

Past experience gives little ground for optimism that such results can be achieved generally in Asia. In some countries—for example, India and Bangladesh—food production per head of population has actually declined. Governments and international aid organizations have at last come to realize that, in future, agriculture rather than industry must be given priority in development and that there is now no more time to lose in the race against famine.

Vast sums of money will have to be invested in land improvement, machinery, irrigation and fertilizer production. Many social and political barriers to the best use of land and animals will have to be removed, and farmers will have to be taught new methods. A greatly improved infrastructure will have to be built for the collection, distribution and storage of harvests, and for the distribution of fertilizer and other requirements for increased yields. Finance will be important but even more essential will be efficient government organization and the introduction of special measures to create a favourable economic climate for agricultural development.

A critical element in raising food production will be the availability of low-cost sources of energy. Oil will be particularly important, because most Asian countries will be heavily dependent upon petrol and diesel driven transport and machinery for agriculture. The cost of energy is also an important component in the price of fertilizers, which will have to be used in greatly increased quantities if significant growth in production is to be achieved. For the rich countries the steadily rising cost of fuel will be an inconvenience, but for the poor it could make the difference between sufficiency and massive starvation.

The difference between the developed Western countries and Asia in the capacity to produce food is wide. In non-communist Asia the production per head has been static or has declined in the years since 1961, whereas in the West it has risen by 1·2 per cent. The countries who already have plenty of food are growing more and more, while the poor are getting hungrier.

The food surplus in Western countries, particularly in North America, has been used to some extent to make up the deficiencies of the poor countries. Some has been given in the form of aid, but this usually amounts only to about ten per cent of their needs. The remaining ninety per cent must be bought on the world market and since 1972 prices, partly as a result of the increase in energy costs, have risen steeply. The dependence of the Asian countries on imports to maintain even the present low standards has increased at the same time that the cost has risen. A vicious circle is thus created: as more resources have to be expended on importing food fewer are available for the development of home production.

The geographical location of the poor countries of Asia is itself a handicap. Agricultural production in tropical zones is more difficult than in the grain-producing areas of the temperate zones. It is harder to maintain soil fertility in heavy rainfall areas, and there is a higher incidence of pests and diseases. The problems of storage, processing and distribution are also greater. Losses occurring in storage reach ten per cent or more of the crop.

The problems of China are basically similar to those in other parts of Asia. It has an estimated population of 850 million, and an annual increase of about 15 million. But because of the emphasis placed on agricultural development by the communist régime food production has kept pace with population growth. Over the past decade imports of food grains have been at about two per cent of total consumption, as compared with six per cent for India and fifteen per cent for Bangladesh, and it would be possible for China to dispense with overseas supplies without drastically affecting standards of living. It should be capable in the coming years of producing a considerable surplus.

The situation of the Soviet Union is less favourable. Owing to the erratic climate there are wide swings in annual production. At times of harvest failure large supplies of grain have to be imported. This is a serious economic and strategic handicap for Russia, and since it is unlikely that it will be able to ensure sufficient internal production to meet the rising food requirements of the people, it can be expected to pursue policies which will give it secure access to overseas supplies.

The United Nations Food and Agricultural Organisation has

estimated that the requirements of the underdeveloped countries for imported food will double by 1985—from 35 to 70 million tonnes—if present minimal standards are to be maintained. It is improbable that this level will be reached, mainly because the needy countries will not be able to pay for such large quantities. It is, indeed, doubtful whether they will be able to afford the increasing cost of the quantities of food that they buy at present.

The countries which have the highest capability for increasing food production are the rich developed nations of the West, especially the United States, Canada and Australia. In the United States there are still large areas of unused land and it has both the capital and the technology to expand grain production substantially above present levels. Canada and Australia face greater climatic limitations on further expansion, but they also could increase production significantly. In 1975 the grain exports of these three countries totalled 92 million tonnes; there is no doubt that by 1985 they could increase this by another 30 or 40 million tonnes. They could therefore easily supply the extra 35 million tonnes of imports which the FAO believes the underdeveloped countries will need by 1985. But the United States, Canada and Australia will not produce this extra food unless they are paid for it; and it is difficult to see where the money will come from.

At the World Food Conference in Rome in 1974 it was recommended that a minimum of 10 million tonnes a year should be provided in food aid for the developing countries. Even in the unlikely event that it were achieved, such aid would make only a marginal contribution to the problem. In 1975 a special session of the United Nations General Assembly called for the establishment of a world food-grains reserve of 30 million tonnes. It was recognized, however, that there was little likelihood of the early implementation of such an ambitious project and it was at the same time proposed that an interim emergency food-grain reserve of 500 000 tonnes be made available to deal with famine situations in the developing countries.

These measures could not be expected to ensure that periodic famine could be avoided. The provision of haphazard batches of food aid often has the paradoxical effect of reducing production in the recipient countries, because it depresses local prices; but in any case centrally-held grain reserves would have to be more than double the 30 million tonnes proposed by the World Food Conference if they were to be sufficient to even out fluctuations in supply and avert famine.

For the countries of Asia, therefore, neither food imports nor aid obtained from Western countries is likely to meet their needs. They have no alternative, other than starvation, to raising food production in their own countries to levels sufficient for their own minimum requirements.

In the coming decades the imbalance in the world's food supplies will be of great political and strategic importance. The same will be true of the prospective energy shortage, with which it is inextricably related. Shortages of food and energy are likely to coincide in the mid-1980s and adequate production of the former will depend upon adequate supplies, at bearable cost, of the latter.

Because the poor countries at present consume only a small proportion of the world's total energy supplies, little attention is normally given to the serious consequences for them of the recent rises in cost, and the even more damaging effects of the global shortage which is expected to develop in the next decade.

There are widely varying estimates as to the extent of this shortage, and it is argued by some that no actual deficiency will occur. It is almost unanimously accepted, however, that there will be a severe rise in costs. The main reason for this will be not so much the depletion of supplies, as the continuing extravagant use of energy by the Western countries. Enough has happened in the United States and Western Europe since the oil producers of the Middle East raised the price of oil in 1973 to demonstrate that these countries do not have the political will to economize more than marginally on their consumption of energy. At the present time the industrialized countries consume about seventy per cent of total energy supplies, although accounting for only thirty per cent of world population. This disparity is likely not only to continue but to increase.

Oil and natural gas in 1976 represented sixty-six per cent of the total fuel consumed for energy. Their combined share of estimated fuel reserves is, however, only seven per cent. Even if this is an under-estimate it is clear that if oil is consumed at the present rate reserves will inevitably run out. Forecasts as to when this could happen vary, but it seems likely that it will occur by the end of this century or the beginnning of the next.

The world's most plentiful energy resource is coal, representing over seventy per cent of known reserves of fuel. At the present time it contributes only thirty per cent of world energy consumption. It would seem therefore that its use could be greatly expanded. But it causes high levels of pollution which could ultimately have a serious effect on the global environment; and a large part of the reserves would be difficult and costly to exploit.

Other sources of energy are hydro-electricity generation, solar power and nuclear power generation. There has been much discussion of the contributions which these and nuclear fusion (if a feasible process were discovered) could ultimately make to the world's energy needs, and this will not be repeated here. It would be unrealistic, however, to rely on hopes that an energy shortage could be avoided in the next twenty-five years, either by a more rational use of existing fuels or by a scientific breakthrough. The rich countries do not have either the will or the courage to impose drastic economies in energy consumption, and the scientists and engineers still have decades to go before they are likely to solve the problems of producing energy from hydrogen fusion. The only source apart from conventional fuels which is likely to make a useful additional contribution to world energy supplies is power generation by nuclear fission.

Unfortunately the debate in Western countries in regard to the use of nuclear fuel has become highly charged with emotion. In particular, it has become entangled with the problem of the proliferation of nuclear weapons.

There is no longer any effective connection between the expanded use of nuclear fuel for energy and the making of nuclear explosives. Any country with a modest level of technology and a single reactor can now make atomic explosives—as India demonstrated in 1975. The question of whether additional countries will develop nuclear weapons now depends on political and economic factors. The main restraint on proliferation is the fact that an explosive is of little use without delivery systems, and that these are at the present time technologically difficult and therefore costly to produce. The real danger of rapid proliferation in the future is that the means of delivery will become cheaper and more freely available.

The dangers arising from the mining of uranium and the operation of nuclear power stations have been exaggerated. Most of the problems which arose in the experimental stages have been solved and nuclear power generation in itself is one of the safest and least polluting of all the major sources of energy. Some risks still exist—as they do in thermal power stations or in the construction of large dams for water power—but all human endeavour involves danger. The industrial age has exacted a heavy toll in human lives—especially the motor-car—but it cannot be doubted that it has also brought benefits to mankind.

Apart from the mining of uranium and the actual operation of the nuclear power stations, there is the problem of the disposal of waste fuel. This is still said to involve dangers, not only in the present but in the distant future.

There are two aspects to this problem. The waste from an ordinary uranium nuclear reactor is not highly dangerous. It consists mostly of short-lived fission products which decay after a few months. There are also quantities of strontium–90 and caesium–137 which take about sixty years to decay, and small amounts of the so-called actinides, including plutonium, some of which remain radioactive for hundreds of thousands of years. In order to economize in the use of uranium it is, however, considered desirable to process the spent fuel so that it can be re-used; this reduces the bulk of the remaining waste, but it substantially increases the amount of plutonium. Unlike the original waste, this can be readily used for making nuclear explosives but, more important, it increases the problem of finding safe storage for long periods of time.

The second aspect relates to the fast-breeder reactor. The objective in using this type of reactor is again to economize in the use of uranium. It breeds much of its own fuel and the countries who are deficient in uranium resources see it as a means of reducing their dependence on imported fuel. Unfortunately it produces immediately usable weapons-grade plutonium and a long-lived radioactive waste product.

Looking back over the past thirty years, it seems unfortunate that a determined effort was not made earlier to develop the ordinary uranium reactor as a substantial provider of energy. The principal reason this was not done was because of the availability of cheap oil, which has been squandered recklessly by the industrial nations. The uranium reactor could have played an important part in conserving oil resources, and might have been sufficient to carry the world through the energy crisis of the next quarter century. This is now too late. In spite of the anti-uranium movements in Western countries, plutonium fast-breeder reactors are here to stay. If uranium were cheaply and readily available it might slow down their development, but for many countries the only alternative now would be to expose themselves to a crippling energy shortage before the end of the century. The ordinary uranium reactor is no longer regarded as sufficient for their needs, primarily because it does little to relieve their dependence on imported fuel.

In the Soviet Union in 1977 there were eighteen nuclear power stations operating, with another twenty under construction—including fast-breeder reactors. Nuclear plants are also operating in East Germany, Czechoslovakia and Bulgaria, and are under construction in Romania, Hungary and Yugoslavia. In Japan there are thirteen commercial uranium reactors in operation, with eleven under construction and more planned. An experimental fast-breeder reactor was brought into operation in 1977. In Western Europe, including the United Kingdom, there are sixty-eight nuclear power plants in operation, and a fivefold increase is planned by 1985. Experimental fast-breeder reactors are in operation in Britain and France and commercial plants of this type are in the planning stages. In the United States sixty-five uranium nuclear reactors are in commercial operation, and a further 160 are under construction or planned. The Carter administration has forecast that America will need 320 nuclear power plants by the year 2000.

The likely spread of nuclear fuel enrichment and re-processing technologies is regarded as more dangerous in relation to nuclear weapons proliferation than the existence of nuclear reactors. The technologies for enriching uranium for commercial reactors and for re-processing spent fuel can be used for the making of weapons-grade plutonium. At present enrichment plants exist only in the United States, the Soviet Union and the United Kingdom. Most of the enriched fuel used in Western countries and Japan is supplied by the United States, although in recent times some has been made available by the Soviet Union. Some user countries dislike this dependence and are planning the construction of enrichment plants of their own—including France, West Germany and Japan. President Carter's energy policy, which he announced in 1977 shortly after taking office, calls for restraint in the proliferation of enrichment and re-processing technology, but present indications are that this will not be heeded. In addition to building their own enrichment plants, France and Germany are negotiating for the sale of plants to Brazil and Pakistan.

In Western countries public opposition has slowed down the further development of nuclear power generation, but it is difficult to believe that this opposition will continue to be effective once the social consequences of the prospective energy shortage begin to take effect. In any case the expansion in the Soviet Union and eastern Europe will continue; and in Japan it is unlikely that any government would allow public dissent to prevent development of a source of energy which could be essential to the country's survival.

Total energy demand in the non-communist world is likely, at a conservative estimate, to grow at the rate of 4·6 per cent per year until 1980 and is then expected to decline to 3·9 over the longer term. At this rate energy requirements will by 1990 be over eighty per cent more than in 1975. At this time the United States will still consume more than one-third of world energy and Western Europe one-quarter. Japan will need about eight per cent. In the rest of the non-communist world, consisting mostly of the under-developed countries, consumption should rise, if their basic needs are to be met, from under twenty per cent to over thirty per cent. These estimates are based on the assumption that there will be a diminished rate of growth in energy requirements of the advanced countries in the future but that in the case of the underdeveloped countries the present rate of growth will continue as they develop basic production-requiring energy.

If these conservative requirements are to be met, a sharply increased contribution to total supplies will have to be made by *all* forms of energy currently in use. It is inescapable that during the rest of the century oil will be the most important fuel, and it is expected that its contribution will have to increase by 1990 by about seventy per cent. It is physically possible to obtain this, but the cost will undoubtedly be much higher than at present and the rate of depletion of total reserves will be greatly increased. Even at this level it will only represent about half the world's energy needs. The other half will have to be made up by coal (expected to contribute nineteen per cent), gas (fifteen per cent) and nuclear power (eleven per cent). All other forms—hydro-electricity, geothermal, solar heat and synthetic fuels—are expected to produce in total no more than five per cent. Nuclear fusion is not expected to make any contribution before next century.

Although coal is the world's largest energy resource, the problems of raising present production to meet the requirement for nineteen per cent of the total energy needs of the non-communist world will be considerable. It will require an increase from under two billion tonnes to over ten billion tonnes. The costs of bringing less accessible deposits into production, and of preventing dangerous pollution, are likely to be high.

It will be seen that although the contribution required from nuclear energy by 1990 is expected to be no more than eleven per cent, it will be crucial. The absence of this marginal addition would put severe pressure on other forms of energy and would drive costs even higher than they are already expected to go. The affluent countries could no doubt survive the loss, albeit at the cost of reductions in their standards of life, but the consequences for the poor countries could well be to halt development and make it impossible for them to feed their additional millions. Even by 1990 their total consumption of energy will only be small compared to the rich countries, but if their minimum requirements are to be met they will need to receive over thirty per cent of the projected total growth in world energy between 1975 and 1990.

For many millions of the world's people, therefore, the only hope of avoiding starvation in the coming decades is for all sources of energy to be exploited at the optimum. The contribution of nuclear energy will be indispensable, and it is urgent that the remaining problems should be solved and maximum development undertaken. The argument about the safety of nuclear power is an argument for the rich: only they could afford the luxury of doing without it.

Through the clouds of emotional debate it is possible to discern solutions which, although not guaranteeing safety to infinity, will provide as much assurance as is possible in any activity of life. The problem of the disposal of radioactive wastes has not been created by nuclear power generation: it was already with us because of the making of nuclear weapons, which has resulted in the accumulation of many thousands of tonnes of waste. A number of alternative solutions is available, including the solidification of the waste in glass and its storage in geologically stable zones, or in the deep sea. Such methods are unlikely to involve consequences for humanity as bad as those arising from the disposal of fossil fuel wastes in the past—of which the landscapes of parts of South Wales and Pennsylvania are a continuing reminder. Some residual waste products may have a radioactive life of a million years or more, but it seems unnecessary to believe that it will cause inconvenience to creatures living in those times. On present prospects it would be optimistic to assume that the human race, which as Bernard Shaw once remarked is an experiment that may not last, will still be in existence.

It is commonly said in Australia that the poor Asian nations do not need nuclear technology but should rely upon simpler forms of energy generation. This is a supercilious attitude to take towards countries whose industrial technology is in some cases more advanced than our own. It is true that in agriculture their principal need is for oil for transport and farm machinery and that they do not have the capital for extensive grid systems to distribute electricity throughout the countryside. But nuclear power could provide urgently needed electricity for the huge cities which have grown up in Asia, and which will inevitably get larger as populations expand.

It is nevertheless true that the main benefit for the poor countries from the development of nuclear power would be indirect: if the advanced industrial nations used nuclear energy to the maximum possible degree this would release oil for poor countries. The best course for the advanced nations, in fact, would be to develop all alternative forms of energy as rapidly as possible and thus enable the underdeveloped countries to obtain oil on less unfavourable terms.

The communist countries are on the whole more fortunate than the non-communist developing countries in their energy resources. They clearly regard the energy problems facing the Western nations as an advantage to them, and they are no doubt happy to see them exacerbated. Communist propaganda funds are presumably flowing to the anti-uranium movements, as they did to the anti-Vietnam movements (some are the same organizations). A slow-down in economic progress in the West in the next twenty years because of fuel shortages would give the communist countries time to catch up, and improve their prospects of fulfilling their ambition to overtake the capitalist countries by the end of the century. It would also strengthen their position in the competition for influence among the needy countries.

In 1976 the Comecon countries (the Soviet Union and Eastern Europe) were not only self-sufficient in energy resources, but exported the equivalent of six per cent of their internal consumption. They have sixty per cent of proven world reserves of coal, over thirty per cent of the natural gas, and about twelve per cent of the oil. They also have twenty per cent of the world's known reserves of uranium.

Most of these resources are, however, in Russia and, except for Romania, all the Eastern European countries are heavily dependent upon energy imports from the Soviet Union. Russia itself faces increasingly difficult problems, in that the largest reserves of oil, coal and gas are in Siberia and the cost of extracting them is high. According to Soviet plans oil production is supposed to grow by over five per cent per annum up to 1980, natural gas by over eight per cent, and coal by about five per cent. Western observers regard these targets as optimistic, and are doubtful whether they can be maintained in the long term. In a report released by the C.I.A. in April 1977 it was predicted that Russia would by 1985 be obliged to import oil from outside the Comecon block. This could probably be avoided if vast capital investments were made in developing the Soviet Union's own production, but it is clear that it would be an economic advantage to be able to obtain cheaper supplies from overseas. Czechoslovakia and Hungary are already drawing some supplies from the Middle East by way of a pipeline from the Adriatic coast of Yugoslavia, and other Comecon countries are seeking direct deals for supplies with OPEC-producing countries, and with prospective new producers. These arrangements are limited by shortage of foreign exchange and in present circumstances are unlikely to constitute a substantial proportion of Comecon's needs. It is reasonable to suppose that one of Russia's long-term strategic objectives is to secure better access to major overseas sources of fuels.

Russia is, meanwhile, relatively well placed to develop nuclear power. Its uranium reserves are said to be as large as Australia's. The Comecon countries' consumption of nuclear energy is expected to rise to ten per cent of their total energy consumption by 1980, and by a steadily rising percentage in future years. As in the West they will, nevertheless, remain primarily dependent upon oil and coal at least until the beginning of next century. If they succeed in drawing substantial supplies from the outside world this will of course increase the difficulties of the Western countries in meeting their own needs, and also cause additional hardship to the underdeveloped countries.

There is, however, a degree of common interest between Russia and the developing countries which may ultimately have important strategic consequences. It is becoming increasingly clear that Russia cannot achieve standards of living comparable with the West from its own resources: it needs both food and energy from the outside world. The only substantial surpluses that are available are in food from North America, and oil from the Middle East. The underdeveloped countries also need food and oil from these sources and, like the Russians, lack the money to pay for them. If Russia were to use its growing military power to exact from Western and Arab countries a share of the resources they hold, it could expect the support of the poor countries—provided they also received a reasonable proportion.

Western commentators usually discount suggestions that war could occur over resources. This neglects the evidence of history. Peoples faced with starvation have in the past been prepared to take great risks to gain the resources they need, and with the possibility of famine on an unprecedented scale in the next two decades the risk of conflict would seem to be high. The fear of global nuclear war may be a deterrent, but perhaps a diminishingly effective one. The rich nations are not likely to use nuclear weapons in a war for resources, because of the danger of retaliation. If the Soviet Union gave its backing to countries trying to seize either food or energy resources, or territory which produces these things, it seems probable that none of the Western nuclear armed powers —the United States, Britain or France—would dare to intervene.

The vulnerability of the oil-producing countries of the Middle East to Soviet pressure—which could be made effective without actual fighting—has been discussed in Chapter 1. As far as food and energy resources other than oil are concerned the obvious targets are Canada, Australia and (because of its grain-producing capacity) Argentina. Since Canada is protected by the United States nuclear shield it is unlikely to be in much difficulty, at least until a late stage. Argentina's internal political weakness means that it would probably yield fairly quickly to determined Soviet pressure. Since in a good year it produces more grain for export than Australia it would make a useful, although not a large, contribution to the food needs of the poor countries.

What about Australia? It is said that our exports of food are too small to make much difference to the hungry countries and therefore that no one is likely to attack us because of them. But it would be physically possible for us to produce at least fifty per cent more wheat. This would bring our exports up to 18 to 20 million tonnes, which is half the total imports that the non-communist developing countries have required annually in recent years. If pressures other than price were applied Australia could also substantially increase its output of meat, fish and other high-protein foods.

The day may come when the world community takes the view that Australia has an obligation to make a larger contribution to the food and energy needs of the poorer countries, and it might not seem unreasonable to others that the necessary pressures should be applied to oblige us to do so. This need not involve military action unless we were foolish enough to initiate it ourselves—but could take the form of trade sanctions, blockade of shipping, or the severance of air communications. If such actions were undertaken by neighbouring countries in south-east Asia and were backed by a major power such as the Soviet Union or China it is clear that we would have no alternative but to yield.

The most important factor in the future struggle for food will, nevertheless, be American production. The United States normally produces six times as much wheat for export as Australia and it is probable that it would be physically possible for it to produce half as much again. It is therefore capable of producing a grain surplus which would be sufficient in itself to prevent starvation in the food-deficient countries. The question might ultimately arise as to whether the Americans might themselves be subjected to pressure to make food available on terms that these countries can afford.

In the United States the political importance of its capacity to produce large surpluses of food is widely recognized, but it has been seen as a strength rather than a weakness. It is often suggested that it might help to offset the decline in the United States global influence caused by the withdrawal of its military power. Its capacity to offer food is seen as useful in countering Soviet influence among the developing countries, and also as a means of applying pressure, because of its periodic need for large grain imports, to Russia itself.

This might have been a safe weapon for the United States to use while it had global strategic control. Now that it has lost this control it could be double-edged. It could attract retaliation in the form of denial of commodities on which it is now dependent—pre-eminently oil—and it might not have the military means to overcome a blockade of this kind. When in 1973 the then United States Secretary of State, Henry Kissinger, spoke of the possibility of American military action in the event of an attempt by the oil-producing countries of the Middle East to cut off supplies of oil, this was quickly seen as an implausible threat. Since then the strategic position of the United States has weakened further, and it is not conceivable that it could afford to take the risk of going to war to obtain oil supplies.

In 1976–77 there was a conjunction of good harvests in the world and as a consequence there was a tendency to belittle the dangers of future famine. A large wheat surplus developed in North America and the American government ordered a twenty per cent reduction in plantings for the 1977–78 season. International efforts towards the establishment of a world grain reserve were allowed to peter out.

The truth was that the surpluses were artificial. About thirteen hundred million people in the world were still without sufficient food, the majority of them in Asia. The surpluses of 1976–77 increased rather than diminished the likelihood of future famine because it dampened the growth of production in the Western grain-exporting countries. In order to fill the gap between the food available in the poor countries and what the people need an increase in production of four per cent a year would be required in the West. There is little prospect that this will be achieved.

Some Asian countries in recent years have made considerable industrial progress, and this is also often regarded as giving grounds for optimism that the developing countries will be able to cope with their population explosion. The case of India suggests caution: it has achieved a high level of industrial output and in some sectors employs more advanced technology than many Western countries.

Yet during this development the standard of living of the masses of the people has declined and has remained one of the lowest in the world. Because of the foreign exchange earned by the industrial products India has been able to purchase foreign food supplies, and it is therefore argued that without industry the Indian people would be worse off. But India has large areas of arable land which are unused, and in many areas two crops a year could be grown instead of only one; if capital had been put into this kind of development instead of into industry not only would there have been no need for imports, but there would have been sufficient food to provide the people with adequate sustenance.

This is not to say that industrial development of a labour-intensive kind should not be established in the poor countries. Even if agriculture were developed at maximum speed there would still be a large labour surplus available for industry. The prospect of plentiful supplies of low-paid workers is already attracting manufacturing industries to these countries and this process will undoubtedly continue. It can be expected that countries like Indonesia, Malaysia and the Philippines will increasingly engage in mass production of consumer products such as motor-cars, domestic appliances and all but the most advanced types of electronic goods. As Taiwan, South Korea and Singapore have shown, workers with little previous industrial experience can be readily trained for the large-scale manufacture of modern consumer goods. No doubt Western countries will continue to raise tariff barriers against such manufactures but in the end economic realities will result in their production being taken over more and more by those countries where labour is plentiful and cheap.

Another element in the struggle for food resources which is likely to have increasing strategic importance is deep-sea fishing. This contributes only about 70 million tonnes a year as compared with 1300 million tonnes of grain, but it is of critical importance to some countries, notably Japan. Fisheries could be expanded to make a valuable contribution to the food needs of the poorer countries. This possibility is the main reason for the declaration of a two-hundred-mile resources zone by most coastal States. This means, however, that the benefits are unevenly divided—landlocked States have no access to ocean fisheries. Moreover, the overlapping of claimed zones gives rise to tension—as it has already between the Soviet Union and Japan. The possibilities of conflict are likely to increase as deep-sea fisheries are developed. The poorer countries, as usual, will no doubt benefit the least from either coastal or deep-sea fishing.

The mineral resources of the deep-sea bed might also become a source of conflict. No progress has so far been made towards the international regulation of the exploitation of these minerals. Since they do not at present belong to any country it would be feasible and sensible to allocate the benefits to the resource and food deficient countries. There is little hope that international agreement will be secured for this. The wealth is likely to go to those who are the first to develop the necessary technology—which means, of course, the rich countries.

The competition is likely to be all the keener because the world's requirements for minerals is expected to increase enormously by the end of the century. On a conservative estimate of rates of economic growth, consumption of lead is likely to increase by about five times, and that of bauxite, zinc and nickel by over four times. It is estimated that during the last thirty years of the century the world will consume from three to four times as many minerals (including fossil fuels) as have been consumed throughout the whole previous history of civilization.

It is not expected that there will be absolute shortages of metals during this period, although the known reserves of lead and zinc might be exhausted by the year 2000. Iron ore, which in the past has been of great strategic importance, is now regarded as plentiful. But in other metals heavy increases in cost must be expected to keep pace with demand. In the case of copper, lead, zinc and nickel the price in real terms, because of the increasing difficulties of extraction, is likely to rise between two and two and a half times. Like the increasing costs of food and energy, these rises will bear most heavily on the poor countries.

Metals are, however, another area in which the Russians and the developing countries may be able to make common cause. The opportunity for this exists particularly in Africa. An account was given in Chapter 2 of the expansion of Russian influence in east and central Africa and it may be relevant to Soviet activities that the African countries produce many important minerals. The Soviet Union itself has large reserves of most metals but, like its fossil fuels, they are becoming more costly to extract. The other Comecon countries would benefit from greater access to the plentiful African supplies. There are already signs that the Russians are prepared to offer on a barter basis machinery and other industrial goods in exchange for minerals. They are also prepared to make a bargain which several African countries find increasingly tempting—to barter arms for minerals.

The advantage to Russia would lie not only in giving them access to more economical supplies than are available in their own territory: it would give them an additional means of pressure on Western countries. African supplies of cobalt and chrome are particularly important. The world's largest producer of cobalt is Zaire, and this is one of the reasons for the concern shown in the West at the support the Russians gave in 1977 to the insurrection in the south of that country. The United States requires substantial imports of cobalt for its industry and its principal source is Zaire. Since the other biggest producers in the world are Russia and Cuba it is easy to see that the communist bloc might have good prospects of gaining a controlling influence over this metal.

Russia produces over one-quarter of the world's chrome. Another quarter is produced by South Africa and about ten per cent by Rhodesia; if Russia ultimately gained control over the output of these two countries—whose political futures must be regarded as uncertain—the consequences for the West would be serious.

It would not be necessary for the Russians completely to block the supply of such metals to Western countries; price increases resulting from partial withholding or diversion of supplies could have damaging effects on the economies of Western countries. The Soviet bloc has not so far gained as much influence in other key producing areas as in Africa, but its objective is undoubtedly to do so—including especially south-east Asia—and if and when it does it will have greatly extended its economic and strategic power.

Suggestions of this kind are customarily dismissed in Western countries as alarmist. But they only seem so because of the widespread illusion that Western domination of the world is here to stay. In the next quarter of a century a period of dangerous global instability, in which Western interests will inevitably suffer, is now inescapable. If humanity were united and well-governed it would have a reasonable chance of surviving the crisis, but this would require the maximum development of agricultural and energy resources and their distribution without regard to political boundaries. The extravagant use of existing supplies by Western countries would have to cease, and new resources would have to be channelled to where they are most needed. The infrastructure for the production, distribution and storage of food—and energy—would have to be vastly improved in the heavily populated countries. Social obstacles to the efficient use of resources would have to be overcome: Western societies would have to adapt to a more austere way of life and Asian societies would have to abandon customs which prevent the best use of available food. Environmentalists would have to balance the cost of preventing pollution against the need to avoid famine: preserving the quality of life may be important for the rich, but for the poor the problem will be to preserve life itself. Concern for the welfare of distant generations would have to be tempered by concern for the generation at present being born—whose chances of dying of starvation are about one in five. Governments and peoples would have to stop being fearful of minor dangers and come to grips with real ones. The empty rhetoric of international conferences would have to be replaced by substantial action.

It would be unrealistic to expect any of these things to be done. The political divisions in the world remain deep and irreconcilable; and the indifference in rich countries towards the poor has deepened since the onset of the current economic crisis. Western societies are preoccupied with allegedly humanitarian concerns which are infinitely remote from the masses of people who live in daily uncertainty as to where their next meal will come from. Compassion in affluent societies does not extend beyond their own boundaries. Talk is everywhere the easy substitute for action.

If disaster is as inevitable as it seems, who is likely to come off best?

Obviously the communist countries are in the best position. The Soviet Union has an average national income of less than one-third of Australia's, but it has the largest armed forces the world has ever seen. It would be historically unprecedented if it did not use this military power to redress the balance of global wealth in its favour. The Chinese level is probably a third of that of the Russians, and it is militarily much weaker. But the Chinese also are determined to catch up with the West—as they say, by the end of the present century. They have the advantage of internal unity and discipline, and have begun to equip themselves with modern forces and weapons. Their sheer numbers—more than a third of the population of Asia—adds powerfully to their influence. Although they will not during the present century have the strategic influence of the Russians, they are determined to develop sufficient strength to safeguard and enhance their own economic interests.

Least able to cope with the coming crisis will be the countries of south and south-east Asia. With a few exceptions they have weak political structures, high population densities, high birth-rates and divisive social customs. All will need substantial outside help if they are to maintain even their present low standards of life.

It cannot, of course, be assumed that the communist powers will take the opportunities presented to them. Unlike the Western countries, they do not have large surpluses to offer; but the real problem for the poor countries is not so much lack of resources as the inability to exploit them. If the communist powers could help them to do this they could themselves share in the results and secure the basic raw materials which their own economies will increasingly need.

It might be thought that the record of the Russians in running their own economy does not suggest that they would do better at running others. On the other hand the Western methods on which the Asian countries have relied during the past century have clearly failed, and the Russians are unlikely to do worse. There is already a considerable degree of interdependence between the Soviet Union and a number of developing countries—especially India and the countries of black Africa—and it is certain that this will grow. The Russians would be the last to neglect economic weapons in their efforts to extend their global influence, and there is plenty of evidence that their strategy in this field is carefully co-ordinated with their political and military aims. It is in truth unlikely that their ultimate aim is territorial conquest: their objective, rather, is to gain for themselves control over the world's wealth. In this sense at least they are true followers of Marx.

The communist Chinese undoubtedly nourish the same ambition. In the economic arena, as in the military, they are at present greatly inferior to the Russians. They do not have industrial goods for barter, nor can they supply large quantities of modern weapons. On the other hand they are more self-sufficient in food than the Russians and they have an asset of great potential importance in the economically influential Chinese groups that are spread throughout south-east Asia. But for the rest of this century they will be unable to compete with the Russians on equal terms: in economics they will have to follow the same defensive strategy as in the military field: they will have to try to prevent the Russians from cutting off their access to resources which they must have if they are to have any chance of catching up with Russia, let alone with the West. In practice this means that China must prevent, if it can, the Soviet Union from gaining control over the productive capacity of Japan, or of the resources of south-east Asia. The coming struggle for resources is in essence, therefore, the same as the struggle for strategic control; and the competition between China and the Soviet Union will ultimately be decided in the seas and territories running northwards from Australia to Japan.

10

Land of Missed Opportunities

In the modern world the effectiveness of a country's foreign policy depends upon the strength of its economy. A country which is economically dependent on others is inevitably subject to constraints on its internal and external political freedom. This is also true of those countries which, though inherently rich, have lost economic flexibility and adaptability.

Australia is in the latter class. We have one of the highest standards of living in the world and an enormous range of resources; but because of the structural rigidities in our economy we are restricted in our pursuit of policies which are essential to our survival as a fully independent nation.

Our most damaging failure is in the field of trade. Contrary to widespread belief, Australia exports a relatively low proportion of its national output. As the Industries Assistance Commission pointed out in its 1976/77 annual report (p. 23) the ratio of exports to total gross product is much lower than that of such countries as Sweden, Canada, France and the United Kingdom. This is primarily due to the lack of competitiveness of our manufacturing industries, which is in turn the result of the high tariff protection they enjoy. Our future security depends upon co-operation with our neighbours in south-east Asia and the Pacific, but our protectionist policies have made it impossible for us to develop mutually beneficial trade relations with them. In trade we are a bad neighbour and this has engendered resentment in all the countries in the region—from New Zealand to Thailand. We try to soften this resentment with gobbets of aid, but these are too small to make any significant difference to countries whose pressing need is access to overseas markets.

There was much argument in 1977 about the restrictions placed by the Australian government on imports of clothing and footwear from Asian countries, the consequence of which is that the Australian people are obliged to pay for clothing made in Australia up to five times as much as for better articles which could be obtained overseas. The Australian Industries Assistance Commission pointed out, to the annoyance of the Fraser government, that it was economically absurd for Australia to produce such articles at all; but this example is not the worst, nor the most important. It is merely one symptom of a widespread condition of Australian industry: it is trapped in the technologies of the last generation. These technologies are now being adopted by countries with large reserves of low-cost manpower. Workers with little or no education can now be organized for the mass production of consumer goods ranging from transistor radios to cars, and it is no longer possible for countries like Australia to compete with them. Many of our manufacturing industries can only survive if tariff walls are made steadily higher, and if we are content to accept declining standards of living.

Most Australians are apparently content to do so. There is an alliance between the trade unions (some of them led by self-styled communists) and employers to hold down the real earnings of the workers. The unions have in effect accepted, in contradiction to their supposed role, that the way to solve Australia's economic difficulties is to hold down real wages; and whenever there is a move to transfer resources to more efficient industry they fiercely resist. Manufacturers therefore have no need for innovation: they are protected both from competition and from effective trade union pressure. The consequence is that they are among the most incompetent and least enterprising in the world.

Australia spends a relatively high proportion of its gross national income on education. It has a completely literate work force, which is under-paid and under-employed. It produces the same kind of manufactures, although of lesser quality, as those produced by men and women workers taken straight from the farm lands of Asia. Australian workers are given ten or more years of expensive education in order to spend their lives mindlessly tending old-fashioned machinery.

The real failure is that of the educated élite. Tertiary education in Australia has since the end of World War II been extravagantly financed from public funds. One of its purposes, presumably, was to produce scientists, engineers and business administrators who could keep Australia in the front rank of technology; whose trained minds could imaginatively adapt modern methods to Australian requirements; and who could develop the means to exploit the resources of Australia not only for our own benefit but for the rest of the world. They have clearly failed. In all fields we have come to rely more than ever on ideas derived from overseas—and then not on the latest ideas but those which are already being superseded. With one or two exceptions the universities are closed circles of self-important academics addressing themselves to apathetic students. When they look beyond the confines of their own institution they take up issues like non-proliferation of nuclear weapons or anti-apartheid: since these are issues about which Australia can do nothing it is easier to support them than to face our own faults and deficiencies. And so Australian science, engineering, sociology, law and culture stagnate.

The contrast with a country like Sweden is instructive. It has a population of eight and a quarter million, compared with our fourteen million. It has only one important mineral—iron ore—compared with our huge reserves of fuels and minerals. We have an area of nearly eight million square kilometres, while the Swedes have about half a million, less than ten per cent of which is arable land. They have no oil, coal or natural gas. Their only important natural resource is timber.

Notwithstanding this relatively poor endowment Sweden's standard of living, measured in national income per head, is the highest in the world. Why is this? The main reason is that in the past thirty years the Swedes have constantly developed their industry to keep it in the front line of technology. They produce and export supersonic aircraft, the most advanced electronic equipment, nuclear-power generators, computers and highly sophisticated chemical products. Their motor-cars and trucks, made by only two firms, are among the best in the world. At the end of World War II Sweden's exports consisted mainly of raw materials and semi-manufactures—wood pulp, iron ore, and iron. Thereafter there was a steady shift towards processed commodities and manufactures. By 1975 these made up eighty per cent of exports. High-class engineering products comprised fifty per cent.

In 1976 and 1977 Sweden was faced with considerable economic difficulties and these were widely reported in the press of less successful countries. In spite of these difficulties, however, its level of unemployment and rate of inflation remained among the lowest in the world.

There is a painful contrast between Sweden's record and Australia's. In 1975 our total exports were only about two-thirds of Sweden's, and of these foodstuffs, unprocessed minerals and other raw materials represented over two-thirds. Semi-processed metals —mainly iron and steel and alumina—accounted for six per cent and manufactures, based mainly on relatively primitive technology, twenty-three per cent.

Australia has all the advantages Sweden lacks: abundant home-grown food, virtually unlimited coal, oil, natural gas, and even sunshine. It has more iron ore than Sweden, and in addition large reserves of almost every mineral important to modern industry. Sweden has proportionately fewer students in tertiary education than Australia and a smaller proportion of national income is spent on all education. We should, therefore, have a better educated population than Sweden; certainly our economic failures cannot be blamed on lack of schooling.

An important clue to Sweden's success is that its tariff policies have traditionally been liberal. Swedish import duties are among the lowest in the world. Moreover, Sweden resorts only sparingly to non-tariff protectionist devices—to which Australian governments are greatly addicted—such as import licensing and quotas. This means that Swedish enterprises have always been obliged to face the stimulating winds of foreign competition. They have responded with vigour and imagination and have put their small country in the first rank of industrial powers.

Australian entrepreneurs and managers take little interest in advanced technology, and when they do it is only to borrow it from others, rather than develop it themselves. Government instrumentalities behave in the same way: the Telecommunications Commission buys computerization systems for its telephones from Sweden. It is never thought to ask why, if the Swedes can make these, cannot the Australians? The government aircraft factory is proud of having developed a small aircraft based on turbo-jet technology. Why can it not make a supersonic jet fighter like the Swedish Viggen? The answer is that Australian management and Australian governments are dedicated to the mediocre. The manufacturers do well out of their second-rate industries and the workers prefer secure jobs to high real incomes. Ambitions are small, both in the boardroom and on the workshop floor.

The system may be reaching the point of breakdown. Australian-made motor-cars cost about three times their overseas value and they can only be sold if the government not only accords them the highest rate of tariff protection in the world but also imposes import quotas on the import of foreign cars. Even then unemployment in the industry is increasing. The same is happening in the electrical goods industries and in the textile manufacturing industry. Throughout Australia declining industries are employing fewer workers at diminishing real wages.

This process will go on. Even if agriculture is developed to the maximum in the poor Asian countries the urban work force will at least double. They are already producing an extensive range of high quality goods and they will be increasingly able to pour them into the world markets at much lower prices than Australia will have any hope of matching. Moreover they will produce for themselves the manufactures which we at present export to them. In 1977 the ASEAN countries complained about their limited access to the Australian market and pointed out that the balance of trade was over two to one in our favour. They can take heart from the fact that this is likely to be a passing phenomenon. They will soon be able to produce, or buy more cheaply elsewhere, the goods that they at present buy from us. Even if they do not retaliate against our protectionist policies by imposing restrictions on the import of our goods, economic realities will progressively erode our share of their markets or, indeed, of any other markets.

Australia has hitherto been able to afford this economic folly because of the lucky discoveries of minerals. By selling these straight out of the ground to other countries we have been able to afford excessive prices for our own manufactures, and to regard with indifference our declining competitiveness in international trade. But the practical consequence is that we have regressed to an earlier stage of our economic life; we are again becoming acutely vulnerable to swings in world prices for metals, fuels and foodstuffs. We are partly cushioned by the sheer range of our raw materials, but our economic health is in the hands of others. While our Asian neighbours are moving forwards into the industrial age we are slipping back to the stage of a primary producing country, with a manufacturing sector which is the modern equivalent of cottage industry.

There is a dawning realization in Australia that something is wrong. Many Australian economists are enmeshed in doctrinal disputes which echo European and American arguments between the monetarists, the neo-Keynesians and the neo-Marxists, and therefore throw little helpful light on Australia's structural problems. An exception is Dr Clive T. Edwards, who was in 1977 appointed as economics adviser to the Minister for Foreign Affairs (unfortunately with no apparent effect on government policy). In a paper published in 1976 he wrote:

> Australia is at a critical turning point. We can either emerge from our parochialism or submerge ourselves in that parochialism. Australia is a rich country but it has a frightening tendency to rest on its largely fortuitously gained laurels . . . The pressure groups supporting the *status quo* are well-organised and very strong. They include not only the various manufacturing lobby groups but also the powerful trade unions. In addition, Australia's population is ageing rapidly. By contrast with most of Asia, fertility is very low in Australia. As a population ages it becomes less innovative, less industrious, less flexible, less mobile and more concerned with social security . . . Certainly the mineral discoveries will go ahead, but continued parochialism will ensure that Australia realises only part of its potential growth and, of the part realised, a major proportion will be sacrificed by a continued inefficient use of available resources.

In spite of this pessimism Dr Edwards has had the courage to propose a long-range plan for reducing tariff protection and for encouraging the development of economically efficient industries. Support is being given to his arguments by the reports issued by the Industries Assistance Commission (which was established by the Whitlam government to review Australia's system of tariff protection). It produced a series of excellent reports on the weaknesses of Australian manufacturing industries and the need to restructure them. These were greatly resented by the Fraser government and new legislation was passed which was aimed at discouraging the Commission's outspokenness. Nevertheless its reports are there for all to read who have some concern about the country's economic decline, and eventually they may lead to an attempt at improvement (see the reading list on p. 220).

Sweden's experience suggests what the first step should be. Programmes for re-training the unemployed were begun in that country immediately after the war and these gradually evolved into a thorough-going manpower training scheme. There was also provision for resettlement allowances which were aimed at stimulating the transfer of labour from weak firms and areas of declining employment to expanding industries. Governments developed a 'labour market policy' which was designed both to help individuals to find work, and the progressive firms to obtain manpower. Over 100 000 people are enrolled each year in the training programmes.

In addition to allowances made to the workers, grants are given to firms who are prepared to train personnel in new skills instead of laying them off. This facilitates their ultimate transfer to other jobs. The scheme is applied mostly to workers who are unemployed or threatened with unemployment, but re-training is also available for those who have jobs but who are prepared to learn trades in which there is a shortage of manpower. Expenditure on the whole scheme is running at the rate of A$400 million per year. This represents about 2·5 per cent of the country's gross national product and it is an investment that has kept Sweden among the world's most advanced industrial nations. Australia has no such comprehensive programme. There is a National Employment and Training Scheme but its funds are tiny and its activities are not related to an overall policy of industrial development. There are apprenticeship and youth training schemes, but the effect of these is minimal.

It is absurd to argue that we could not afford a scheme on Swedish lines. The Industries Assistance Commission reported in 1977 that protection for the textiles, clothing and footwear industries cost A$800 million per year, or A$200 for each Australian household. To re-train the entire work force in these industries would cost a fraction of this.

This would not be worth while if there were no new industries into which the re-trained workers could be moved. This is where the ignorance and lack of enterprise of the Australian managerial class is a great handicap. The only hope is that multi-national companies can be persuaded to provide the necessary skills and initiative. But even here the record has been unsatisfactory. Because of government policy the foreign car companies have set up in Australia high-cost industries which produce low-grade vehicles. We should have had one car manufacturer who aimed at producing the best possible product. We have the largest supplies of bauxite in the world, and if the industry were properly organized we could produce the cheapest aluminium. Instead two multi-national concerns are encouraged to develop uncompetitive industries behind high tariff protection.

The government seems to have been obsessed by notions about the dangers of monopoly, which might be appropriate to powerful economies like the United States but are irrelevant to countries like Australia. Opposition to monopoly is based on the argument that it prevents competition, but the Australian government in any case prevents competition by giving high protection to all comers. Our major export industries should be consolidated, not fragmented.

They would not then need tariff protection and could compete on equal terms with the outside world.

An obvious line of advance for Australia would be to go much further in processing the raw materials we export. Bauxite should be converted into aluminium, natural gas into petro-chemical products, iron ore into high-grade steels, and so on. Some of this is being done, but in a half-hearted and uneconomical way. It is said that such processing industry requires large amounts of capital, and this is true; this is why the help of the multi-national corporations is necessary. It is also said that such enterprises are not large employers of labour; this is also true, but fortunate, because if the Australian economy were efficiently organized our worst handicap would be shortage of labour. In any case such processing industries would be only the beginning. We should also develop engineering industries which operate on the most advanced frontiers of technology. It is too late to follow on with today's technology; we are so far behind that our only hope is to leap-frog to tomorrow's. Rather than making television sets we should make highly sophisticated electronic equipment; instead of import-ing computerized communications systems we should make them ourselves and export them to others; in place of motor-car engines we should develop jet and rocket propulsion for aircraft and missiles. Our uranium ores should be the basis for a complete nuclear-processing and engineering industry. We should take the world's most advanced technology and add to it. Sweden has shown how it can be done.

Instead of contemplating our uranium deposits like terrified rabbits we should see them as offering an opportunity to carry us into the modern world. We should not merely mine and export uranium oxide; we should develop the technologies to re-process it and to dispose of the nuclear waste. This would be working on the frontiers of technology, and there would be risks. But they are not greater than human ingenuity has overcome in the past, and there is no reason to doubt that they can be overcome in the future. Australia has an opportunity to lead the way in finding the solutions.

Such developments should not be left to private enterprise or market forces. One of our objectives should be to make uranium fuel available to the world at the most economical cost, thereby helping to keep down the price of energy and release oil for the countries most in need of it. Instead of seeking the highest possible market price for our uranium we should sell it at a price that would do no more than cover real costs, including a reasonable return to the mining companies. Re-processing facilities and waste disposal should be offered on the same basis.

If Australia developed its uranium deposits in this coherent way we could have a positive influence on the problem of the proliferation of nuclear weapons. We could supply uranium oxide on condition that it be re-processed only in our own plants. This would ensure that none of it could be diverted to the making of nuclear explosives. Similarly we could insist that all waste be solidified and buried in earthquake-free zones of the Australian continent—again ensuring that it was not used for warlike or terroristic purposes.

These would be heavy responsibilities and we could not handle them alone. We should call on the International Atomic Energy Agency for help. One of the functions of the I.A.E.A., as laid down in its Statute, is particularly relevant to such an enterprise. Article III (A)(2) gives the organization the power:

> To make provision, in accordance with this Statute for materials, services, equipment, and facilities to meet the needs of research on, and development and practical application of, atomic energy for peaceful purposes, including the production of electric power, with due consideration for the needs of the underdeveloped areas of the world.

Because of the unwillingness of national governments to make the necessary resources available to the organization, activity under this article has hitherto been of marginal importance. We could open up a new phase of international co-operation by asking the I.A.E.A. to set up in Australia an organization which would take responsibility for all the safety aspects of uranium development, and also to assist in ensuring that the best use is made of it for the production of energy—giving special attention, as the I.A.E.A. Statute requires — to the needs of the developing countries (for example in providing electricity for their bursting cities and their new industries).

In Australia the discussion of nuclear energy has been focused unduly on the Fox reports. These were produced after large expense of time and money but gave little enlightenment. The first report reproduced basic information about nuclear physics, readily available in standard text books, and for the rest presented a confused mixture of sound and unsound scientific opinions. The Royal Commission which produced the reports was requested to advise on the environmental effects of one proposed uranium mining development but went far beyond its authority. A great deal of imprecise information was given about issues which certainly exist but which will not be affected by whether or not Australia exports uranium oxide—namely the proliferation of nuclear weapons, and the possibilities of the seizure of nuclear materials by terrorists. Attempts were made to forecast world requirements for uranium fuel and to estimate market prospects for Australian supplies, but since they were based on incomplete assumptions the results were meaningless.

Of the fifteen recommendations of the first report all were statements of the obvious except the first and the last. The first stated, in the double negatives beloved by judges, that 'the hazards of mining and milling, if those activities are properly regulated and controlled, are not such as to justify a decision not to develop Australian uranium mines'. It might have been thought that this disposed of the matter, but because the first report had not, in fact, touched on the proper subject of the Commission's enquiry and in order to keep itself in business it was recommended that no decision be taken until a second report was presented. This took another nine months.

Recommendation 15 of the first report was one of serious importance. It stated that 'the policy of the government should take into account the importance to Australia, and the countries of the world, of the position of developing countries concerning energy needs and resources'. In fact, the report gives no serious considera-tion to the contribution Australia might make to meeting the energy needs of developing countries: its whole approach is based upon the assumption that the basis on which uranium mining should be developed was the maximum commercial advantage to Australia. Questions as to how Australia might contribute to the welfare of others were not faced. Our responsibilities for the re-processing of fuel and the storage of nuclear waste were brushed aside, as was the contribution which we might make to keeping down the cost of energy to the developing countries.

In the conclusions to its second report the Fox Commission makes seemingly authoritative assertions about the future, but they are guesswork. One of the more foolish relates to the energy problems of the developing countries and reveals how little serious thought was given to them. It states (p. 320):

> At present, and for at least fifteen to twenty years, most developing countries have, and will have, relatively little need for uranium; their requirements for electricity production can be met more cheaply and more satisfactorily from conventional fuels.

This statement shows no recognition of the fact that the market for energy is now a total world market, and includes the communist bloc; or that the price of 'conventional' fuels must rise rapidly in the next few years and in fifteen or twenty years will, on present projections, be catastrophically high for the developing countries; or that although they must have oil for their transport needs, they will urgently need some other form of fuel for electrical generation; or that if engineering and financial factors were allowed to operate unhindered it would be possible to build nuclear power generators for the crowded cities of Asia within five to ten years; or that the cost of energy of all kinds to the poor countries will be increased to the extent that *any* form of fuel is withheld from the world market. Finally, the conclusion takes no account of the fact that any projections about the need for uranium depend on whether, and under what conditions, the absolutely critical supplies of Middle East oil will continue to be available.

What the Fox report was really saying was not that the developing countries did not need uranium fuel, but that they should not be allowed to have it. This is typical of the attitude of the rich countries towards the poor, and its persistence will be an important element in pushing the developing countries, as their standards continue to deteriorate, towards extreme action. (The attitude taken towards the welfare of the Australian Aboriginal community was very similar. Much attention was properly given to the protection of their rights, but the emphasis was not on what they wanted, but on what was thought to be good for them.)

Another assumption in the Fox Report is that no harm would be done by denying Japan access to our uranium. Japan's lack of indigenous fuels and its dependence upon overseas supplies is as likely as any other factor to be a cause of war in the next twenty-five years. It is in Australia's interests more than others that Japan should never again be faced with the choice of being economically strangled or going to war. To the extent that Australia could provide the Japanese with an assured source of fuel we would be making a significant contribution to stability in our own region. Even in economic terms it would be natural and desirable that most of our uranium exports should go to the Japanese: it would diminish their call on the world's conventional fuel supplies, making these more readily available to poorer countries, and it would also help to ensure that Japan could continue to provide the engineering products which the developing countries of Asia will need.

Doubt has been thrown on the good faith of the anti-uranium movements in Australia because of the moral ambiguity of their arguments. The real problem seems to be confusion of thought, rather than an attempt to mislead—confusion to which the Fox reports have contributed. One prominent member of the anti-uranium movement repeatedly said that if Australia withheld its uranium from the world's markets this would drive up the cost of energy, and that this would be desirable because it would lead to the conservation of fuel. Since the burden of rising energy costs falls most heavily on the poor the immorality of this approach is clear.

But the remark was not based so much on ill-intent as on a lack of understanding of where Australia's real responsibilities lie. Behind the rhetoric about the proliferation of nuclear weapons and the dangers to future generations— about which Australia in any case can do nothing—the Fox Commissioners, the pro-uranium lobby and the anti-uranium movements have had one basic approach in common: they have been concerned only with what is best for Australia. In effect all aim at increasing the cost of Australian uranium. If it were genuinely accepted that Australia had in-escapable responsibilities to the rest of the world, not only because of its uranium resources but because of its rich deposits of other fuels and of a vast range of minerals, the whole nature of the debate would change. Instead of trying to turn our backs on the future we might even have courage to go forward to meet it.

Assuming that such a change of heart occurred, the first step would be for the Australian government to invite the International Atomic Energy Agency to send a commission of experts to Australia to advise on the following:

1. At what rate should the mining and export of Australian uranium proceed to make the maximum contribution to meeting the prospective world energy shortage, and to ensure that it is available at the lowest possible price?
2. What re-processing facilities could be established in Australia (including advice on the most desirable technology, the best safety arrangements and the most advantageous siting of plants)?
3. The practicability of insisting that uranium exported from Australia should be re-processed in Australia, and all waste returned for final treatment and storage.
4. The availability of geologically safe sites in Australia for the storage of radioactive wastes, bearing in mind the desirability of storing not only wastes derived from Australian uranium, but from the nuclear power reactors of countries, especially in the developing world, who do not have the means to store it.
5. The possibility of the establishment in Australia of a Permanent Commission of the I.A.E.A. to supervise the

re-processing and storage operations to ensure that they meet the requirements of the Nuclear Non-proliferation Treaty, the safeguards laid down under its own Charter, and also the purposes of Article III(A)(2) (quoted above).

An initiative of this kind, if resolutely carried through, would at last give Australia a positive say in the regulation of nuclear developments. It would set an example which the world badly needs in bringing the increasingly chaotic situation under control, and might lead to the adoption by other countries of similar arrangements. Notwithstanding the current disputation the world cannot, and will not, turn its back on nuclear power. The communist countries are pressing ahead with all possible speed; Japan could not afford to deny itself this source of energy, and the same is true in varying degrees of West Germany and other fuel-deficient countries; and United States' increasingly dangerous dependence on imports of foreign oil makes it inevitable that it will shortly resume full-scale development of nuclear energy. Australia has an opportunity to contribute to ensuring that these developments could go forward without disaster.

Acceptance of our responsibilities in nuclear development would be of great assistance in enabling us to leap-frog to the front rank of technology. Our expensive research and training schools of physical sciences would at last be able to contribute something to the advancement of Australian industry. The mastering of the latest techniques in the re-processing and handling of nuclear wastes would enable us to contribute to the progress of nuclear science in a wide range of related fields. The Swedes export nuclear equipment and technology; so might we, perhaps specifically adapted for our neighbouring region. Instead of trying to compete with the ASEAN countries in low-grade engineering products we could perhaps sell them equipment for their power stations, and computerized control systems for their new industries. We might even sell sophisticated equipment to China, in addition to our annual quotas of wheat. In order that these countries could pay for these things we would have to open our own markets to their cars, trucks, television sets, domestic appliances, textiles and clothing. Our own standards of living would rise, unemployment would be replaced by labour shortages, and we could resume the task of populating this empty continent.

The resources of the sea are another field in which we could make an important contribution to the exploitation of the world's natural wealth for the benefit of mankind. The continental shelf which we have already claimed is far larger than we can effectively exploit or defend; and the same will be true of the two-hundred-mile fishing zone which, in imitation of others, we will soon proclaim.

Because of the failure to find other solutions there is a growing trend towards the acceptance of such claims by the world community. But they only benefit States with coastlines, and the rich States more than the poor ones. The land-locked States receive no benefit. Australia would have nothing to lose if it offered to open up areas of the continental shelf and the two-hundred-mile fishing zone for exploitation for the benefit of the resources-deficient and the land-locked countries.

Proposals have been made for over a decade for the establishment of an international agency to develop the mineral resources of the deep sea on a basis that would share them equitably among all nations, but the reluctance of the wealthy nations to yield control over resources which for the foreseeable future only they are likely to have the technology to exploit has meant that no agreement has been possible. Australia has, as usual, played a passive role. It should, instead, press for the early creation of such an agency, even if this displeases our rich friends. It should also propose that the agency should have power to exploit areas of continental shelves and fishing zones which are not being developed by countries laying claim to them. These could be much more use in the coming period of critical shortages than the deep sea, if only because the necessary technologies for exploitation are already known. International capital would have to be mobilized for such undertakings, but this should not present insuperable difficulties: some of the surpluses accumulated by the oil-producing nations might be guided in this direction, and the World Bank and the Asian Development Bank might find this a more productive outlet for their resources than some of their present commitments. Australia's contribution could be to provide base facilities and other local support. This would cost us little and there might even be a flow on of technology and of locally generated industry.

A principal objective of any such initiatives in the field of resources should be to improve our relations with our immediate neighbours in south-east Asia and the South Pacific and they should be associated with such moves at all stages.

In 1977 we signed the Asian Regional Co-operative Agreement of the I.A.E.A., of which our neighbours are also signatories. This provides a framework for co-operative research, development and training in nuclear science and technology. If we proceeded with the development of our uranium industry this could be used to give real substance to nuclear co-operation with these countries. The agreement cuts across ideological barriers and it would be eminently fitting that consultations regarding our own developments should be carried out under its auspices.

Proposals for the exploitation of our two-hundred-mile fishing zone could be first discussed in the South Pacific Forum. At a meeting held in Port Moresby in August 1977 Australia agreed to participate in the South Pacific Regional Fisheries Agency. This has modest research, data collection and advisory functions, and because of the weakness of our own fisheries industry Australia has little to contribute. If we opened areas of our two-hundred-mile zone for the benefit of the Pacific Islands fishing industry, and perhaps offered base and training facilities on our own territory, the agency could be involved in the planning and execution of the concept. This might contribute more to the future well-being of the islands than our present grant aid, which is thinly spread over the whole area, and over a wide range of marginal enterprises.

Australia is the fortunate possessor of enormous natural wealth, far beyond its own needs or its capacity to develop. It has a unique opportunity, without cost to its own people and, indeed, ultimately to their great advantage, to take initiatives for the equitable sharing of the resources of the southern hemisphere, including the uranium of northern Australia, the oil and gas of the continental shelves, the fish of the two-hundred-mile coastal zones, and also the minerals, fish and fresh water of the Antarctic (as proposed in Chapter 5).

If we do nothing it should not be taken for granted that we will be left undisturbed with this wealth. Since we can neither develop it nor defend it the time may come when, fittingly and with the likely approbation of other nations, it will be taken from us.

11

Defending the Indefensible

It has never been the custom for Australian defence ministers to explain to the taxpayers the concepts on which the vast annual expenditure of their money is based. These are regarded as too complex for ordinary human understanding, and as best left to military and civilian experts to decide in private.

The Australian people have traditionally acquiesced in this attitude and have never sought to enquire whether, in fact, their betters know what they are doing. The time has come when such an enquiry should be made, because it is now very apparent that the defence experts are themselves confused about Australia's strategic situation, and are spending large sums of money without any clear idea of our real defence needs.

The attitude that the people should be told nothing was carried by D. J. Killen to its extreme in his statement to Parliament as Minister for Defence on 22 September 1977. He announced that expenditure in 1977–78 would be $2343 million, and made a boast of the fact that this represented an increase of one per cent in real terms over the actual outlay in 1967–77. He said that a major review had been made of the international security outlook, and that 'certain unfavourable developments' had been noted. He added that, nevertheless, 'we judged our prospects on balance to be favourable', but no details were given as to how this sanguine judgement was reached. The rest of his speech consisted of an account of various defence projects and items of equipment, strung together in a way that made systematic analysis impossible.

Killen remarked that contingency studies had been made in the Department of Defence which had focused on the defence of Australia. If members of parliament were relieved to know that defence officials had not been entirely inactive they showed no signs of it. He then told parliament that 'it would not expect me to give an account of these studies'. The sharp reaction which such a comment would have provoked in the U.S. Congress, or in almost any other Western parliament can be imagined; but the apathy of the Australian parliament was undisturbed. He said that he sympathized with those who found the process by which the Australian forces were developed too complex to grasp, but he commended to members, in the unlikely event that they wanted further information, the White Paper on Australian Defence which had been published in November 1976. He said that this was 'a declaration of the government's aims and intentions' and remained 'the basic reference for discussion of our national defence'.

This paper would place no strain on the members' intelligence. It proposes expenditure of 12 000 million dollars over a five-year period but offers only simple generalizations about why such large sums should be spent and what weapons and equipment should be bought.

No doubt responding to the wishes of the government of the day, the defence authorities gave the paper a determinedly optimistic slant. Apart from some nervous references to the Soviet Union it saw no serious threats to Australian security. It suggested that military conflict in our own region could only occur in a conjunction of circumstances which was unlikely to develop. It asserted that Australia could by its 'own policy and effort . . . insure against uncertainties . . . that could produce situations' with which it might have to deal on its own. From a later remark it is clear, however, that it was not intended to suggest that we would be capable of defending ourselves in a real war: it was said that 'our alliance with the United States gives substantial grounds for confidence that in the event of a fundamental threat to Australia's security, United States' military support would be forthcoming'.

The paper made a number of other optimistic assumptions. It was taken for granted that the United States would continue to hold its own in competition with the Soviet Union—although it was conceded that this would depend on 'the political will' of the American people and the NATO countries. The likelihood of major war between Russia and China was virtually ruled out, as also were renewed fighting in Korea, or an armed conflict over Taiwan. Japan was said to be 'most unlikely' to change its policy of limiting its military development. China and India were regarded as being unlikely to take action affecting Australian security in 'the foreseeable future'. It was also stated—astonishingly in view of India's development of a nuclear explosive—that 'there are no signs of significant movement towards acquisition of nuclear weapons in the region of Australia's primary concern'.

Much is made in the White Paper, and by Killen in his speech to parliament, of the contribution made by the Australian intelligence organizations to these assessments. The paper stated that our capabilities and arrangements for meeting our intelligence requirements were good, and that we drew 'considerable benefit from arrangements developed over many years with co-operating countries'. Killen told parliament that developments since the paper was issued had been closely watched by 'our intelligence community' and that they did not call for any change in the basic assessment.

It is not possible to ascertain from published figures the full extent of the funds spent on Australia's many intelligence organizations, but it must be considerable—and it will be significantly increased when yet another body is in operation, as a consequence of the Hope Commission's report, under the Prime Minister. The unrealistic forecasts which this community invariably produces— of which typical examples have been given above—brings into question whether it is worth the money spent on it. It might be asked, indeed, whether its tendency to provide governments with the assessments they want to hear, and to support them with material drawn from foreign sources, is not itself a danger to the national interest. Intelligence communities often become so absorbed in their incestuous inter-service relationship that they lose contact with the real world; this certainly seems to have happened in the case of the Australian 'intelligence community'.

Valuable financial savings could be made in this area. On top of the military intelligence organizations, which are of course essential, is a superstructure of civilian bodies which has repeatedly given bad advice to governments. The government should reduce this to a small bureau and attach it to the Department of Foreign Affairs—where international political intelligence properly belongs.

An organization which *is* at present attached to the Department of Foreign Affairs but does not belong there, is the Australian Secret Intelligence Service. This was established in an attempt to join in the spy game, but its activities were too amateurish and half-hearted to be effective. After William McMahon inadvertently revealed its existence while he was Prime Minister, there was hope that it might be wound up, but unfortunately it was given a new lease of life by the Hope Royal Commission on Intelligence and Security, which recommended in 1977 that it be continued and that it should remain attached to the Department of Foreign Affairs.

Judge Hope shares with many Australian officials and politicians a vast over-estimation of the value of clandestine intelligence services, and the consequence of his recommendations will be an *increase* in expenditure on these organizations and an expansion of their powers.

If Australia were a neutral and truly independent country it would have little need for secret intelligence. The expensive organizations which we maintain are not for the protection of our own secrets, but those of the United States. Much was made by Hope of the activities of intelligence officers attached to foreign embassies, but their main role is to monitor the defence relationship between Australia and the United States and penetrate, if possible, secret American activities in Australia. If it were not for the American alliance we might be able to rid ourselves of both the K.G.B. and the C.I.A.

Another unfortunate result of the Hope Commission report is that ASIO will not only go on but be expanded. He exposed many of the weaknesses of the organization, but he said that these had been, or were being, remedied. Enough is known about its recent activities to indicate that he was wrong. The leopard has not, and will not, change its spots.

The original reason for the creation of ASIO was political—to combat communism in Australia and to prevent the infiltration of communist agents from overseas. It may be doubted whether such an enterprise was ever necessary—the Australian people have always shown themselves remarkably resistant to Marxist infection —but certainly it is no longer so. Some highly publicized trade union leaders call themselves communists, but they show little knowledge of Marx, and no revolutionary ambitions. ASIO's evident interest in their activities is, if anything, a help in consolidating their support among their followers. They are Luddites rather than Marxists and by holding down the real wages of the workers they promote the interests of the industrialists and the Liberal Party; but it would be absurd to blame any of this on agents of the communist powers.

Although ASIO's anti-communist role has diminished it has

found other political work to do. It was at first reluctant to concern itself with extremists of the right as well as the left, but under the Whitlam government it was persuaded to interest itself in the activities of the anti-Tito elements among Croatian and Serbian migrants in Australia. Its effect in curbing these activities has not been measurable; in so far as they have diminished it has been because of more effective police measures. For the rest, the organization devotes itself to building up fat files of hearsay and gossip on politicians, academics and public servants, and to keeping under surveillance persons whom it dislikes.

Clandestine political intelligence organizations are sometimes regarded as a necessary evil. But all such bodies tend to corruption. They are inevitably staffed from among the less balanced members of the community and because they operate without supervision they extend their activities into illicit fields. It is, therefore, essential that periodically they should be broken up and re-organized. ASIO has outlived its original purpose and could be disbanded without harm to the national interest. Its files, which might perhaps be first reviewed by a committee of Labor politicians, could be burnt, or deposited with the National Archives. Functions which have accrued to it in regard to the security checking of migrants should be transferred to the Special Branch of the Australian Police.

A specious argument put forward for retaining ASIO is that it is needed to combat terrorism. This is essentially a criminal activity and the task of countering it should not be left to a political intelligence organization—least of all to an incompetent one—but should be a matter for the police. The Australian police force should be equipped with the most modern means for combating terrorism and should be encouraged to extend its co-operation with the police forces of other countries—communist as well as non-communist. The Baader–Meinhof hijacking in October 1977 of a Lufthansa aircraft was defeated with the co-operation of the government of the Peoples' Socialist Republic of Somaliland. This co-operation could not have been secured by an anti-communist security organization like ASIO. Modern terrorism ignores ideological boundaries and those who have the responsibility for combating it must do likewise.

Secret intelligence activities have an unhealthy fascination for some people and it is clear that Mr Justice Hope was not immune. His reports have set back for some years the prospect of a dismantling of the present extravagant system; but it must be hoped that politicians of all parties will eventually realize that it is against their interests that clandestine organizations should exist which are in effect outside the law.

In previous chapters of this book an attempt has been made to give an account of the real world as it is at present and to describe some possible developments in the next twenty-five years. Some of the deductions I have made are arguable, but the facts are not. In summary those that directly affect Australian security are:

The decline of the United States from its position of global dominance (exemplified by the statements of its leaders and by the structure of its armed forces);

the expansionist moves of the Soviet Union (again exemplified by the statements of its leaders and by the structure of its armed forces, including the enormous expansion of its navy); and

the evident determination of the post-Mao régime to turn China into a military superpower.

The Australian defence authorities are not completely unaware of what is going on. The White Paper of November 1976 notes that 'the U.S.S.R. has achieved essential nuclear strategic equivalence with the United States and competes with the United States as a global power', and that 'the U.S.S.R. now has the capability to project military power into a distant region'. It adds that the changes that have occurred 'constitute a fundamental transformation of the strategic circumstances that governed Australia's security throughout most of its history' but concludes that 'change does not necessarily mean insecurity'.

This comfortable opinion seems plausible only because neither the White Paper nor the Minister for Defence mentioned other important changes: the increasing superiority of Russian forces in Europe over the NATO forces, not only in conventional arms but also in the tactical nuclear field; the acceptance by the United States of a position of permanent naval inferiority to the Russians in the Indian Ocean; the acknowledged inability of the United States navy to control the western Pacific, or indeed any waters outside the North American strategic zone, except the Mediterranean (and even this is no longer certain); and the progressive withdrawals of American forces from South Korea, Taiwan and the Philippines.

As far as China was concerned the White Paper announced that there had been a major intelligence re-assessment of this country. The results, if any, were not revealed. There is no mention of the active spread of Chinese influence through northern Burma, Bangladesh and into north-east India; or of China's strong presence in

Kampuchea; or of its continuing activities in Africa. If any forecast was made of the future consequences of the determination of the post-Mao régime to modernize its armed forces it was not disclosed.

It may be true, although it certainly cannot be taken for granted, that no military danger to Australia will, as a result of these developments, emerge in the next few years. But it cannot be doubted that during the coming quarter of a century we will be faced with difficulties and dangers quite different from those of the past. We can expect to survive these only if we prepare now to meet them.

It is impossible to discover anywhere in the publications of the Department of Defence, or in the statements of cabinet ministers, any realistic discussion of these dangers, or any coherent ideas about how Australia will be defended. In other democratic countries the structure of the armed forces and the total defence organization is related to a comprehensive strategic and defence doctrine, which is publicly presented and debated. In Australia such a doctrine simply does not exist. Our forces are haphazardly put together on the basis of ideas partly from the last war and partly from the period of our dependence on the United States. Large sums are annually committed to the purchase of weapons systems, and to the development of facilities, without any explanation being given as to why these will be needed and what specific purposes they will serve.

An excuse often given for avoiding explanation is that this would require the discussion of 'contingencies' in which enemies would have to be named, and that this would be diplomatically undesirable. This notion is more current in the Department of Defence than in the Department of Foreign Affairs. There is no real diplomatic difficulty; countries do not have to be named, and even if they are, serious offence need not be caused. It is no offence to the present government of Japan to discuss the hypothesis that it might one day be succeeded by a government which would acquire nuclear weapons; it is a hypothesis that is now discussed in Japan itself. President Suharto would not be greatly offended if Indonesia's neighbours took account of the possibility that a future government of Indonesia might return to a policy of confrontation with its neighbours: realistic consideration of the circumstances in which it might occur would strengthen Suharto's own efforts to avoid them.

The essential requirement is, in any case, not to identify particular contestants but to assess realistically the possibilities of conflict, where it is likely to occur, and what weapons and forces are likely to be involved.

All that can be found in the Defence White Paper are casual generalizations which do not seem to have any relationship to the structure and organization of the Australian defence forces. In the section of the paper headed 'Areas of Australia's Primary Strategic Concern' it is stated:

> For practical purposes, the requirements and scope for Australian defence activity are limited essentially to the areas close to home—areas in which the deployment of military capabilities by a power potentially unfriendly to Australia could permit that power to attack or harass Australia and its territories, maritime resources zone and rear lines of communication. These are our adjacent maritime areas; the South West Pacific countries and territories; Papua New Guinea; Indonesia; and the South East Asian region.

This at least indicates that the defence authorities accept that despatch of all our forces to distant theatres of war, as occurred in the first and second world wars, should not be repeated. But nothing is said about the kind of Australian armed forces which would be needed if we were to engage in 'defence activity' in, for example, the south-east Asian region. In the chapter headed 'Australia's Defence Requirements', effective activity seems in fact ruled out; it is stated that 'in our contemporary circumstances we no longer base our policy on the expectation that Australia's Navy or Army or Air Force will be sent abroad to fight as part of some other nation's force, supported by it'. It seems that if we sent any units into this region it would have to be as a composite 'Australian Defence Force' consisting of all three arms—without regard, apparently, to what units were needed, and also whether we could deploy a balanced and self-sufficient force (which we certainly could *not* do at the present time).

This notion is a reflection of the currently fashionable doctrine that Australia no longer needs 'forward defence'. All the major political parties, and most defence commentators, now seem to believe that the role of the armed forces is to protect Australia from direct attack, and that the idea that we should help our neighbours to keep the enemy away from our shores is out of date. In future we will not support the defence forces of our neighbours in a way related to their needs; nor, presumably, will we maintain the links between our services and theirs which would be essential to effective co-operation in a crisis.

This is folly. The only practicable defence for Australia (or for New Zealand) is forward defence. The Australian people do not have the resources or the numbers to protect the country from direct attack; we can be defeated by the naval and air forces of a hostile power without a soldier being landed on our shores. Our only hope of security lies in co-operating with our neighbours in defending the whole region of south-east Asia and the south-west Pacific.

In view of the inability of defence experts to provide a defence policy it is up to laymen to try to do so. I have in previous chapters of this book sought to give an account of the changes in the world strategic balance that have already taken place, and to forecast future developments of direct importance to Australia's security. The conclusion which I believe can be drawn from this survey is that the strategically critical region of the world in the next quarter of a century will be the nexus of islands and waterways—lying to the north of Australia—which joins the Indian Ocean to the South China Sea and thence to the Pacific. My reasons for believing this are: that it is likely to be the eventual focus of the competition between the Soviet Union and China; that the resources of the region will be of increasing global importance; that because of the vast increases in population that will occur in the next twenty-five years it is likely to be an area of severe political instability; and, finally, that the survival of Japan will depend on whether or not this region falls under the domination of a power hostile to its interests.

A starting point for an Australian strategic doctrine would be that the survival of Australia also will depend upon keeping this region free from the domination of any hostile power. It would immediately follow that first priority should be given to co-operation for the defence of the whole region with the other countries in it: Indonesia, Singapore, Malaysia, Thailand, Cambodia, Vietnam, Laos, Taiwan and the Philippines.

Merely to list the names of the countries is to indicate the difficulties involved. Australia, because of its discriminatory racial and economic policies, and also to a lesser extent because of its reputation over the past thirty-five years of being a tool of the United States, is distrusted in all these countries. At the diplomatic level we have some friendly contacts, but dislike is the prevailing attitude among most politicians and many of the people. The fact that this dislike is not always openly expressed should not delude us into believing otherwise. Our aid programmes, which might otherwise have won us useful friends, have been overshadowed by our rigid protectionist policies; and our attitude of moral self-righteousness, which is regarded as unseemly in view of our own history, has given great offence to the proud and sensitive leaders of the newly independent nations of the region.

In the days when we could rely on the protection of a great power we could afford to be indifferent to the opinion of our neighbours: in future our security will depend on their good will. It will be difficult to earn it, but it is urgent that the attempt be made.

Among our neighbours there are also deep enmities but progress is being made towards overcoming these. Indonesia, Singapore, Malaysia, Thailand and the Philippines (who form the Association of South East Asian Nations) are working in growing harmony, and although divisive issues still exist all the present governments are determined that they will not be allowed to interfere with overall co-operation.

Great difficulties persist in bringing into the area of co-operation the States of Indo–China (Vietnam, Cambodia and Laos) and Taiwan. The inclusion of all these countries would be indispensable to a coherent system of regional security because of their strategic locations, and because each could become the bridgehead for a power hostile to the other countries in the region. Moreover their economic resources could eventually make an important contribution to the growth of the whole region. Many problems will have to be overcome before close co-operation is possible between these countries and the ASEAN group, but it is possible to hope that awareness of mutual interest will gradually bring them together.

The ASEAN countries are at present careful to disclaim any intention of setting up a regional security organization, and this is understandable in view of their historical differences. As co-operation develops in the economic and political field, it seems possible that sufficient mutual trust will develop to enable the creation of a co-operative defence structure. It is already recognized by a number of important leaders that economic progress is of little avail unless national independence can be protected; and also that none of the countries in the region is capable of providing adequately for its own security. Bilateral consultations on defence problems and joint exercises are already taking place and eventually it may be possible for the governments concerned to broaden these activities into a collective defence system.

If and when this happens Australia should seek to participate, hopefully in the company of New Zealand. Since the only real prospect of keeping ourselves secure lies in military co-operation with the countries of south-east Asia the Australian armed forces should be designed for that purpose above any other.

In order to discover what weapons, equipment and forces would be needed it is necessary to consider the kind of conflict which might occur in the region. In World War I the predominant new weapon was the tank and in World War II the aircraft. In the next war it will be the missile. Development of this weapon is proceeding over a range and at a pace which is forcing a re-assessment of the whole structure of conventional armed forces.

The balance between NATO and the Warsaw Pact forces is still an important element in the global equilibrium. In Europe the missile is changing the balance in favour of the Warsaw forces. These forces have always been larger in numbers than NATO, and have the advantages of fully integrated command, standardization of equipment, internal lines of communication and a relatively short defence perimeter. In the West these advantages are regarded as being offset by the superiority of the equipment of the NATO forces, and by the option of being able to use tactical nuclear weapons if a breakthrough were achieved by the conventional forces of the Warsaw Pact.

These advantages no longer exist for NATO. The Warsaw forces are now acquiring precision-guided weapons of the most advanced kind, and would be able to initiate an attack on NATO forces with tactical nuclear weapons. It is no longer credible— if indeed it ever was—that the Soviet bloc would unleash a conventional attack on Western Europe in the certainty that it would be countered with nuclear weapons; they are now in a position to use from the outset missiles armed with tactical nuclear warheads which can be launched from the air or from the ground. The only counter the NATO forces would have would be to attack with tactical nuclear weapons the launching sites and the principal centres of military concentration in Eastern Europe. At present most NATO tactical nuclear missiles are of too short range to do this. No doubt this deficiency will be repaired in the coming years, but for the present Western Europe's only hope of survival in the face of an attack by the Warsaw countries would be for the United States to launch a strategic nuclear attack on the Soviet Union. It seems, therefore, that the West is caught in the dilemma which the NATO forces were constructed specifically to avoid: namely that Western Europe cannot at present be defended without escalation to global nuclear war.

It is unlikely that the Warsaw forces will, in fact, launch an attack on Western Europe, but the present situation considerably enlarges the freedom of action of the Soviet Union. Its own western boundaries are secure, and the preoccupation of the United States and other NATO countries with re-establishing effective equilibrium with the Warsaw forces will inhibit them from taking resolute action elsewhere in the world. This means that other countries who may be faced with Russian pressure will have to protect themselves on their own as best they can.

The development by the U.S.S.R. of a structure of forces designed to assist its global expansion has been described in earlier chapters (pages 30–35). The importance of its submarines and mine–laying capability for the control of the world's shipping lanes is obvious. It has been developed with the clear intention of limiting the control of the high seas by the United States navy. As has been said, it represents in particular a great danger to the American aircraft carriers. In 1976 the United States had two nuclear-powered carriers in operation (over 90 000 tons) and eleven conventionally powered carriers (ranging from 64 000 to 87 000 tons). These are the backbone of the American navy: on them primarily rests the ability of the United States to police the world's oceans. But there is increasing fear in the United States that these carriers have become ineffective in the face of nuclear submarines, as the capital ships of the past did in the face of aircraft.

The relevance of this to the situation in the Indian Ocean is clear. Even if the Americans were to station a carrier task force at the base being developed at Diego Garcia (which is unlikely) it could be immobilized by the Soviet underwater fleet. This means that the American force could do little to protect commercial and other shipping in the Indian Ocean—whether plying in the region of the Persian Gulf and the Red Sea or the Bay of Bengal and the Malacca Strait. To recover control of the Indian Ocean, and the waterways to and from it, the United States would have to deploy a highly sophisticated anti-submarine force consisting of a wide range of ships and aircraft. Since the American government has declared that the Indian Ocean is not a region of strategic priority to the United States it is unlikely to do this.

The danger which is most likely to be faced by Australia and the countries of south-east Asia in the next quarter of a century is precisely the interdiction of shipping passing through the waterways connecting the Indian and Pacific Oceans. Is there a realistic possibility that we could counter this danger?

Certainly not if we acted individually, or sought to rely on our existing hodge-podge of conventional weapons and forces. But the arrival of the missile era does give us a chance. The counter to the missile-firing submarine is the anti-submarine missile. What we would need are ships, submarines and aircraft capable of launching these missiles.

It must be remembered, however, that the threat would not only come from submarines. The Soviet Union has a large force of surface craft which are ideally suited for the interdiction of shipping —including the Kiev class carriers, which are only half the size of the Americans, but which carry vertical-take-off aircraft and are heavily armed with missiles, and a wide range of modern missile-armed cruisers and destroyers. The counter to these ships is the same—missile-firing submarines, ships and aircraft.

It needs also to be remembered that the Soviet Union is not the only possible threat in the next twenty-five years. If China or Japan (or both in alliance) sought to pre-empt Russian interdiction of the Malacca Strait they might believe that their best course would be to take control of the region themselves. To do so they would need the same kind of weapons the Russians have already developed, and if the countries in the region wished to maintain their freedom from the Chinese and Japanese no less than from the Russians, they would need the same counter forces.

None of the countries in the region have at the present time anything like the right kind of forces. The most heavily armed country, Indonesia, has three submarines armed only with conventional torpedoes, some obsolete frigates without missiles, and a collection of smaller vessels. It has some fast patrol boats armed with surface-to-surface missiles, but in 1976 only twelve were operational. The air force has about forty operational aircraft, none armed with missiles. The army has a large quantity of guns and armour but, as far as is known, no effective missile capability.

Malaysia has two frigates and eight fast patrol boats equipped with missiles; and an air force with thirty-one combat aircraft and no missiles. The Philippines forces have some American equipment, including 104 combat aircraft, but again practically no missile capability. Singapore has six fast patrol boats with surface-to-surface missiles and some modern fighter aircraft armed with air-to-air missiles.

Australia has six diesel submarines which are armed only with conventional torpedoes. (Advanced precision-guided torpedoes have been ordered but unfortunately we will be dependent on the United States for supplies.) There is a useful force of nine destroyers armed with the Australian-made Ikara anti-submarine missiles, and with surface-to-air and surface-to-surface missiles. The air force has 120 combat aircraft (including the expensive F111) but no missile capability. The most valuable air component is the maritime reconnaissance squadron which is equipped with the long-range Orion aircraft (of which there are ten in operation and ten more on order). There is also a maritime reconnaissance squadron equipped with twelve obsolescent Neptune aircraft. The army has no missile capability except for one battery of surface-to-air missiles which is effective only in daylight and for which there is no conceivable use.

The New Zealanders have four frigates armed with surface-to-air missiles, but no effective anti-submarine capability. They have, however, a useful maritime reconnaissance squadron equipped with up-to-date Orion aircraft.

All the countries mentioned have other forces and equipment, some of considerable size, but they would have little use in the kind of conflict that, as I believe, is likely to break out in the next twenty-five years.

It would be a task of some complexity to define the scale and structure of the forces which would be sufficient to keep secure the region of south-east Asia and the south-west Pacific. That it would be within the combined capacity of these countries to build up such forces cannot be doubted. They would not need to be vast: nuclear-powered aircraft carriers, expensive fighter aircraft, or heavy armour and weapons for land war would not be needed. Essentially what would be required would be platforms for anti-submarine, anti-shipping and anti-aircraft precision-guided missiles. These platforms would include submarines (diesel-electric rather than nuclear-powered because of their silence), guided-missile destroyers and frigates, and long-range missile-armed aircraft. In addition, since aerial surveillance is the key to anti-submarine and anti-shipping warfare, a large number of long-range reconnaissance aircraft would be needed, equipped with the most modern detection devices.

The total annual expenditure on defence of the five ASEAN countries is about 3000 million dollars. Taiwan spends about 1000 million. The expenditure of Vietnam is not known, but it is probably also in the region of 1000 million. Australia's expenditure is about 2250 million and New Zealand's 210 million. In total the annual expenditure in the whole region is at least 7500 million dollars. Much of this money is at present spent on maintaining unnecessary ground forces or on the purchase of inappropriate equipment. If, say, one quarter of it could be devoted over a five-year period to building up a regional defence structure a formidable force could be assembled.

There is some useful basic equipment already in existence and this could be equipped for sea-control purposes at relatively little cost. Australia, for example, has at present twenty-two F111C aircraft which, as now equipped, are not usable in any conflict in which we are likely to be involved. If they were equipped for long-range reconnaissance and armed with precision-guided missiles they would be a valuable addition to a regional force. Similarly with the Oberon submarines: because of their silent operation these would be excellent in an anti-shipping role, but only if they were adequately armed with modern missiles.

No doubt the other countries in the area have considerable numbers of ships and aircraft which could also be adapted to serve as missile platforms or be used for long-range reconnaissance.

The waters which would have to be controlled by the regional force would include the eastern side of the Bay of Bengal, the Indian Ocean to the west of Australia, the Malacca Strait, the Java Sea, the Timor Sea, the South China Sea and the waters and straits lying between the South China Sea and the Pacific Ocean.

This is a large area geographically and the first requirement would be to keep it under continuous aerial surveillance. Excellent aircraft are now available for such purposes. The job could be done by squadrons of Orion aircraft based at Djakarta, Singapore, Bangkok, Taipei, Manila and Darwin, operating on interlocking flight patterns.

The next requirement would be for flotillas of submarines and destroyers which could be summoned quickly to investigate signs of hostile activity and to intervene if necessary with appropriate force. It would be desirable for such flotillas to be deployed in strategic locations at all times.

Finally squadrons of long-range missile-armed attack aircraft would be needed to intervene in any engagement for which the flotillas were not adequate, or for which they could not arrive in time. These squadrons could be deployed throughout the region in the same way as the reconnaissance aircraft.

Careful study would be required before a firm estimate could be given of the numbers of aircraft, warships and submarines that would be required for these purposes. A force which would have a formidable deterrent effect would, however, be one consisting of:

50 diesel submarines
100 destroyers and frigates (all carrying helicopters)
1000 fast patrol craft
100 long-range attack aircraft
100 long-range reconnaissance aircraft.

All would be equipped with precision-guided missiles. Some small aircraft carriers, with vertical-take-off aircraft and armed helicopters, might be useful, but if sufficient long-range attack aircraft were strategically placed throughout the region they would not be a high-priority requirement. A valuable item would be an Airborne Warning and Control System (which is an aircraft being developed by Boeing in the United States with sophisticated electronic equipment which would provide an airborne platform for the surveillance of a wide area). Another useful aircraft might be the Grumman 'Hawkeye', which can maintain surveillance over a large area and is less expensive. These could also provide a means for commanding and controlling surface forces. All arms should be capable of operating on the same integrated tactical basis as that developed in recent years by the Soviet navy.

An important element in maintaining the long-term effectiveness of such a force would be that the essential equipment should be produced within the region. The combat effectiveness of most of the armed forces of the individual countries, including Australia, is at present crippled by dependence upon logistic support from outside powers. It would be futile to build up a combined force which was similarly dependent.

There are no physical reasons why all the equipment listed above could not be produced within the region. There is a large steel-making and ship-building capacity, and several countries are technologically capable of producing aircraft. Basic electronics industries already exist and they could be developed to more advanced levels.

Ideally Australia should be able to play the leading role in producing the sophisticated equipment that would be necessary for a combined force. Given our expensively educated manpower we should have no difficulty in manufacturing the advanced electronic equipment for precision missiles and for the computerized monitoring systems necessary for surveillance. We could make these not only for our own use but for sale to our regional allies. Instead of importing modern technology we should develop it for ourselves and for export.

The policy of closing down our own ship-building industry, and purchasing ships and submarines from overseas should be reversed. We should, instead, build not only our own requirements but our neighbours'. Aircraft frames can readily be built elsewhere in the area, but there is no reason, except for the incompetence of our industrial managers, why Australia could not produce advanced jet engines. It is absurd to argue, as is often done, that we cannot do these things because of the high cost of Australian labour. Real incomes are low by comparison with other affluent countries. If management were efficient the productive capacity of Australian labour could be sharply increased, and workers could be attracted to advanced engineering enterprises, of the kind necessary to produce modern military equipment and munitions, by the offer of high wages.

Another reason given for not producing advanced equipment is that our own internal needs are too small. This also is nonsense: other small countries have found world-wide markets for their sophisticated engineering products. This kind of myopia is reflected in the Defence White Paper. It states that

> current strategic circumstances would not support diversion of sufficient resources from other national priorities to overcome this technological gap (between Australia and those countries which can produce modern weapons systems), even if it were feasible and the higher cost of the small number of equipment items required could be justified.

The 'other national priorities' presumably include protecting the ability of foreign corporations to manufacture in Australia low-grade motor-cars and domestic appliances and thereby to waste the country's manpower and material resources. The possibility that Australia might follow the example of such countries as Sweden and Switzerland in designing and exporting sophisticated defence equipment seems never to have crossed the minds of our defence planners—or of our industrialists or politicians.

Although the defence support industries in Australia have been allowed to decline to a pitiful level and research and development for military purposes is run on a shoe string, there are some pointers to what could be done if a determined and imaginative effort were made. The Nomad aircraft and the Ikara missile were produced in Australia and have found markets overseas. What is needed is a jump to the high levels of technology. We should now manufacture, for example, anti-shipping missiles like the American-designed Harpoon, a sea-skimming missile with an over-the-horizon capability which evades radar protection by approaching the target at a very low altitude, and which can be launched from ships, submarines and aircraft.

The weapon of the future, however, is the long-range surface-skimming cruise-missile. This is being developed by the United States as part of its strategic force. In this role it will be armed with nuclear warheads, but it can also be used with conventional explosives. The technology required for its production should be well within the capability of a country like Australia, and American sources suggest that such missiles could be made for about 500 000 dollars each. Even if this is an under-estimate it is clear that they would be much less expensive than aircraft like the F111. Existing designs have a range of 2500 miles, and it is believed that this could be considerably extended. If they were acquired in sufficient numbers by a south-east Asian regional defence force they would greatly strengthen its ability to keep a potential enemy at a safe distance from the region. They would have added deterrent effect in that it would be possible, in some circumstances, to strike at the homeland of a hostile power.

The facilities built in Australia by the Americans for satellite communications and surveillance would also be useful in maintaining a watch over all the activities in the area of potentially hostile powers. The installations would have to be taken over by the Australian government and operated for the benefit of ourselves and neighbouring countries. As I have suggested elsewhere, these facilities could serve as a means of supervision of a zone of neutrality in the Indian Ocean and the south-west Pacific. The establishment of such a zone is a distant hope rather than a present possibility, but meanwhile the stations could be used to contribute to the defence of the region. At present they do no more than link us to the strategic defence of the United States and thus expose us, in the event of global war, to nuclear attack. Unfortunately the Fraser government acquiesced in leaving them in American hands. In 1977 the agreement in regard to the Defence Space Research Facility at Pine Gap came up for renewal and an opportunity existed for negotiating an arrangement which would have more regard to Australia's security interests. The agreement was renewed as it stood for ten years, and the opportunity was allowed to pass, astonishingly without protest by the Labor Party. The agreement concerning the United States Naval Communications Centre at Northwest Cape will not expire until 1988, so that essential control over these two important facilities will be denied to Australia for another decade.

For Australia to move out of the past technological era into the present would require considerable capital investment, and much of this would have to be diverted from the private sector. Considerable savings could, however, be found within the defence budget. These could be invested in research and development, in the rehabilitation of existing defence support industries, and in the establishment of pilot enterprises for the production of the more sophisticated components.

In recent years large sums have been spent on weapons and equipment which have no visible role in the defence of Australia. If the White Paper is any guide it is proposed to spend even larger sums over the next five years.

Nearly one hundred million dollars have been spent on the purchase of one hundred German-built Leopard tanks. No explanation has been given by the defence authorities or by the government as to what these will be used for. Even if there were an invasion of Australia—which is the least likely contingency—it is very doubtful whether they would be able to contribute anything to the country's defence. They cannot be transported by air, so it is unlikely that they could be brought into action before the battle was over. Even if they were they would not last long: they have no missiles and would soon be knocked out by a modern attacking force. The only justification given for buying them was that it was necessary for the army, in the current jargon of the defence authorities, 'to keep up with the state of the art'. Even this claim was untrue: the model bought was already obsolescent and was being superseded overseas by the Leopard Mark II and by the British-designed Chieftain tank.

Other equipment for land warfare which it is proposed to buy are new 105 mm howitzers and 155 mm medium guns. The numbers and amount of money to be spent are not disclosed; neither are the uses, if any, to which they would be put.

The greatest extravagance which is likely to occur in the next five years is in the air force: it is proposed to replace the present obsolescent Mirage tactical fighters, of which there are forty-eight in service, with more modern fighter aircraft. No information is given as to why these aircraft are needed, although there has been much discussion as to whether the new aircraft should be designed for aerial combat or for the support of ground troops, or both. They would only be useful in either role if there were a direct invasion of Australia, or perhaps of one of our allies. (Two Mirage squadrons are stationed at Butterworth, presumably to assist if needed in resisting an attack on Malaysia, although nothing explicit is ever said as to why they are there.) Such operations are, however, only conceivable *in extremis*—when the battle for the defence of the region has already been lost. Our neighbours are as little defensible against invasion as is Australia itself. In the event of such an attack the only sensible course would be to destroy the aircraft before the enemy captured them.

In the navy the most conspicuous extravagance is the maintenance in operation of the H.M.A.S. *Melbourne*. Its only surviving purpose seems to be to act as flagship for the commander-in-chief of the naval forces. It could not be risked in combat: its maximum speed is twenty knots and it has no effective missile defences. It is supposed to provide 'air defence at sea, reconnaissance and surveillance, and anti-submarine warfare'. It is most unlikely that it could engage in any of these activities in waters where there was a hostile modern submarine or destroyer.

There was for some time the possibility that *Melbourne* would be replaced by another conventional carrier of a similar type. Fortunately this is now unlikely, but the present vessel is to be maintained in service until 1985. Plainly the most sensible course would be to take it out of service without further delay. Ultimately it might be worth while to replace it with a small Australian-built carrier capable of carrying vertical-take-off aircraft and helicopters, but this would depend upon whether it could contribute usefully to regional defence.

If all the equipment demands of the Australian services were carefully scrutinized in the light of a realistic strategic doctrine, big savings could be made which could be diverted to more useful purposes, including the subsidization of technologically-advanced defence industries. The 100 million dollars wasted on Leopard tanks could have been given to the government aircraft factory to develop a cruise-missile. The money earmarked for new fighters could instead be spent on more Orion long-range reconnaissance aircraft, or on equipping the F111s with armaments which would at last give them a useful role. Instead of providing the army with heavy weapons which could only be used in Australia, it should be reorganized into marine-type forces, equipped with the most advanced tactical missiles and air-transportable equipment. It should be given its own transport aircraft. In order to economize in the purchase of equipment, training and planning should be on the basis of using in an emergency the wide-bodied aircraft owned by Qantas for the transport of troops—and if necessary the smaller aircraft owned by the domestic airlines. Because of its highly developed air services Australia is well-placed for air transport and, as in other countries, the commercial aircraft available should be regarded as an integral part of our defence infrastructure. Whenever new aircraft are bought by the airlines they should be required to take account of this defence role and ensure that their equipment is quickly adaptable to army use. Commercial pilots should be suitably trained and made reserve officers in the armed services. The co-operation of the many flying clubs in Australia could also be enlisted and they could be encouraged to play their part in providing the mobility which is the nation's over-riding defence requirement.

The bureaucratic superstructure of the defence forces is excessive and useful funds could be saved by dismantling large sections of it. When the Fraser government came to power the foreign service, which in peace time is more important to the security of the country than the defence services, was damagingly reduced, but the defence department was virtually untouched. The professional forces are barely sufficient for present needs and would have to be expanded if realistic roles for them were developed, but large numbers of civilians who sit at their elbows could be transferred to more useful work.

The situation is particularly unsatisfactory at the top level. Senior public servants have been placed in positions in which they overshadow the chiefs of the armed services, not only in policy matters but also in the actual running of the services. This arrangement arose partly because of the failure of the senior professional officers to bring their ideas up to date and develop effective policies, and might have been justified if the civilian officials had produced realistic defence doctrines appropriate to our present needs. Their failure to do this is sufficiently demonstrated by the Defence White Paper of November 1976, with all its evasions, misjudgements and incoherencies.

Of the 1200 million dollars which, according to the Defence White Paper, should be spent on defence in the five-year period 1977 to 1981, one half will be for pay and allowances for service and civilian staffs. There were in 1976 nearly 32 000 civilians compared with 68 000 service men and women. Half the civilians were attached to the headquarters defence staffs (including the intelligence community) and it is in this area that there is the most scope for savings. It would not be unrealistic to assume that these could be reduced by about 5000 people. This would mean a saving to the defence budget over the five-year period of 200 million dollars.

In the equipment field it is proposed that a sum of 2320 million dollars should be spent. If inappropriate equipment like tanks, heavy field guns and tactical fighter aircraft were deleted from the list, and if the development of a naval base at Cockburn Sound (the need for which has never been convincingly explained) were abandoned, the saving could be in the region of 1000 million dollars. This would not be a net saving: most of it would need to be used for the purchase of additional long-range aircraft, submarines, ships and missiles. It is possible to envisage, however, that small funds could be saved out of the proposed expenditure for the other essential requirement for Australia's defence—investment in research and development of advanced technology.

Savings from the existing budgetary proposals would clearly not be sufficient for the full redevelopment of our defence industries. Because of our present backwardness whole new industrial complexes would have to be created. Planned defence expenditure for the next five years will, however, run at only about 2·5 per cent of the gross national product. In most other affluent countries it is between 3·5 to 5 per cent. Britain spends 4·8 per cent; the Netherlands 3·9 per cent; Norway 3·6 per cent and Sweden about 4 per cent. For the United States it is as high as 6·5 per cent.

For a country as vulnerable as Australia it would not be unreasonable to devote 3·5 per cent of its national product to defence. This would add 1000 million dollars annually to the defence budget. If most of this were invested in defence support industries our security prospects would indeed be improved. Given appropriate support by private capital we could provide ourselves with mobile fighting forces which would be equipped with advanced weapons systems made in Australia; these forces could be the nucleus of a regional defence organization realistically designed to preserve the security of south-east Asia and the south-west Pacific; and we could provide our allies with the means to build up their forces for the same purpose. We might even make a profit out of it. If we established sophisticated engineering industries for the production of defence equipment there would be a flow on to Australian industry as a whole which might at last lift us into the modern era of technology.

As a country with modern engineering industries and defence forces, Australia could clearly play a very different role in international relations from its present one. Instead of competing with the economies of our neighbours we could provide the high technology which they will need. Our role would then be seen as a useful one and this could ultimately lead to our being accepted as a trusted partner in promoting the security and welfare of the region.

These suggestions are put forward to illustrate what might be possible, but not, I must confess, in any expectation that they are likely to be adopted. I sketched some of them in *The Last Domino* but concluded that it would be optimistic to expect that Australians would change their traditional attitudes sufficiently to enable these proposals to be realized. Since then the prospect has worsened. One of the most conservative and isolationist governments in our history is in power; the Labor Party is dominated, with a few exceptions, by men whose economic views and racial attitudes go back a century; a new political party has come into being whose policies are the quintessence of traditional Australian middle-class opinions; neurotic concern with side issues has swamped consideration of real internal and international problems; and our standing overseas is at its lowest since the war. The population is ageing and our national arteries have already hardened. Most disappointingly, the younger generation clings to the clichés of its elders, has little interest in radical new ideas, and no vision of the future.

Time will not wait for us to catch up: the chance to do so may already have passed. Life for Australia and the Australians will go on, but the future is unlikely to be what we would have chosen or our descendants will enjoy.

Reading List

Soviet Military Strategy, Marshal V. D. Sokolovsky, 1968 edition, ed. Harriet Fast Scott, Stanford Research Institute, 1975.

Red Star Rising at Sea, translations and commentaries on articles by Admiral S. G. Gorshkov, 1972–73, United States Naval Services Institute, 1974.

On Watch, Admiral Elmo R. Zumwalt, Jnr., Quadrangle, New York, 1976.

Precarious Security, General Maxwell D. Taylor, W. W. Norton & Co., New York, 1976.

The Control of Naval Armaments, Barry M. Blechman, Brookings Institution, Washington, 1975.

The Persian Gulf and Indian Ocean in International Politics, ed. Abbas Amirie, Institute for International Political and Economic Studies, Tehran, 1975.

An Area of Darkness, V. S. Naipaul, Andre Deutsch, 1964.

Papua New Guinea's Improvement Plan 1973–74, Central Planning Office, Port Moresby, 1973.

New Zealand at the Turning Point, Sir Frank Holmes and others, Government Printer, Wellington, New Zealand, 1976.

Japan's Nuclear Option, John E. Endicott, Praeger, New York, 1975.

Treaties Between China and Foreign Countries, Huang Yueh–po and others, Commercial Press, Shanghai, 1935.

History of Diplomacy Between China and Russia, Ho Han–wen, Chung Hua, Shanghai, 1935.

History of Taiwan, Chung Hua, Taipei, 1955.

A Record of Taiwan, Ho Lien–kuei and Wei Hui–lin, Chung Hua, Taipei, 1962.

The International Legal Status of Formosa, Frank P. Morello, M. Nijhoff, The Hague, 1966.

Taiwan in China's Foreign Relations 1836–1974, Sophia Su–fei Yen, Shoe String Press, Connecticut.

The Future of the World Economy: A Study on the Impact of Prospective Economic Issues and Policies on the International Development Strategy, United Nations, 1976.

Energy Information Handbook, prepared by U.S. Congressional Research Service, Washington, July 1977.

Structural Change in Australia
Structural Change and Economic Interdependence
Some Issues in Structural Adjustment
    Papers issued by Industries Assistance Commission, Australian Government Publishing Service, 1977.

Index